A Student's Seneca

A Student's Seneca

Ten Letters and Selections from
De providentia and *De vita beata*

With Notes and Commentary by
M. D. Usher

University of Oklahoma Press : Norman

Also by M. D. Usher

Homeric Stitchings: The Homeric Centos of the Empress Eudocia (Lanham, Md., 1998)

Homerocentones Eudociae Augustae (Stuttgart, 1999)

Wise Guy: The Life and Philosophy of Socrates (a children's picture book) (New York, 2005)

Library of Congress Cataloging-in-Publication Data

Seneca, Lucius Annaeus, ca. 4 B.C–65 A.D.
    [Selections. 2006]
    A student's Seneca: ten letters and selections from De providentia and De vita beata / notes and commentary by M. D. Usher.
      p. cm.
    Texts in Latin; introduction, notes and commentaries in English.
    Rev. and expanded ed. of: Letters of Seneca / Seneca; selected, with notes and commentary, M. D. Usher. Newburyport, MA: Focus Pub., 2000.
    Includes bibliographical references.
    ISBN 0-8061-3744-4 (pbk.: alk. paper)
    1. Seneca, Lucius Annaeus, ca. 4 B.C–65 A.D.—Correspondence.
2. Philosophers—Rome—Correspondence. 3. Conduct of life—Early works to 1800. 4. Philosophy—Early works to 1800. 5. Ethics—Early works to 1800. 6. Latin language—Readers. I. Usher, Mark David, 1966– II. Seneca, Lucius Annaeus, ca. 4 B.C–65 A.D. Epistulae morales ad Lucilium. Selections. III. Seneca, Lucius Annaeus, ca. 4 B.C–65 A.D. De providentia. Selections. IV. Seneca, Lucius Annaeus, ca. 4 B.C–65 A.D. De vita beata. Selections V. title.
    PA6661/A7U84 2006
    878'.010—dc22   2005053845

1   2   3   4   5   6   7   8   9   10

Contents

Preface

This edition of selections from Seneca's prose works is a revised and expanded version of an edition first issued by Focus Publishing in 2000. As the title suggests, it is meant primarily to help beginning students engage Seneca's Latin with understanding and pleasure. If it is asked "Why Seneca?" I would respond that he is, in my view, an ideal author to read once one has completed a full course in Latin grammar and syntax. Seneca's sentences are short and crisp, and the cleverness of his style is readily appreciated, even by the novice. His works are also full of interesting arguments, pleasant commonplaces, and bold metaphors, many of which are already vaguely familiar to students from other contexts. What is more, Seneca writes primarily about the philosophic way of life. His works are thus—by design—universal in scope and psychological in orientation, making the appreciation of them somewhat less dependent on a student's knowledge of the historical context in which they were composed. In short, I find that Seneca appeals to the aesthetic sensibility of today's students and satisfies their linguistic needs and expectations as well. In fact, one of my students (with no knowledge of the function of the *sententia* in Silver Latin) once dubbed him a "Master of Segue," suggesting that Seneca may yet take his rightful place in this beguiling era of electronic entertainment, conspicuous consumption, and other psychical distractions.

∞

This edition contains ten of the shorter letters to Lucilius and selections from two of Seneca's essays (also called dialogues).[1] Most of the letters included here are also available in other student editions: Walter Summers's *Select Letters of Seneca*, (first published in 1910 by Macmillan and since reissued by Bristol Classical Press); Anna Lydia Motto's *Seneca's Moral Epistles* (Bolchazy Carducci Publishers, 2001; previously published by Scholar's Press, 1985); and C. D. N. Costa's *Seneca: 17 Letters* (Aris & Phillips, 1988). Each of these editions is excellent in its own way. The rationale for including some of the same material here is quite simply that the letters in question were well chosen in the first place and are among the most interesting and accessible of Seneca's oeuvre. Where this edition differs from others is in the detail, analysis, emphasis, and in the arrangement of its parts.

From the essays I have taken extended, continuous passages from the *De providentia* and the *De vita beata*. While each of these works as wholes do form (more or less) an extended argument, many readers of Seneca will agree with Quintilian (*Inst. Or.* 10.1.131) that he lends himself to excerption with little harm done. (As Quintilian says, *quod utinam ipse fecisset!*). Among student editions, both essays appear in their entirety in John F. Hurst and Henry C. Whiting's long out-of-print *Seneca's Moral Essays* (American Book Company, 1884), and a couple of short excerpts in John Lawless's *The Virtues of a Stoic: Selections from Seneca's Philosophical Works* (Classical Association of New England, 1994). The whole of *De vita beata* appears, with translation and some commentary, in Costa's *Seneca: Four Dialogues* (Aris & Phillips, 1994).

∽

The text of this edition is basically that of the Loeb, and I personally have no quarrel with it (nor will the beginning Latinists for

---

1. On the term *dialogus* applied to these treatises, see Miriam T. Griffin, *Seneca: A Philosopher in Politics* (Oxford: Clarendon, 1976), 13ff. and 412ff.

whom this edition is intended).[2] The letters are not arranged in ascending numerical order but are grouped loosely by theme and, with pedagogical interests in mind, by length and degree of difficulty. At the head of each letter and essay—and for the elided portions of the essays—I offer a brief summary or interpretation in English. The Commentary consists of line-by-line notes on grammar, style, syntax, and content. My aim in writing the notes was to be helpful, and to draw attention to interesting things that might otherwise be overlooked. (Doubtless, I will have overlooked some interesting things myself.) Grammatical references are to Allen and Greenough's *New Latin Grammar* (1931; reprint, Caratzas, 1998), which is also available online at the Perseus Project Web site (www.perseus.tufts.edu) and in a book-form revision by Anne Mahoney (Focus, 2001). For further information about rhetorical tropes I refer students to the second edition of Richard Lanham's *A Handlist of Rhetorical Terms* (University of California Press, 1991), which provides definitions, discussion, and excellent examples of classical figures from literature in English. For the occasional lexical matter I cite the big Lewis and Short lexicon— not only because I like it, but because it is one of the best Latin dictionaries readily available to students in abridged form. (See further "How to Use This Edition.")

∞

Any expert on Seneca will quickly see that students will need to look elsewhere for substantial bibliography. For starters I suggest,

2. *Seneca: Epistles*, ed. and trans. by Richard M. Gummere (based on the text of O. Hense) Loeb Classical Library vols. 75–77; *Seneca: Moral Essays*, ed. and trans. by John W. Basore (based on the text of E. Hermes), Loeb Classical Library vols. 214, 254. I have, however, made some minor changes in punctuation and orthography. Critical texts with apparatus of all the works included here may be found in L. D. Reynolds, *L. Annaei Senecae ad Lucilium Epistulae Morales*, 2 vols. (Oxford: Clarendon, 1965) and *L. Annaei Senecae Dialogorum Libri Duodecim* (Oxford: Clarendon, 1977).

x *Preface*

in addition to recent works listed in *L'Année philologique*, Anna Lydia Motto's annotated *Seneca: A Critical Bibliography, 1900–1980: Scholarship on His Life, Thought, Prose, and Influence* (Hakkert, 1989). Motto's alphabetical index to Seneca's prose works, *Guide to the Thought of Lucius Annaeus Seneca* (Hakkert, 1970), is also a wonderful resource. Excellent treatments of the life and times of Seneca include Miriam T. Griffin's *Seneca: A Philosopher in Politics* (Clarendon, 1976) and, translated from the French, Paul Veyne's *Seneca: The Life of a Stoic* (Routledge, 2003). Relevant material can also be mined from G. D. Williams's recent commentary on Seneca's *De otio* and *De brevitate vitae* (Cambridge University Press, 2003). On Stoicism, F. H. Sandbach, *The Stoics* (Chatto and Windus, 1975; reprint, Hackett, 1994) and A. A. Long, *Hellenistic Philosophy* (University of California Press, 1986), pp. 107–209, are both excellent. (Sandbach's pages 149–62 deal specifically with Seneca.) Tad Brennan's invigorating new book, *The Stoic Life: Emotions, Duties, and Fate* (Oxford University Press, 2005), is especially accessible to students. *The Cambridge Companion to the Stoics*, edited by Brad Inwood (Cambridge University Press, 2003), provides a comprehensive and authoritative account of current trends and controversies in Stoic studies. For translations of and technical commentary on Stoic texts, pages 158–437 in volume 1 of Long and Sedley's *The Hellenistic Philosophers* (Cambridge University Press, 1987) are indispensable. On Seneca's style and its influence, Summers's introduction is still superb. Motto's treatment of style (*Seneca's Moral Epistles,* pp. xix–xxiii) is also very good and friendlier to students. On the larger issue of the relationship of ancient philosophy to modern life, see Pierre Hadot, *Philosophy as a Way of Life: Spiritual Exercises from Socrates to Foucault* (Blackwell, 1995) or, an even more congenial treatment, Alain de Botton, *The Consolations of Philosophy* (Vintage Books, 2000; pp. 73–112 deal specifically with Seneca). Any of these works will get interested students well on their way.

Acknowledgments

It is a pleasure to thank several friends, students, and colleagues for their various contributions to this edition of Seneca. First and foremost, I would like to thank R. Scott Smith, whose careful and conscientious reading of the manuscript and whose close acquaintance with Seneca and the Latin language improved this book considerably. I am likewise indebted to the various comments, corrections, and suggestions of my colleagues Brian Walsh and Robert Rodgers, and to the reports of three anonymous referees. My friend Mike Ford, with whom I had the pleasure of reading Seneca several years ago, kindly provided the illustration that appears on the cover, and much excellent discussion besides. Thanks, too, to Pippa Letsky for doing a fine job of copyediting the manuscript. If, in spite of the efforts of all of these individuals, any errors of fact or judgment still lurk within these pages, they are of course my own responsibility.

Finally, I would like to extend a special thank-you to my students at the University of Vermont on whom this edition was "betatested": Rozenn Bailleul-LeSuer, Erin Burke, Angela DiGiulio, Colin Dowling, Cory Elliott, Alison McCarthy, and also Allison McCarthy, Elisa Pepicelli, Alexis Ressler, Andrew Siebengartner, and Rachel Thomas. Their success with Seneca confirms my original hunch that he would be—and indeed is—an excellent author for budding Latinists.

Introduction

LIFE

Lucius Annaeus Seneca was born during the reign of Augustus at Cordoba, Spain, between 4 and 1 B.C.E. He came from a reasonably well-off and talented family. His nephew—the son of his younger brother, Mela—was the poet Lucan, famous for his epic on the battle between Caesar and Pompey at Pharsalia (*De bello civili*). Seneca's older brother, Novatus (later adopted by the senator Junius Gallio, whose name he eventually took), appears in the *Acts of the Apostles* (18:12) as the proconsul of Achaia. Seneca's father, known as the Elder Seneca, was a lifelong enthusiast of rhetoric. As a youth, the Elder Seneca had studied the art of public speaking in Rome, and toward the end of his life he compiled two important manuals on rhetorical theory and practice, the *Controversiae* and *Suasoriae*, both of which survive. We know little about Seneca's mother, Helvia, who stayed behind in Spain to manage the family's estates when the Elder Seneca brought their son to Rome to be educated, though from Seneca's *Consolatio ad Helviam matrem*, written on the occasion of his father's death, it is clear she was a capable person of considerable character. Seneca himself married a younger woman named Pompeia Paulina and had a son by her, but we know surprisingly little about either of them.

Seneca lived most of his life in Rome, where he had a well-connected aunt and uncle who seem to have helped in supporting him in the early years. As a young man, he traveled with them to Egypt and on the return voyage survived a shipwreck in which he witnessed his uncle's death. Seneca's aunt continued to support his causes at Rome and played an important role in getting him elected to the usual entry-level positions in government that all aspiring Roman gentlemen held in the course of their political careers. Seneca was heavily influenced by his father's passion for rhetoric, which was at once a pastime and, within the larger framework of Roman education, the central subject of study that prepared young men for a public career. In his early teens, Seneca began to study more intensively with Papirius Fabianus, a versatile scholar who not only taught him a great deal about prose style but, more importantly, converted him to the philosophic way of life.

Unlike Cicero, Seneca's interest in philosophy steered him away from an active political career. Seneca did not enter politics until he was well past the age of thirty, about ten years behind most young men of his social class, though he did hold various lower offices of state and was eventually inducted into the Senate. Poor physical health was also a constant problem and no doubt reinforced his natural inclination toward intellectual pursuits. Seneca appears to have suffered from some form of asthma, which in turn made him prone to other bronchial disorders, including tuberculosis. As a practicing philosopher with a weak constitution, he adopted an austere lifestyle, abstaining from the culinary luxuries of his day such as oysters, mushrooms, and wine. He took cold baths to fortify himself and slept on a hard bed.

The first forty years of Seneca's life were thus unexceptional. He published some philosophical essays and acquired a decent reputation in literary circles as a scholar and stylist, but he was little more than a cultivated private citizen. In the year 41, however, this all changed. The emperor Gaius (Caligula) was assassinated in that year, and his uncle Claudius was hailed as emperor in his stead. Previously, in 39, Gaius had banished his own sister Julia Livilla on charges of adultery with her brother-in-law. Upon his accession, Claudius recalled Julia, but she was soon accused of adultery again by Claudius's scheming wife, Messalina—this time with Seneca. It is unclear whether Seneca was guilty of this offense (adultery was a common charge leveled against potential rivals at court—in this case Julia, not Seneca), but he was convicted nonetheless and relegated to the island of Corsica, where he lived in exile for eight years. Intellectually, this was a productive, if introspective, period for Seneca, who spent most of his time reading and writing. When Claudius divorced Messalina and married his niece Agrippina, Seneca was recalled—"on account of his scholarly reputation," according to the historian Tacitus—to be the tutor of Claudius's new stepson, Lucius Domitius Ahenobarbus, the young Nero, then twelve years old. Seneca was thus suddenly and inextricably thrust into imperial family affairs.

Given Nero's enthusiasm for sub-imperial pursuits like singing, dancing, acting, and chariot racing, Seneca's task was—by default— more to inculcate restraint than to impart any positive moral influence. When Nero became emperor in 54 at age seventeen, Seneca's official role as court tutor shaded into an unofficial position as the emperor's advisor and speech writer. At first, together with Sextus Afranius Burrus, the head of the imperial bodyguard, Seneca helped preserve and extend a period of good government begun under Claudius by keeping Nero's domineering mother in check and by putting a good public face on Nero's private amusements. But as time wore on, Nero's passions tended more and more toward debauchery and crime. In 55, he killed Claudius's natural son and potential heir, Brittanicus, by poison. In 59, he tried to have his mother, Agrippina, murdered at sea in a plot involving a collapsible boat. When that failed, he sent assassins to finish the job as she slept in her bed—a spectacular end to what many regarded as an incestuous relationship.

Seneca's position vis-à-vis these and the many other incredible crimes of Nero's reign is difficult to assess. He himself tells us nothing. What is certain is that he continued to compose philosophical essays and somehow managed to amass a considerable fortune during this period, in spite of any misgivings. By the time his colleague Burrus died in 62, however, Seneca was eager to go into retirement. He asked to be allowed to do so at least twice, offering to hand over all his assets to the imperial purse. Although official permission was never granted, he seems to have spent his last years on the periphery. By 64, the year of the infamous fire at Rome and the mass execution of Christians, Seneca had fallen out of favor and had withdrawn completely. In 65, he was implicated with his nephew Lucan and others in a conspiracy to assassinate Nero and was ordered to commit suicide, a final vignette from Seneca's life that has been immortalized by Tacitus (*Annals* 15.62–64).

That Seneca offers posterity no apologies, justifications, or exposés for the years he spent at Nero's court has troubled many readers, both ancient and modern.[1] On first glance, the ascetic moralist we meet in his letters and essays is difficult to reconcile with the wealthy spokesman for Nero's regime. But any person well acquainted with his or her own humanity will understand that it is also difficult to extricate oneself from circumstances beyond one's control. Moreover, as a Stoic, Seneca believed "that the goodness of an intention or principle of action must be evaluated independently of a man's achieving some desirable result." The wise man, the Stoics were fond of saying, "having done everything in his power, does not feel pity or regret" (Long p. 198, citing *Stoicorum Veterum Fragmenta* iii 450–52). The moral of Seneca's Letter 28—*animum debes mutare, non caelum* ("change your way of thinking, not your surroundings")—is advice he himself appears to have taken to heart. Although he was well aware of the philosopher's political responsibilities and seems to have acted upon them as far as he could, ultimately Seneca resigned himself to a life of philosophical introspection and detachment. In doing so, he felt he was focusing on what was really important.

---

1. One intriguing exception is *De vita beata* 17–27, included in this volume, where Seneca responds (albeit in the abstract) to specific charges that philosophers do not practice what they preach.

PHILOSOPHY

Stoicism was by far the most popular and influential school of thought at Rome. While there are of course highly technical elements in any philosophical system, it bears saying outright that philosophy in antiquity—Stoicism especially—was not primarily an "academic" subject studied only by professionals. As we learn from Seneca's Letter 44 (included in this volume), philosophy is for everyone, and the Stoics could count among their greatest sages not only Seneca, but a Greek ditch-digger who began his career as a boxer (Cleanthes), a handicapped slave from Phrygia (Epictetus), and the Roman emperor Marcus Aurelius.

The Stoics took their name from the *Stoa Poikilē*, "The Painted Porch" in the Athenian agora, a public building where the school's founder, Zeno of Citium, habitually discussed his ideas with the young men of the city beginning in the early third century B.C.E. Citium was an ancient Phoenician city on Cyprus, and one of the remarkable things about Stoicism is that its earliest proponents came from the margins of the Greek world. Chrysippus, for example, the most prolific and influential of Stoic teachers, hailed from the city of Soli on the coast of southeastern Turkey. Indeed, when Diogenes the Cynic (himself from the northern reaches of modern Turkey) proclaimed himself a *cosmopolitēs*, a "citizen of the world," he was marking what was to become a decidedly universalist trend in philosophical thinking in the centuries after Plato and Aristotle. Alexander the Great's conquests in Greece, Asia Minor, and the Near East coincided with this intellectual trend and contributed to the spread of Greek philosophical ideas throughout the Mediterranean. These ideas made their way to Rome in the wake of Rome's conquest of the Greek world in the second century B.C.E. Stoic teachers like Panaetius of Rhodes and Posidonius of Apamea (in Syria), both of whom spent time teaching in Rome, were especially influential figures here. Among notable Romans of the Republican period, Cicero and Cato the Younger were deeply affected by Stoicism. Seneca is in a very real way their intellectual heir.

To its adherents, Stoicism offered an internally coherent body of thought that provided its followers with a detailed account of the universe, an elaborate theology, sophisticated theories of cognition and language, and a practical morality. The Stoics themselves presented their system as a tripartite division into logic, physics, and ethics. Among the many organic images they used to describe the interdependence of parts in their philosophy is that of an egg, where logic is the shell, ethics the white, and physics the yolk. The Stoics understood what is true of any sound philosophical system—that logic, physics, and ethics are fundamentally interrelated. Seneca shows a deep interest in all three areas of inquiry, but like the Stoics generally, he was concerned above all with ethics and the practical task of living a virtuous life. Rather than trying, as it were, to crack any philosophical eggs here, let me simply invite the reader to consider aspects of Stoic philosophy as they crop up in the works collected in this volume. Many of Seneca's appeals require no technical knowledge of Stoicism. (Nor indeed are those appeals necessarily unique to Stoicism.) In those few places where the argument depends on such knowledge, explanations will be found in the Notes and Commentary.[2]

STYLE

Seneca was famous in antiquity and throughout the early modern period for his "sententious" or "pointed" style. These words are mildly technical terms that describe an author's choice and positioning of words and his use of various acoustic effects in

2. See in particular the notes and cross references at *natura*, Letter 60.3; *vivit is qui . . . se utitur,* Letter 60.4; *secundum naturam vivere*, Letter 5.4; *providentia, maximum bonum condicionis humanae*, Letter 5.8; *supra fortunam*, Letter 44.5; *patet exitus . . . licet fugere,* De providentia 6.7; *erubescitis, De providentia* 6.9; *haec quae indifferentia vocamus*, *De vita beata* 22.4.

order to point out or underscore his meaning. Essentially it is a style characterized by cleverly worded one-liners. The rhetorical styles of Abraham Lincoln ("You may fool all of the people some of the time; you can even fool some of the people all of the time; but you cannot fool all of the people all of the time"), John F. Kennedy ("Ask not what your country can do for you, but what you can do for your country"), or Winston Churchill ("Never in the field of human conflict was so much owed by so many to so few") provide classic examples. But it is not merely a presidential style affected by august politicians. It is also the style of modern advertising ("Eat to get slimmer") and pop lyrics ("Home is anywhere you hang your head," Elvis Costello). Nor is it a style only for men. Consider, for example, this vigorous paragraph from Camille Paglia:

> Woman does not dream of transcendental or historical escape from natural cycle, since she *is* that cycle. Her sexual maturity means marriage to the moon, waxing and waning in lunar phases. Moon, month, menses: same word, same world. The ancients knew that woman is bound to nature's calendar, an appointment she cannot refuse. The Greek pattern of free will to hybris to tragedy is a male drama, since woman has never been deluded (until recently) by the mirage of free will. She knows there is no free will, since she is not free. She has no choice but acceptance. Whether she desires motherhood or not, nature yokes her into the brute inflexible rhythm of procreative law. Menstrual cycle is an alarming clock that cannot be stopped until nature wills it.[3]

Not only is the sentiment of this passage shot through with Stoic ideas (for example, the emphasis, directly expressed or implied, on Fate, accepting one's circumstances, living according to Nature), the style is also completely Senecan and provides a fitting introduction in English to Seneca's Latin style. (Latin examples of

3. Camille Paglia, *Sexual Personae: Art and Decadence from Nefertiti to Emily Dickinson* (New York: Vintage Books, 1991) 10.

many of the techniques pointed out below are identified and explained in the Notes and Commentary.)

Note first the sonorous repetition of *x, m, o, n, s,* and *w* sounds in the first two sentences of Paglia's tirade ("Her sexual maturity means marriage to the moon, waxing and waning in lunar phases. Moon, month, menses: same word, same world"). Note also how the second sentence does not so much expand the thought of the first as illustrate it with a clever etymological play on the Latin word *menses* (month), to which both "menstrual" and "moon" are related. Note, too, the effect of the pun "word . . . world," which, reinforced by the repetition of the word "same," serves to universalize the particular, even to the point of exaggeration. The phrase "nature's *calendar, an appointment* she cannot refuse" is a transposition of the more familiar collocation "an appointment calendar" (which it calls to mind) and takes us into the world of the cheery, obsequious office secretary. Coming from Paglia (an outspoken critic of idealistic feminism), this sentence is a wicked jab at the "career woman" and the naïve belief that the ability to break out of traditionally female roles in society is necessarily conducive to greater personal freedom, happiness, or power. The sentence "Menstrual cycle is an *alarming clock*" contains a similar workaday pun (one instantly thinks of "alarm clock"—and perhaps, by extension, given the context, of the familiar phrase "*biological* clock") that reinforces the point, especially with the use of the word "dream" in the opening sentence. Taken together, these rhetorical features add muscle, tone, color, and humor to what might have been a bald run of declarative sentences.

As with Seneca, one can appreciate the sheer intelligence and ingenuity of the style without necessarily being persuaded by the author's arguments or conclusions. I would suggest, however, that a sententious author's striving after rhetorical effect is not just a style of *writing*, but a style of *thought* that revels in hyperbole, paradox, and ambiguity. In Seneca's case, this derives in part from his commitment to Stoicism, where paradoxes and linguistic ambiguity were central concerns. But it also reflects his interest in poetry. It is no accident that Seneca the philosopher was also an accomplished poet, the author of at least eight tragedies, and that he freely incorporates into his prose poetic words and forms that were avoided in Cicero and Caesar's day. Indeed, Seneca is something of a prose counterpart to the Latin poet Lucretius (ca. 99–ca. 55 B.C.E.), who once compared his presentation of Epicurean philosophy through poetry to the age-old trick of spreading honey around the rim of a cup of bitter medicine so that children will drink it (*De rerum natura* 1.936–50). Seldom has the bitter pill of philosophy had such attractive packaging as it does here.

How to Use This Edition

No one likes being told what to do. Nonetheless, there are some things one should observe in order to get the most out of this edition. First, it is highly recommended that students read the passages, beginning with the Letters, in the order presented here, for the reasons cited in the Preface, but also because grammatical and rhetorical features explained once (or twice, or thrice) are not always explained again in subsequent notes. To be sure, there are many cross-references in the notes, but it is hoped these serve more to jog the reader's memory, and that linguistic competence and familiarity with Seneca's style will increase in the course of using this book. With this goal in mind, it is important that students take the trouble to look up the references to Allen and Greenough (abbreviated as A&G—the numbers refer to sections, not pages), read the explanations and examples given there, and consider it something of a study technique. It may make for slower reading at first, but the returns will come fast and furious. The reader should also become conversant with the grammatical and stylistic terminology used in the notes. If one is to talk about language, one needs to acquire a vocabulary to do so.

Second, while quite a number of words and phrases are glossed in the notes and a vocabulary is provided for the selections included here, students should be encouraged to look up words in a real dictionary. Good dictionaries cite examples of the various constructions and idiomatic meanings a word or phrase may have, and knowing how to use a dictionary is an important step in getting students out of their textbooks and into the Latin language itself. This is especially important for students reading Seneca, for

Seneca loves to play on the meanings of words and phrases. Without a dictionary, such nuances would not be appreciated or even identified as such. I suggest that students obtain a copy of Charlton Lewis's *An Elementary Latin Dictionary* (Oxford University Press), which is an abridgement of an excellent larger dictionary known familiarly as "Lewis and Short" (occasionally referred to in the notes as L&S). Both are available through the Perseus Project Web site (www.perseus.tufts.edu). The *Oxford Latin Dictionary* is also excellent and easy to use.

The Vocabulary at the end of this book is intended primarily for quick and handy reference—to keep readers from feeling bogged down. (See further "A Note on the Vocabulary".) Only the basic meanings of words are provided. I have tried to weed out egregiously irrelevant meanings, but students will still need to exercise some linguistic *ingenium* in choosing the best meaning for a given context. (If in doubt, or dissatisfied with the information I give, consult a real dictionary!)

Latin Texts

Letters

LETTER 60

This letter is a fitting introduction to typical Senecan/Stoic themes and illustrates many points of Seneca's style in short space. Thinking persons, he argues, should not let family and friends tell them what to do. Parents and friends pray for things that are actually harmful to those who have chosen to pursue a life in philosophy. And why do we pray for things at all, S. asks, when Nature provides us with what is sufficient for life? The animals, who do not pray, know their place in the world. We sink beneath them when we overreach—in fact, in our extravagant ways of life, we are like the living dead.

SENECA LUCILIO SUO SALUTEM:

Queror, litigo, irascor. Etiamnunc optas quod tibi optavit   1
nutrix tua aut paedagogus aut mater? Nondum intellegis
quantum mali optaverint? O quam inimica nobis sunt vota
nostrorum! Eo quidem inimiciora quo cessere felicius. Iam
non admiror si omnia nos a prima pueritia mala sequuntur;
inter execrationes parentum crevimus. Exaudiant di nostram quoque pro nobis vocem gratuitam.

Quousque poscemus aliquid deos ita quasi nondum ipsi   2 *not yet*
alere nos possimus? Quamdiu sationibus implebimus magnarum urbium campos? Quamdiu nobis populus metet?
Quamdiu unius mensae instrumentum multa navigia et quidem non ex uno mari subvehent? Taurus paucissimorum
iugerum pascuo impletur; una silva elephantis pluribus
sufficit; homo et terra et mari pascitur. Quid ergo? Tam   3

3

insatiabilem nobis natura alvum dedit, cum tam modica corpora dedisset, ut vastissimorum edacissimorumque animalium aviditatem vinceremus? Minime. Quantulum est enim quod naturae datur! Parvo illa dimittitur. Non fames nobis ventris nostri magno constat, sed ambitio. Hos itaque, ut ait Sallustius, "ventri oboedientes," animalium loco numeremus, non hominum, quosdam vero ne animalium quidem, sed mortuorum. Vivit is qui multis usui est; vivit is qui se utitur. Qui vero latitant et torpent sic in domo sunt quomodo in conditivo. Horum licet in limine ipso nomen marmori inscribas: MORTEM SUAM ANTECESSERUNT. VALE.

4

LETTER 5

In this letter S. argues that ostentatious acts of self-denial interfere with the true aims of philosophy, which are to change a person's internal motivations. The thought is dense, the sentences terse. In sections 1–6, S. establishes a dichotomy between external and internal qualities that culminates in a discussion of wealth, toward which he recommends a psychological indifference. In section 7 and following, he shifts his focus to a discussion of the close, even causal, connection between hope and fear. Unlike other animals, human beings are dominated by these emotions because of our sense of time, which we exercise in our capacity for forethought and memory. Following the philosopher Hecato, S. concludes that if we cease to hope we will cease to fear, and that it is better to live fully in the present, where fear and hope are ineffectual.

SENECA LUCILIO SUO SALUTEM:

Quod pertinaciter studes et, omnibus omissis, hoc unum agis, ut te meliorem cotidie facias, et probo et gaudeo, nec tantum hortor ut perseveres, sed etiam rogo. Illud autem te admoneo, ne eorum more qui non proficere sed conspici cupiunt facias aliqua quae in habitu tuo aut genere vitae

1

notabilia sint. Asperum cultum et intonsum caput et negle-   2
gentiorem barbam et indictum argento odium et cubile
humi positum et quicquid aliud ambitionem perversa via
sequitur evita. Satis ipsum nomen philosophiae, etiam si
modeste tractetur, invidiosum est; quid si nos hominum
consuetudini coeperimus excerpere? Intus omnia dissimilia
sint; frons populo nostra conveniat. Non splendeat toga; ne   3
sordeat quidem. Non habeamus argentum in quod solidi
auri caelatura descenderit, sed non putemus frugalitatis
indicium auro argentoque caruisse. Id agamus, ut meliorem
vitam sequamur quam vulgus, non ut contrariam; alioquin
quos emendari volumus fugamus a nobis et avertimus.
Illud quoque efficimus, ut nihil imitari velint nostri, dum
timent ne imitanda sint omnia.

Hoc primum philosophia promittit: sensum communem,   4
humanitatem et congregationem. A qua professione dissimilitudo nos separabit. Videamus ne ista per quae admi-
rationem parare volumus ridicula et odiosa sint. Nempe
propositum nostrum est secundum naturam vivere; hoc
contra naturam est: torquere corpus suum et faciles odisse
munditias et squalorem adpetere et cibis non tantum vilibus
uti sed taetris et horridis. Quemadmodum desiderare deli-   5
catas res luxuriae est, ita usitatas et non magno parabiles
fugere dementiae. Frugalitatem exigit philosophia, non
poenam. Potest autem esse non incompta frugalitas. Hic
mihi modus placet: temperetur vita inter bonos mores et
publicos; suspiciant omnes vitam nostram, sed agnoscant.

"Quid ergo? eadem faciemus, quae ceteri? Nihil inter   6
nos et illos intererit?" Plurimum. Dissimiles esse nos vulgo
sciat qui inspexerit propius. Qui domum intraverit nos
potius miretur quam supellectilem nostram. Magnus ille est
qui fictilibus sic utitur quemadmodum argento. Nec ille
minor est qui sic argento utitur quemadmodum fictilibus.
Infirmi animi est pati non posse divitias.

Sed ut huius quoque diei lucellum tecum communicem,   7
apud Hecatonem nostrum inveni cupiditatum finem etiam
ad timoris remedia proficere. "Desines," inquit, "timere, si
sperare desieris." Dices: "Quomodo ista tam diversa pariter
eunt?" Ita est, mi Lucili: cum videantur dissidere, coniuncta sunt. Quemadmodum eadem catena et custodiam et
militem copulat, sic ista quae tam dissimilia sunt pariter
incedunt: spem metus sequitur. Nec miror ista sic ire;   8
utrumque pendentis animi est, utrumque futuri exspectatione solliciti. Maxima autem utriusque causa est quod non
ad praesentia aptamur, sed cogitationes in longinqua
praemittimus. Itaque providentia, maximum bonum condicionis humanae, in malum versa est. Ferae pericula quae   9
vident fugiunt; cum effugere, securae sunt; nos et venturo
torquemur et praeterito. Multa bona nostra nobis nocent;
timoris enim tormentum memoria reducit, providentia
anticipat. Nemo tantum praesentibus miser est. VALE.

LETTER 43

*In this letter, S. uses the lighthearted occasion of some rumor
about Lucilius that has reached him in Rome to comment on the
inherent moral pitfalls one faces in a status-based culture. S.
argues that one should not gauge the amount of responsibility one
has to live a moral life by one's social standing, which is relative
(for there is always someone, somewhere, more important than
you). Rather, it is incumbent upon each individual to live a good
life according to his or her own conscience, regardless of whether
anyone is watching.*

SENECA LUCILIO SUO SALUTEM:

Quomodo hoc ad me pervenerit quaeris, quis mihi id te   1
cogitare narraverit quod tu nulli narraveras? Is qui scit
plurimum, rumor. "Quid ergo?" inquis. "Tantus sum ut

possim excitare rumorem?" Non est quod te ad hunc locum
respiciens metiaris; ad istum respice in quo moraris. Quic-   2
quid inter vicina eminet magnum est illic ubi eminet. Nam
magnitudo non habet modum certum; comparatio illam aut
tollit aut deprimit. Navis, quae in flumine magna est, in
mari parvula est. Gubernaculum, quod alteri navi magnum,
alteri exiguum est.

Tu nunc in provincia, licet contemnas ipse te, magnus es.   3
Quid agas, quemadmodum cenes, quemadmodum dormias,
quaeritur, scitur; eo tibi diligentius vivendum est. Tunc
autem felicem esse te iudica, cum poteris in publico vivere,
cum te parietes tui tegent, non abscondent, quos plerumque
circumdatos nobis iudicamus non ut tutius vivamus, sed ut
peccemus occultius. Rem dicam ex qua mores aestimes   4
nostros: vix quemquam invenies qui possit aperto ostio
vivere. Ianitores conscientia nostra, non superbia opposuit;
sic vivimus ut deprendi sit subito adspici. Quid autem
prodest recondere se et oculos hominum auresque vitare?
Bona conscientia turbam advocat; mala etiam in solitudine   5
anxia atque sollicita est. Si honesta sunt quae facis, omnes
sciant; si turpia, quid refert neminem scire, cum tu scias?
O te miserum, si contemnis hunc testem! VALE.

LETTER 84

*This letter is a profound meditation on the process and purpose of
reading. S. argues that reading keeps one from being self-absorbed
and that good readers are engaged in a dialogic relationship with
their texts. S. argues further that the act of writing itself should be
a reflex of careful reading—in fact, S. models that for us in this letter. Above all, he is concerned that we make knowledge our own. As
usual, S. is not shy about mixing metaphors to illustrate his point,
or about shifting quickly from one analogy to another. Section 11
and following comprises a general exhortation to philosophy in*

which S. leaves his central point behind. Note, however, how the letter ends as it began with reference to a journey. It is almost as if we are meant to imagine S. writing this letter en route as he is carried through town on a litter.

SENECA LUCILIO SUO SALUTEM:

Itinera ista quae segnitiam mihi excutiunt et valitudini   1
meae prodesse iudico et studiis. Quare valitudinem adiuvent vides: cum pigrum me et neglegentem corporis litterarum amor faciat, aliena opera exerceor; studio quare
prosint indicabo: a lectionibus nihil recessi. Sunt autem, ut
existimo, necessariae, primum ne sim me uno contentus,
deinde ut, cum ab aliis quaesita cognovero, tum et de
inventis iudicem et cogitem de inveniendis. Alit lectio
ingenium et studio fatigatum, non sine studio tamen,
reficit. Nec scribere tantum nec tantum legere debemus;   2
altera res contristabit vires et exhauriet (de stilo dico),
altera solvet ac diluet. Invicem hoc et illo commeandum est
et alterum altero temperandum, ut quicquid lectione collec-
tum est stilus redigat in corpus. Apes, ut aiunt, debemus   3
imitari, quae vagantur et flores ad mel faciendum idoneos
carpunt, deinde quicquid attulere, disponunt ac per favos
digerunt et, ut Vergilius noster ait,

   . . . liquentia mella
   stipant et dulci distendunt nectare cellas.

De illis non satis constat utrum sucum ex floribus ducant   4
qui protinus mel sit, an quae collegerunt, in hunc saporem
mixtura quadam et proprietate spiritus sui mutent. Quibusdam enim placet non faciendi mellis scientiam esse illis,
sed colligendi. Aiunt inveniri apud Indos mel in harundinum foliis, quod aut ros illius caeli aut ipsius harundinis
umor dulcis et pinguior gignat. In nostris quoque herbis
vim eandem sed minus manifestam et notabilem poni,

quam persequatur et contrahat animal huic rei genitum. Quidam existimant conditura et dispositione in hanc qualitatem verti quae ex tenerrimis virentium florentiumque decerpserint, non sine quodam, ut ita dicam, fermento quo in unum diversa coalescunt.

Sed ne ad aliud quam de quo agitur abducar, nos quoque   5
has apes debemus imitari et quaecumque ex diversa lectione congessimus separare (melius enim distincta servantur), deinde adhibita ingenii nostri cura et facultate in unum saporem varia illa libamenta confundere, ut etiam si apparuerit unde sumptum sit, aliud tamen esse quam unde sumptum est appareat. Quod in corpore nostro videmus sine ulla opera nostra facere naturam (alimenta, quae   6
accepimus, quamdiu in sua qualitate perdurant et solida innatant stomacho, onera sunt; at cum ex eo quod erant, mutata sunt, tum demum in vires et in sanguinem transeunt), idem in his quibus aluntur ingenia praestemus, ut quaecumque hausimus non patiamur integra esse, ne aliena sint. Concoquamus illa; alioqui in memoriam ibunt, non in ingenium. Adsentiamur illis fideliter et nostra faciamus, ut unum quiddam fiat ex multis, sicut unus numerus fit ex singulis, cum minores summas et dissidentes computatio una comprendit. Hoc faciat animus noster: omnia quibus est adiutus, abscondat; ipsum tantum ostendat quod effecit.   8
Etiam si cuius in te comparebit similitudo quem admiratio tibi altius fixerit, similem esse te volo quomodo filium, non quomodo imaginem. Imago res mortua est.

"Quid ergo? Non intellegetur cuius imiteris orationem, cuius argumentationem, cuius sententias?" Puto aliquando ne intellegi quidem posse, si imago vera sit; haec enim omnibus quae ex quo velut exemplari traxit formam suam impressit, ut in unitatem illa competant. Non vides quam   9
multorum vocibus chorus constet? Unus tamen ex omnibus redditur; aliqua illic acuta est, aliqua gravis, aliqua media.

Accedunt viris feminae; interponuntur tibiae. Singulorum   10
illic latent voces, omnium apparent. De choro dico quem
veteres philosophi noverant; in commissionibus nostris
plus cantorum est quam in theatris olim spectatorum fuit.
Cum omnes vias ordo canentium implevit et cavea aena-
toribus cincta est et ex pulpito omne tibiarum genus or-
ganorumque consonuit, fit concentus ex dissonis. Talem
animum nostrum esse volo: multae in illo artes, multa prae-
cepta sint, multarum aetatum exempla, sed in unum
conspirata.

"Quomodo," inquis, "hoc effici poterit?" Adsidua inten-   11
tione; si nihil egerimus nisi ratione suadente. Hanc si
audire volueris, dicet tibi. Relinque ista iamdudum ad quae
discurritur. Relinque divitias, aut periculum possidentium
aut onus. Relinque corporis atque animi voluptates; molli-
unt et enervant. Relinque ambitum; tumida res est, vana,
ventosa; nullum habet terminum, tam sollicita est ne quem
ante se videat quam ne quem post se. Laborat invidia et
quidem duplici; vides autem, quam miser sit, si is cui
invidetur et invidet.

Intueris illas potentium domos, illa tumultuosa rixa salu-   12
tantium limina? Multum habent contumellarum ut intres,
plus cum intraveris. Praeteri istos gradus divitum et magno
adgestu suspensa vestibula; non in praerupto tantum istic
stabis, sed in lubrico. Huc potius te ad sapientiam derige
tranquillissimasque res eius et simul amplissimas pete.
Quaecumque videntur eminere in rebus humanis, quamvis   13
pusilla sint et comparatione humillimorum extent, per dif-
ficiles tamen et arduos tramites adeuntur. Confragosa in
fastigium dignitatis via est; at si conscendere hunc verticem libet, cui se fortuna summisit, omnia quidem sub te
quae pro excelsissimis habentur, aspicies, sed tamen venies
ad summa per planum. VALE.

LETTER 56

*Full of humor and rich in detail, this letter is a consolation to any-
one who has tried to study in a dormitory. In S.'s case, it is the
noise of a bathhouse downstairs that poses the problem, which,
after a lengthy and bathetic account of the sources of noise, S.
proposes to solve—much to the reader's surprise—by moving out
of town. Interspersed (of course) are philosophical reflections on
the causes of mental distraction, and in the end the letter becomes
an exhortation to Lucilius to turn inward in his search for peace
and quiet.*

SENECA LUCILIO SUO SALUTEM:

Peream, si est tam necessarium quam videtur silentium   1
in studia seposito. Ecce undique me varius clamor circum-
sonat. Supra ipsum balneum habito. Propone nunc tibi
omnia genera vocum quae in odium possunt aures adduc-
ere: cum fortiores exercentur et manus plumbo graves iactant, cum aut laborant aut laborantem imitantur, gemitus
audio, quotiens retentum spiritum remiserunt, sibilos et
acerbissimas respirationes; cum in aliquem inertem et hac
plebeia unctione contentum incidi, audio crepitum inlisae
manus umeris, quae prout plana pervenit aut concava, ita
sonum mutat. Si vero pilicrepus supervenit et numerare
coepit pilas, actum est. Adice nunc scordalum et furem
deprensum et illum cui vox sua in balineo placet. Adice
nunc eos qui in piscinam cum ingenti impulsae aquae sono
saliunt. Praeter istos quorum, si nihil aliud, rectae voces   2
sunt, alipilum cogita tenuem et stridulam vocem, quo sit
notabilior, subinde exprimentem nec umquam tacentem,
nisi dum vellit alas et alium pro se clamare cogit; iam libari
varias exclamationes et botularium et crustularium et
omnes popinarum institores mercem sua quadam et insignita modulatione vendentis.

"O te," inquis, "ferreum aut surdum, cui mens inter tot   3
clamores tam varios, tam dissonos constat, cum Chrysippum nostrum adsidua salutatio perducat ad mortem." At
mehercules ego istum fremitum non magis curo quam fluctum aut deiectum aquae, quamvis audiam cuidam genti
hanc unam fuisse causam urbem suam transferendi, quod
fragorem Nili cadentis ferre non potuit. Magis mihi videtur   4
vox avocare quam crepitus. Illa enim animum adducit,
hic tantum aures implet ac verberat. In his quae me sine
avocatione circumstrepunt essedas transcurrentes pono et
fabrum inquilinum et serrarium vicinum, aut hunc qui ad
Metam Sudantem tubulas experitur et tibias, nec cantat, sed
exclamat.

Etiamnunc molestior est mihi sonus qui intermittitur   5
subinde quam qui continuatur. Sed iam me sic ad omnia
ista duravi, ut audire vel pausarium possim voce acerbis-
sima remigibus modos dantem. Animum enim cogo sibi
intentum esse nec avocari ad externa; omnia licet foris
resonent, dum intus nihil tumultus sit, dum inter se non rix-
entur cupiditas et timor, dum avaritia luxuriaque non dis-
sideant nec altera alteram vexet. Nam quid prodest totius
regionis silentium, si adfectus fremunt?

Omnia noctis erant placida composta quiete   6

falsum est. Nulla placida est quies nisi quam ratio composuit. Nox exhibet molestiam, non tollit, et sollicitudines
mutat. Nam dormientium quoque insomnia tam turbulenta
sunt quam dies. Illa tranquillitas vera est in quam bona mens
explicatur. Aspice illum cui somnus laxae domus silentio   7
quaeritur, cuius aures ne quis agitet sonus, omnis servorum
turba conticuit et suspensum accedentium propius vestigium ponitur; huc nempe versatur atque illuc, somnum
inter aegritudines levem captans. Quae non audit audisse se   8
queritur. Quid in causa putas esse? Animus illi obstrepit.

non est = it is not possible (sometimes)

The fact that you consider this person to be peaceful even if the body lies down

this (his mind) want to sothel

it's his treason that must be calmed down
of this hay't be curbed/divided aswl *which is not what*

Hic placandus est, huius compescenda seditio est, quem
you judge to be calm *calm* *if the body lies* *mean*
non est quod existimes placidum, si iacet corpus. Interdum
calm is inquiet
quies inquieta est. // *sometimes rest is unrestful.*

Et ideo ad rerum actus excitandi ac tractatione bonarum
artium occupandi sumus, quotiens nos male habet inertia
sui impatiens. Magni imperatores, cum male parere mili-   9
tem vident, aliquo labore compescunt et expeditionibus
detinent; numquam vacat lascivire districtis nihilque tam
certum est quam otii vitia negotio discuti. Saepe videmur
taedio rerum civilium et infelicis atque ingratae stationis
paenitentia secessisse; tamen in illa latebra in quam nos
timor ac lassitudo coniecit interdum recrudescit ambitio.
Non enim excisa desit, sed fatigata aut etiam obirata rebus
parum sibi cedentibus. Idem de luxuria dico quae videtur   10
aliquando cessisse, deinde frugalitatem professos sollicitat
atque in media parsimonia voluptates non damnatas, sed
relictas petit, et quidem eo vehementius, quo occultius.
Omnia enim vitia in aperto leniora sunt; morbi quoque tunc
ad sanitatem inclinant, cum ex abdito erumpunt ac vim
suam proferunt. Et avaritiam itaque et ambitionem et cetera
mala mentis humanae tunc perniciosissima scias esse, cum
simulata sanitate subsidunt.

Otiosi videmur, et non sumus. Nam si bona fide sumus,   11
si receptui cecinimus, si speciosa contemnimus, ut paulo
ante dicebam, nulla res nos avocabit, nullus hominum avi-
umque concentus interrumpet cogitationes bonas, soli-
dasque iam et certas. Leve illud ingenium est nec sese   12
adhuc reduxit introrsus quod ad vocem et accidentia erigitur. Habet intus aliquid sollicitudinis et habet aliquid con-
cepti pavoris quod illum curiosum facit, ut ait Vergilius
noster:

et me, quem dudum non ulla iniecta movebant
tela neque adverso glomerati ex agmine Grai,

quem
cuius

nunc omnes terrent aurae, sonus excitat omnis
suspensum et pariter comitique onerique timentem.

Prior ille sapiens est quem non tela vibrantia, non arietata   13
inter se arma agminis densi, non urbis impulsae fragor terri-
tat. Hic alter imperitus est, rebus suis timet ad omnem crepitum expavescens, quem una quaelibet vox pro fremitu
accepta deicit, quem motus levissimi exanimant; timidum
illum sarcinae faciunt. Quemcumque ex istis felicibus ele-   14
geris, multa trahentibus, multa portantibus, videbis illum
"comitique onerique timentem."
    Tunc ergo te scito esse compositum, cum ad te nullus
clamor pertinebit, cum te nulla vox tibi excutiet, non si
blandietur, non si minabitur, non si inani sono vana cir-
cumstrepet. "Quid ergo? Non aliquando commodius est et   15
carere convicio?" Fateor. Itaque ego ex hoc loco migrabo.
Experiri et exercere me volui. Quid necesse est diutius tor-
queri, cum tam facile remedium Ulixes sociis etiam adversus Sirenas invenerit? VALE.

LETTER 28

*We are citizens of the world, S. declares, who should not be
psychologically tied to time and place. In this letter, S. develops
a series of nautical metaphors and analogies to emphasize the
point that travel will—in and of itself—bring no peace of mind to
an anxious soul. Whether we travel out of boredom or the perceived need for recreation, we travel with the Self in tow. When, in
section 6, S. imagines the most anxiety-ridden place on earth, he
naturally thinks of the Roman Forum, which leads him to consider
the wise man's attitude toward politics. Ultimately, following the
example of Socrates, S. advocates a form of conscientious non-
participation.*

SENECA LUCILIO SUO SALUTEM:

Hoc tibi soli putas accidisse et admiraris quasi rem   1
novam, quod peregrinatione tam longa et tot locorum varietatibus non discussisti tristitiam gravitatemque mentis?
Animum debes mutare, non caelum. Licet vastum traie-
ceris mare, licet, ut ait Vergilius noster,

terraeque urbesque recedant,

sequentur te quocumque perveneris vitia. Hoc idem quer-   2
enti cuidam Socrates ait: "Quid miraris nihil tibi peregrina-
tiones prodesse, cum te circumferas? Premit te eadem
causa quae expulit." Quid terrarum iuvare novitas potest?
Quid cognitio urbium aut locorum? In inritum cedit ista
iactatio. Quaeris quare te fuga ista non adiuvet? Tecum
fugis. Onus animi deponendum est; non ante tibi ullus
placebit locus. Talem nunc esse habitum tuum cogita,   3
qualem Vergilius noster vatis inducit iam concitatae et
instigatae multumque habentis in se spiritus non sui:

Bacchatur vates, magnum si pectore possit
excussisse deum.

Vadis huc illuc ut excutias insidens pondus quod ipsa iactatione incommodius fit, sicut in navi onera immota minus
urgent, inaequaliter convoluta citius eam partem in quam
incubuere demergunt. Quicquid facis, contra te facis et
motu ipso noces tibi; aegrum enim concutis.

At cum istud exemeris malum, omnis mutatio loci   4
iucunda fiet; in ultimas expellaris terras licebit, in quolibet
barbariae angulo conloceris, hospitalis tibi illa qualiscumque sedes erit. Magis quis veneris quam quo interest, et
ideo nulli loco addicere debemus animum. Cum hac persuasione vivendum est: "Non sum uni angulo natus; patria mea
totus hic mundus est." Quod si liqueret tibi, non admirareris   5

nil adiuvari te regionum varietatibus in quas subinde priorum taedio migras. Prima enim quaeque placuisset, si
omnem tuam crederes. Nunc non peregrinaris, sed erras et
ageris ac locum ex loco mutas, cum illud quod quaeris,
bene vivere, omni loco positum sit. Num quid tam tur-   6
bidum fieri potest quam forum? Ibi quoque licet quiete
vivere, si necesse sit. Sed si liceat disponere se, conspec-
tum quoque et viciniam fori procul fugiam. Nam ut loca
gravia etiam firmissimam valitudinem temptant, ita bonae
quoque menti necdum adhuc perfectae et convalescenti
sunt aliqua parum salubria. Dissentio ab his qui in fluctus   7
medios eunt et tumultuosam probantes vitam cotidie cum
difficultatibus rerum magno animo conluctantur. Sapiens
feret ista, non eliget, et malet in pace esse quam in pugna.
Non multum prodest vitia sua proiecisse, si cum alienis
rixandum est. "Triginta," inquit, "tyranni Socraten circum-   8
steterunt nec potuerunt animum eius infringere." Quid
interest quot domini sint? Servitus una est. Hanc qui contempsit in quantalibet turba dominantium liber est.

Tempus est desinere, sed si prius portorium solvero. "Ini-   9
tium est salutis notitia peccati." Egregie mihi hoc dixisse
videtur Epicurus. Nam qui peccare se nescit corrigi non
vult; deprehendas te oportet antequam emendes. Quidam   10
vitiis gloriantur; tu existimas aliquid de remedio cogitare
qui mala sua virtutum loco numerant? Ideo quantum potes,
te ipse coargue, inquire in te; accusatoris primum partibus
fungere, deinde iudicis, novissime deprecatoris. Aliquando
te offende. VALE.

LETTER 44

In this letter, S. urges Lucilius not to make too much—or too little—
of his station in life. If we trace our family trees back far enough,
he argues, we will arrive at a time before culture in which all men

and women stood on equal footing. Noble birth and wealth are accidents over which we have no control and are themselves no guarantors of happiness. To illustrate this, S. subtly evokes the image of the Wheel of Fortune by which human fortunes rise and fall. The possession of a sound mind trained in philosophy is the only constant in human life—and philosophy, no respector of persons, is open to all. Throughout this letter, S. employs the rich vocabulary and nomenclature that Romans used to mark status in society and gives it an ethical cast.

SENECA LUCILIO SUO SALUTEM:

Iterum tu mihi te pusillum facis et dicis malignius tecum   1
egisse naturam prius, deinde fortunam, cum possis eximere
te vulgo et ad felicitatem hominum maximam emergere. Si
quid est aliud in philosophia boni, hoc est, quod stemma
non inspicit. Omnes, si ad originem primam revocantur, a
dis sunt. Eques Romanus es, et ad hunc ordinem tua te per-   2
duxit industria; at mehercules multis quattuordecim clausa
sunt; non omnes curia admittit; castra quoque quos ad
laborem et periculum recipiant fastidiose legunt. Bona
mens omnibus patet, omnes ad hoc sumus nobiles. Nec
reicit quemquam philosophia nec eligit; omnibus lucet.
Patricius Socrates non fuit. Cleanthes aquam traxit et rig-   3
ando horto locavit manus. Platonem non accepit nobilem
philosophia, sed fecit. Quid est quare desperes his te posse
fieri parem? Omnes hi maiores tui sunt, si te illis geris
dignum; geres autem, si hoc protinus tibi ipse persuaseris,
a nullo te nobilitate superari. Omnibus nobis totidem ante   4
nos sunt; nullius non origo ultra memoriam iacet. Platon ait
neminem regem non ex servis esse oriundum, neminem
servum non ex regibus. Omnia ista longa varietas miscuit
et sursum deorsum fortuna versavit. Quis est generosus?   5
Ad virtutem bene a natura compositus. Hoc unum intuendum est; alioquin si ad vetera revocas, nemo non inde est

ante quod nihil est. A primo mundi ortu usque in hoc tempus perduxit nos ex splendidis sordidisque alternata series. Non facit nobilem atrium plenum fumosis imaginibus. Nemo in nostram gloriam vixit nec quod ante nos fuit nostrum est; animus facit nobilem cui ex quacumque condicione supra fortunam licet surgere.

Puta itaque te non equitem Romanum esse, sed libertinum: potes hoc consequi, ut solus sis liber inter ingenuos. "Quomodo?" inquis. Si mala bonaque non populo auctore distinxeris. Intuendum est non unde veniant, sed quo eant. Si quid est quod vitam beatam potest facere, id bonum est suo iure. Depravari enim in malum non potest. Quid est ergo in quo erratur, cum omnes beatam vitam optent? Quod instrumenta eius pro ipsa habent et illam, dum petunt, fugiunt. Nam cum summa vitae beatae sit solida securitas et eius inconcussa fiducia, sollicitudinis colligunt causas et per insidiosum iter vitae non tantum ferunt sarcinas, sed trahunt; ita longius ab effectu eius quod petunt semper abscedunt et quo plus operae impenderunt, hoc se magis impediunt et feruntur retro. Quod evenit in labyrintho properantibus; ipsa illos velocitas implicat. VALE.

6

7

LETTER 47

This important letter offers two main arguments for the humane treatment of slaves. The first argument—that slaves are persons— is made negatively and consists of a detailed description of the decadent, inhuman lifestyles of Roman masters. We are all slaves, S. argues, in our unthinking addiction to pleasure and power. Only the man who is master of himself is truly free. The other argument is based on expediency: it is in masters' best interest to treat their slaves well. This second point is supported, as in Letter 44, by an appeal to the unpredictable element of chance in determining the course of human lives.

SENECA LUCILIO SUO SALUTEM:

Libenter ex is qui a te veniunt cognovi familiariter te   1
cum servis tuis vivere. Hoc prudentiam tuam, hoc erudi-
tionem decet. "Servi sunt." Immo homines. "Servi sunt."
Immo contubernales. "Servi sunt." Immo humiles amici.
"Servi sunt." Immo conservi, si cogitaveris tantundem in
utrosque licere fortunae.

Itaque rideo istos qui turpe existimant cum servo suo   2
cenare. Quare, nisi quia superbissima consuetudo cenanti
domino stantium servorum turbam circumdedit? Est ille
plus quam capit, et ingenti aviditate onerat distentum ventrem ac desuetum iam ventris officio, ut maiore opera
omnia egerat quam ingessit. At infelicibus servis movere   3
labra ne in hoc quidem, ut loquantur, licet. Virga murmur
omne compescitur, et ne fortuita quidem verberibus
excepta sunt, tussis, sternumenta, singultus. Magno malo
ulla voce interpellatum silentium luitur. Nocte tota ieiuni
mutique perstant.

Sic fit ut isti de domino loquantur quibus coram domino   4
loqui non licet. At illi quibus non tantum coram dominis
sed cum ipsis erat sermo, quorum os non consuebatur,
parati erant pro domino porrigere cervicem, periculum
imminens in caput suum avertere; in conviviis loquebantur,
sed in tormentis tacebant. Deinde eiusdem arrogantiae   5
proverbium iactatur, totidem hostes esse quot servos. Non
habemus illos hostes, sed facimus.

Alia interim crudelia, inhumana praetereo, quod ne
tamquam hominibus quidem, sed tamquam iumentis abu-
timur. Cum ad cenandum discubuimus, alius sputa detergit,
alius reliquias temulentorum subditus colligit. Alius pre-   6
tiosas aves scindit; per pectus et clunes certis ductibus circumferens eruditam manum frusta excutit, infelix qui huic
uni rei vivit, ut altilia decenter secet, nisi quod miserior est
qui hoc voluptatis causa docet quam qui necessitatis discit.

Alius vini minister in muliebrem modum ornatus cum   7
aetate luctatur; non potest effugere pueritiam, retrahitur,
iamque militari habitu glaber retritis pilis aut penitus evulsis tota nocte pervigilat, quam inter ebrietatem domini ac
libidinem dividit et in cubiculo vir, in convivio puer est.
Alius, cui convivarum censura permissa est, perstat infelix   8
et expectat quos adulatio et intemperantia aut gulae aut linguae revocet in crastinum. Adice obsonatores quibus
dominici palati notitia subtilis est, qui sciunt cuius illum rei
sapor excitet, cuius delectet aspectus, cuius novitate nauseabundus erigi possit, quid iam ipsa satietate fastidiat, quid
illo die esuriat. Cum his cenare non sustinet et maiestatis
suae deminutionem putat ad eandem mensam cum servo
suo accedere. Di melius!

Quot ex istis dominos habet! Stare ante limen Callisti   9
dominum suum vidi et eum qui illi impegerat titulum, qui
inter reicula mancipia produxerat, aliis intrantibus excludi.
Rettulit illi gratiam servus ille in primam decuriam coniec-
tus in qua vocem praeco experitur; et ipse illum invicem
apologavit, et ipse non iudicavit domo sua dignum. Dominus Callistum vendidit; sed domino quam multa Callistus!

Vis tu cogitare istum quem servum tuum vocas ex isdem   10
seminibus ortum eodem frui caelo, aeque spirare, aeque
vivere, aeque mori! Tam tu illum videre ingenuum potes
quam ille te servum. Variana clade multos splendidissime
natos, senatorium per militiam auspicantes gradum, fortuna depressit, alium ex illis pastorem, alium custodem
casae fecit. Contemne nunc eius fortunae hominem in
quam transire, dum contemnis, potes.

Nolo in ingentem me locum immittere et de usu servo-   11
rum disputare, in quos superbissimi, crudelissimi, contumeliosissimi sumus. Haec tamen praecepti mei summa est:
sic cum inferiore vivas quemadmodum tecum superiorem
velis vivere. Quotiens in mentem venerit, quantum tibi in

servum liceat, veniat in mentem tantundem in te domino
tuo licere. "At ego," inquis, "nullum habeo dominum."   12
Bona aetas est; forsitan habebis. Nescis qua aetate Hecuba
servire coeperit, qua Croesus, qua Darei mater, qua Platon,
qua Diogenes?

Vive cum servo clementer, comiter quoque, et in ser-   13
monem illum admitte et in consilium et in convictum. Hoc
loco adclamabit mihi tota manus delicatorum: "nihil hac re
humilius, nihil turpius." Hos ego eosdem deprehendam
alienorum servorum osculantes manum. Ne illud quidem   14
videtis, quam omnem invidiam maiores nostri dominis,
omnem contumeliam servis detraxerint? Dominum patrem
familiae appellaverunt, servos, quod etiam in mimis adhuc
durat, familiares. Instituerunt diem festum, non quo solo
cum servis domini vescerentur, sed quo utique; honores illis
in domo gerere, ius dicere permiserunt et domum pusillam
rem publicam esse iudicaverunt.

"Quid ergo? Omnes servos admovebo mensae meae?"   15
Non magis quam omnes liberos. Erras si existimas me
quosdam quasi sordidioris operae reiecturum, ut puta illum
mulionem et illum bubulcum; non ministeriis illos aes-
timabo, sed moribus. Sibi quisque dat mores, ministeria
casus adsignat. Quidam cenent tecum quia digni sunt,
quidam ut sint. Si quid enim in illis ex sordida conversa-
tione servile est, honestiorum convictus excutiet. Non est,   16
mi Lucili, quod amicum tantum in foro et in curia quaeras;
si diligenter adtenderis, et domi invenies. Saepe bona materia cessat sine artifice; tempta et experire. Quemadmodum
stultus est qui equum empturus non ipsum inspicit, sed
stratum eius ac frenos, sic stultissimus est qui hominem aut
ex veste aut ex condicione, quae vestis modo nobis circum-
data est, aestimat.

"Servus est." Sed fortasse liber animo. "Servus est."   17
Hoc illi nocebit? Ostende quis non sit; alius libidini servit,

alius avaritiae, alius ambitioni, omnes timori. Dabo consularem aniculae servientem, dabo ancillulae divitem, ostendam nobilissimos iuvenes mancipia pantomimorum! Nulla servitus turpior est quam voluntaria.

Quare non est quod fastidiosi isti te deterreant, quo minus servis tuis hilarem te praestes et non superbe superiorem; colant potius te quam timeant. Dicet aliquis nunc me   18 vocare ad pilleum servos et dominos de fastigio suo deicere, quod dixi "colant potius dominum quam timeant." "Ita," inquit, "prorsus: colant tamquam clientes, tamquam salutatores?" Hoc qui dixerit obliviscetur id dominis parum non esse quod deo sat est. Qui colitur, et amatur; non potest amor cum timore misceri. Rectissime ergo facere te iudico   19 quod timeri a servis tuis non vis, quod verborum castigatione uteris; verberibus muta admonentur.

Non quicquid nos offendit et laedit. Sed ad rabiem nos cogunt pervenire deliciae, ut quicquid non ex voluntate respondit iram evocet. Regum nobis induimus animos.   20 Nam illi quoque obliti et suarum virium et inbecillitatis alienae sic excandescunt, sic saeviunt, quasi iniuriam acceperint, a cuius rei periculo illos fortunae suae magnitudo tutissimos praestat. Nec hoc ignorant, sed occasionem nocendi captant querendo; acceperunt iniuriam ut facerent.

Diutius te morari nolo; non est enim tibi exhortatione   21 opus. Hoc habent inter cetera boni mores: placent sibi, permanent. Levis est malitia, saepe mutatur, non in melius, sed in aliud. VALE.

LETTER 62

S. offers here a succinct statement of philosophic self-reliance as he has come to understand it through the example of the philosopher Demetrius. The wise man does not avoid the important business of moral and intellectual development by "keeping busy."

Moreover, when demands are made on his time by others, he does not relinquish his primary moral responsibility to himself.

SENECA LUCILIO SUO SALUTEM:
Mentiuntur qui sibi obstare ad studia liberalia turbam   1
negotiorum videri volunt; simulant occupationes et augent et
ipsi se occupant. Vaco, Lucili, vaco et ubicumque sum, ibi
meus sum. Rebus enim me non trado, sed commodo, nec
consector perdendi temporis causas. Et quocumque constiti
loco, ibi cogitationes meas tracto et aliquid in animo salutare
converso. Cum me amicis dedi non tamen mihi abduco, nec   2
cum illis moror quibus me tempus aliquod congregavit aut
causa ex officio nata civili, sed cum optimo quoque sum; ad
illos, in quocumque loco, in quocumque saeculo fuerunt,
animum meum mitto. Demetrium, virorum optimum,   3
mecum circumfero et, relictis conchyliatis, cum illo seminudo loquor, illum admiror. Quidni admirer? Vidi nihil ei
deesse. Contemnere aliquis omnia potest, omnia habere
nemo potest. Brevissima ad divitias per contemptum divitiarum via est. Demetrius autem noster sic vivit, non
tamquam contempserit omnia, sed tamquam aliis habenda
permiserit.VALE.

LETTER 18

Like our Mardi Gras, the Roman festival to the god Saturn, the Saturnalia, was a time when the rules of society were temporarily suspended and its structures inverted. Amid general feasting and heavy drinking, slaves were served at table by their masters, gifts (and clothes) were exchanged, and everyone wore the felt cap of freedom (see note on 47.18). In this letter, S. proposes an inversion of his own—that Lucilius balance this occasion of licence and feasting with fixed times of self-restraint, even fasting. In support of his argument, S. cites the example of the hedonist philosopher

Epicurus. Rehearse for poverty in times of prosperity, S. argues,
so that you will be immune to the weapons of fortune when they
strike.

SENECA LUCILIO SUO SALUTEM.

December est mensis, cum maxime civitas sudat. Ius
luxuriae publicae datum est. Ingenti apparatu sonant
omnia, tamquam quicquam inter Saturnalia intersit et dies
rerum agendarum. Adeo nihil interest ut non videatur mihi
errasse, qui dixit olim mensem Decembrem fuisse, nunc
annum.

Si te hic haberem, libenter tecum conferrem quid existimares esse faciendum: utrum nihil ex cotidiana consuetu-
dine movendum an, ne dissidere videremur cum publicis
moribus, et hilarius cenandum et exuendam togam. Nam
quod fieri nisi in tumultu et tristi tempore civitatis non sole-
bat, voluptatis causa ac festorum dierum vestem mutavimus. Si te bene novi, arbitri partibus functus nec per
omnia nos similes esse pilleatae turbae voluisses nec per
omnia dissimiles; nisi forte his maxime diebus animo
imperandum est, ut tunc voluptatibus solus abstineat, cum
in illas omnis turba procubuit; certissimum enim argumentum firmitatis suae capit, si ad blanda et in luxuriam tra-
hentia nec it nec abducitur. Hoc multo fortius est ebrio ac
vomitante populo siccum ac sobrium esse, illud temperan-
tius, non excerpere se nec insigniri nec misceri omnibus et
eadem, sed non eodem modo, facere. Licet enim sine luxuria agere festum diem.

Ceterum adeo mihi placet temptare animi tui firmitatem
ut ex praecepto magnorum virorum tibi quoque praecip-
iam: interponas aliquot dies quibus contentus minimo ac
vilissimo cibo, dura atque horrida veste dicas tibi: "Hoc est
quod timebatur?" In ipsa securitate animus ad difficilia se
praeparet et contra iniurias fortunae inter beneficia firme-

NON EST QUOD: it isn't necessary

tur. Miles in media pace decurrit, sine ullo hoste vallum iacit et (supervacuo labore) lassatur ut sufficere necessario possit. Quem in ipsa re trepidare nolueris, ante rem exerceas. Hoc secuti sunt qui omnibus mensibus paupertatem imitati prope ad inopiam accesserunt, ne umquam expavescerent quod saepe didicissent.

7

Non est nunc quod existimes me dicere Timoneas cenas et pauperum cellas, et quicquid aliud est per quod luxuria divitiarum taedio ludit; grabatus ille verus sit et sagum et panis durus ac sordidus. Hoc triduo et quatriduo fer, interdum pluribus diebus, ut non lusus sit, sed experimentum; tunc, mihi crede, Lucili, exultabis dupondio satur et intelleges ad securitatem non opus esse fortuna; hoc enim quod necessitati sat est, debet irata.

8

Non est tamen quare tu multum tibi facere videaris. Facies enim quod (multa milia servorum,) (multa milia pauperum faciunt) illo nomine te suspice, quod facies non coactus, quod tam facile erit tibi illud pati semper quam aliquando experiri. (Exerceamur ad palum) et ne imparatos fortuna deprehendat, fiat nobis paupertas familiaris. Securius divites erimus, si scierimus quam non sit grave pauperes esse.

9

Certos habebat dies ille magister voluptatis Epicurus quibus maligne famem extingueret visurus an aliquid deesset ex plena et consummata voluptate, vel quantum deesset, et an dignum quod quis magno labore pensaret. Hoc certe in his epistulis ait, quas scripsit (Charino magistratu) ad Polyaenum. Et quidem gloriatur non toto asse se pasci, Metrodorum, qui nondum tantum profecerit, toto. In hoc tu victu saturitatem putas esse? Et voluptas est. Voluptas autem non illa levis et fugax et subinde reficienda, sed stabilis et certa. Non enim iucunda res est aqua et polenta aut frustum hordeacei panis, sed summa voluptas est posse capere etiam ex his voluptatem et ad id se deduxisse, quod

10

eripere nulla fortunae iniquitas possit. Liberaliora alimenta 11
sunt carceris: sepositos ad capitale supplicium non tam
anguste (qui occisurus est pascit.) Quanta est animi magnitudo ad id sua sponte descendere, quod ne (ad extrema) quidem decretis timendum sit! Hoc est praeoccupare tela
fortunae.

    Incipe ergo, mi Lucili, sequi horum consuetudinem et 12
aliquos dies destina quibus secedas a tuis rebus minimoque
te facias familiarem; incipe cum paupertate habere commercium.

    aude, hospes, contemnere opes et te quoque dignum
finge deo.

13

Nemo alius est deo dignus quam qui opes contempsit.
Quarum possessionem tibi non interdico, sed efficere volo
ut illas intrepide possideas; quod uno consequeris modo, si
te etiam sine illis beate victurum persuaseris tibi, si illas
tamquam exituras semper aspexeris.

14

    Sed iam incipiamus epistulam complicare. "Prius,"
inquis, "redde quod debes." Delegabo te ad Epicurum; ab
illo fiet numeratio: "Immodica ira gignit insaniam." Hoc,
quam verum sit, necesse est scias, cum habueris et servum 15
et inimicum. In omnes personas hic exardescit affectus;
tam ex amore nascitur quam ex odio, non minus inter seria
quam inter lusus et iocos. Nec interest ex quam magna
causa nascatur, sed in qualem perveniat animum. Sic ignis
non refert quam magnus, sed quo incidat. Nam etiam maximum solida non receperunt; rursus arida et corripi facilia
scintillam quoque fovent usque in incendium. Ita est, mi
Lucili, ingentis irae exitus furor est, et ideo ira vitanda est
non moderationis causa, sed sanitatis. VALE.

Selections from De providentia

*This essay begins as a theodicy—a justification of the ways of God
to men—and closes with a meditation on suicide. What binds these
apparently disparate themes together is the description of Cato
the Younger's heroic suicide at Utica, North Africa, in 46 B.C.E.,
which S. cites to illustrate his central point—that the gods especially test with hardship those whom they especially love. The
question S. tries to answer here is "Why do good people seem to
suffer bad things?" His answer, illustrated with analogies and
exempla drawn from medicine, athletics, the military, and Roman
history, is that what most people consider a calamity is really not
so but, rather, an opportunity to make progress in virtue.*

Quaesisti a me, Lucili, quid ita, si providentia mundus   1.1
regeretur, multa bonis viris mala acciderent. Hoc commodius in contextu operis redderetur, cum praeesse universis
providentiam probaremus et interesse nobis deum; sed
quoniam a toto particulam revelli placet et unam contradictionem manente lite integra solvere, faciam rem non difficilem, causam deorum agam.

*[S. launches immediately into a digression, pointing to the
order and regularity one finds in the workings of Nature as
evidence of a superintending Providence (the classic Argument from Design). But considering this too large a topic to
tackle, he returns to answering the original question as to
why bad things happen to good people.]*

27

In gratiam te reducam cum diis adversus optimos opti-   1.5
mis. Neque enim rerum natura patitur ut umquam bona
bonis noceant; inter bonos viros ac deos amicitia est conciliante virtute. Amicitiam dico? Immo etiam necessitudo et similitudo,
quoniam quidem bonus tempore tantum a deo differt, discipulus eius aemulatorque et vera progenies, quam parens
ille magnificus, virtutum non lenis exactor, sicut severi
patres, durius educat. [. . .]

Non vides quanto aliter patres, aliter matres indulgeant?   2.5
Illi excitari iubent liberos ad studia obeunda mature, feriatis quoque diebus non patiuntur esse otiosos, et sudorem
illis et interdum lacrimas excutiunt; at matres fovere in
sinu, continere in umbra volunt, numquam contristari,
numquam flere, numquam laborare. Patrium deus habet   2.6
adversus bonos viros animum et illos fortiter amat et
"Operibus," inquit, "doloribus damnis exagitentur, ut verum
colligant robur." Languent per inertiam saginata nec labore
tantum, sed motu et ipso sui onere deficiunt. Non fert ullum
ictum inlaesa felicitas; at cui adsidua fuit cum incommodis
suis rixa, callum per iniurias duxit nec ulli malo cedit, sed
etiam si cecidit de genu pugnat. Miraris tu, si deus ille   2.7
bonorum amantissimus, qui illos quam optimos esse atque
excellentissimos vult, fortunam illis cum qua exerceantur
adsignat? Ego vero non miror, si aliquando impetum capiunt spectandi magnos viros conluctantis cum aliqua
calamitate. [. . .] Ecce spectaculum dignum ad quod respi-   2.9
ciat intentus operi suo deus, ecce par deo dignum, vir fortis
cum fortuna mala compositus, utique si et provocavit. Non
video, inquam, quid habeat in terris Iuppiter pulchrius, si
eo convertere animum velit, quam ut spectet Catonem
iam partibus non semel fractis stantem nihilo minus inter
ruinas publicas rectum. "Licet," inquit, "omnia in unius   2.10
dicionem concesserint, custodiantur legionibus terrae, clas-

sibus maria, Caesarianus portas miles obsideat, Cato qua exeat habet: una manu latam libertati viam faciet. Ferrum istud, etiam civili bello purum et innoxium, bonas tandem ac nobiles edet operas: libertatem quam patriae non potuit Catoni dabit. Aggredere, anime, diu meditatum opus, eripe te rebus humanis. Iam Petreius et Iuba concucurrerunt iacentque alter alterius manu caesi, fortis et egregia fati conventio, sed quae non deceat magnitudinem nostram: tam turpe est Catoni mortem ab ullo petere quam vitam." Liquet mihi cum magno spectasse gaudio deos, dum ille   2.11 vir, acerrimus sui vindex, alienae saluti consulit et instruit discedentium fugam, dum studia etiam nocte ultima tractat, dum gladium sacro pectori infigit, dum viscera spargit et illam sanctissimam animam indignamque quae ferro contaminaretur manu educit. Inde crediderim fuisse parum   2.12 certum et efficax vulnus: non fuit dis immortalibus satis spectare Catonem semel; retenta ac revocata virtus est ut in difficiliore parte se ostenderet; non enim tam magno animo mors initur quam repetitur. Quidni libenter spectarent alumnum suum tam claro ac memorabili exitu evadentem? Mors illos consecrat quorum exitum et qui timent laudant.

[Drawing analogies with unpleasant medical treatments that are administered in order to make a patient well, S. continues by arguing that the things we typically call misfortunes are really not so but are sent by the gods for our moral health. Examples from Greek and Roman history are then offered to illustrate how Fortune chooses only the toughest, bravest men to afflict with adversity in order to test and refine them.]

Avida est periculi virtus et quo tendat, non quid passura   4.4 sit cogitat, quoniam etiam quod passura est gloriae pars est. Militares viri gloriantur vulneribus, laeti fluentem meliori

casu sanguinem ostentant: idem licet fecerint qui integri
revertuntur ex acie, magis spectatur qui saucius redit. Ipsis,   4.5
inquam, deus consulit quos esse quam honestissimos cupit,
quotiens illis materiam praebet aliquid animose fortiterque
faciendi, ad quam rem opus est aliqua rerum difficultate:
gubernatorem in tempestate, in acie militem intellegas.
Unde possum scire quantum adversus paupertatem tibi
animi sit, si divitiis diffluis? Unde possum scire quantum
adversus ignominiam et infamiam odiumque populare constantiae habeas, si inter plausus senescis, si te inexpugnabilis et inclinatione quadam mentium pronus favor
sequitur? Unde scio quam aequo animo laturus sis orbi-
tatem, si quoscumque sustulisti vides? Audivi te, cum alios
consolareris: tunc conspexissem, si te ipse consolatus
esses, si te ipse dolere vetuisses. Nolite, obsecro vos, ex-   4.6
pavescere ista quae di immortales velut stimulos admovent
animis: calamitas virtutis occasio est. Illos merito quis
dixerit miseros qui nimia felicitate torpescunt, quos velut in
mari lento tranquillitas iners detinet: quidquid illis inci-
derit, novum veniet. Magis urgent saeva inexpertos, grave   4.7
est tenerae cervici iugum; ad suspicionem vulneris tiro
pallescit, audacter veteranus cruorem suum spectat, qui scit
se saepe vicisse post sanguinem. Hos itaque deus quos probat, quos amat, indurat, recognoscit, exercet; eos autem
quibus indulgere videtur, quibus parcere, molles venturis
malis servat. [. . .]

*[S. continues with an admonition to eschew luxurious
habits and behavior that would make one soft, then exhorts
Lucilius to consider it a privilege to be chosen by the gods
for special testing. Just so, he argues, commanders hand-
pick only the fittest soldiers for important missions, and
teachers single out only the most promising students for
special instruction. In the following passage, S. contrasts*

Roman decadence with the remarkable, even philosophic self-sufficiency of the barbarian gentes who live beyond the reach of Rome.]

Omnes considera gentes in quibus Romana pax desinit. 4.14
Germanos dico et quicquid circa Histrum vagarum gentium occursat. Perpetua illos hiems, triste caelum premit, maligne solum sterile sustentat; imbrem culmo aut fronde defendunt, super durata glacie stagna persultant, in alimentum feras captant. Miseri tibi videntur? Nihil miserum est 4.15 quod in naturam consuetudo perduxit; paulatim enim voluptati sunt quae necessitate coeperunt. Nulla illis domicilia nullaeque sedes sunt nisi quas lassitudo in diem posuit; vilis et hic quaerendus manu victus, horrenda iniquitas caeli, intecta corpora; hoc quod tibi calamitas videtur tot gentium vita est!

[S. continues with a discussion of what criteria one should apply in order to judge whether something is good or bad or of no moral consequence at all, and he exhorts Lucilius—largely through the example of the philosopher Demetrius (see Letter 62.3)—to consider nothing his own, but as given to him on loan by Fate and the gods. There follows an allegory of Ovid's cautionary tale of Phaethon (Met. 2.63–81), who is willing, according to S. here, even at great cost to himself (in Phaethon's case, self-destruction), to seek the highest realms of virtue. In the following passage, S. speaks directly to his philosophic readers in persona dei *about how fortunate they are to have risen above unthinking persons in the pursuit of virtue.]*

"'At multa incidunt tristia horrenda, dura toleratu.' Quia 6.6
non poteram vos istis subducere, animos vestros adversus omnia armavi: ferte fortiter. Hoc est quo deum antecedatis:

ille extra patientiam malorum est, vos supra patientiam.
Contemnite paupertatem: nemo tam pauper vivit quam
natus est. Contemnite dolorem: aut solvetur aut solvet.
Contemnite mortem: quae vos aut finit aut transfert. Contemnite fortunam: nullum illi telum quo feriret animum
dedi. Ante omnia cavi ne quid vos teneret invitos; patet exi   6.7
tus. Si pugnare non vultis, licet fugere. Ideo ex omnibus
rebus quas esse vobis necessarias volui nihil feci facilius
quam mori. Prono animam loco posui; trahitur, adtendite
modo et videbitis quam brevis ad libertatem et quam expedita ducat via. Non tam longas in exitu vobis quam intrantibus moras posui; alioqui magnum in vos regnum fortuna
tenuisset, si homo tam tarde moreretur quam nascitur.
Omne tempus, omnis vos locus doceat quam facile sit   6.8
renuntiare naturae et munus illi suum impingere; inter ipsa
altaria et sollemnes sacrificantium ritus, dum optatur vita,
mortem condiscite. Corpora opima taurorum exiguo concidunt vulnere et magnarum virium animalia humanae
manus ictus impellit; tenui ferro commissura cervicis
abrumpitur, et cum articulus ille qui caput collumque committit incisus est, tanta illa moles corruit. Non in alto latet   6.9
spiritus nec utique ferro eruendus est; non sunt vulnere
penitus impresso scrutanda praecordia: in proximo mors
est. Non certum ad hos ictus destinavi locum: quacumque
vis pervium est. Ipsum illud quod vocatur mori, quo anima
discedit a corpore, brevius est quam ut sentiri tanta velocitas possit: sive fauces nodus elisit, sive spiramentum aqua
praeclusit, sive in caput lapsos subiacentis soli duritia comminuit, sive haustus ignis cursum animae remeantis interscidit. Quidquid est, properat. Ecquid erubescitis? Quod
tam cito fit timetis diu!"

Selections from De vita beata

What is "the good life"? How can one measure one's success in living it? These are the central topics of this intriguing, highly self-conscious essay. S. begins by establishing that popular opinion on any question cannot be trusted, much less followed. This premise foists an "us-and-them" dichotomy onto the discussion (that is, philosophers versus the general populace), which affects the tone of the rest of the essay. In fact, the bulk of this piece consists of point-by-point answers to charges of hypocrisy. Ultimately S. concludes that, although we should strive for moral perfection in all things, we should also be content, as he says, "not to be on par with the best, but to be better than the bad" (non ut optimis par sim, sed ut malis melior). *Moral progress is gradual: "I am not yet a wise man," S. confides in 17.3. "It is enough for me to eliminate a few of my vices every day"* (hoc mihi satis est, cotidie aliquid ex vitiis meis demere).

Vivere, Gallio frater, omnes beate volunt, sed ad pervidendum quid sit quod beatam vitam efficiat caligant; adeoque non est facile consequi beatam vitam ut eo quisque ab ea longius recedat quo ad illam concitatius fertur, si via lapsus est; quae ubi in contrarium ducit, ipsa velocitas maioris intervalli causa fit. 1.1

Proponendum est itaque primum quid sit quod adpetamus; tunc circumspiciendum qua contendere illo celerrime possimus, intellecturi in ipso itinere, si modo rectum erit, quantum cotidie profligetur quantoque propius ab eo simus ad quod nos cupiditas naturalis impellit. Quam diu quidem passim vagamur non ducem secuti sed fremitum et clamorem 1.2

dissonum in diversa vocantium, conteretur vita inter
errores brevis, etiam si dies noctesque bonae menti labore-
mus. Decernatur itaque et quo tendamus et qua, non sine
perito aliquo, cui explorata sint ea in quae procedimus,
quoniam quidem non eadem hic quae in ceteris peregrinationibus condicio est: in illis comprensus aliquis limes et
interrogati incolae non patiuntur errare, at hic tritissima
quaeque via et celeberrima maxime decipit. Nihil ergo   1.3
magis praestandum est quam ne pecorum ritu sequamur
antecedentium gregem, pergentes non quo eundum est sed
quo itur. Atqui nulla res nos maioribus malis implicat quam
quod ad rumorem componimur, optima rati ea quae magno
adsensu recepta sunt, quodque exempla nobis multa sunt
nec ad rationem sed ad similitudinem vivimus. Inde ista   1.4
tanta coacervatio aliorum super alios ruentium. Quod in
strage hominum magna evenit, cum ipse se populus premit—nemo ita cadit ut non et alium in se adtrahat, pri-
mique exitio sequentibus sunt—hoc in omni vita accidere
videas licet. Nemo sibi tantummodo errat, sed alieni erroris
et causa et auctor est; nocet enim applicari antecedentibus
et, dum unusquisque mavult credere quam iudicare, numquam de vita iudicatur, semper creditur, versatque nos et
praecipitat traditus per manus error. Alienis perimus exemplis: sanabimur, si separemur modo a coetu. Nunc vero stat 1.5
contra rationem defensor mali sui populus. Itaque id evenit
quod in comitiis, in quibus eos factos esse praetores idem
qui fecere mirantur, cum se mobilis favor circumegit:
eadem probamus, eadem reprehendimus; hic exitus est
omnis iudicii in quo secundum plures datur.

   Cum de beata vita agetur, non est quod mihi illud disces- 2.1
sionum more respondeas: "haec pars maior esse videtur."
Ideo enim peior est. Non tam bene cum rebus humanis
agitur ut meliora pluribus placeant: argumentum pessimi
turba est.

[S. continues with a discussion of whom he means by "the mob"—not just low-born, poorly educated persons, but also unreflective careerist ministers at court. External trappings, S. argues, are unimportant. He calls attention rather to the quality of one's soul as the basis for judging character and urges us to pursue only those things that contribute to its improvement, for only these foster a truly happy life. We must, then, turn inward, S. argues, and tap our spiritual and intellectual resources if we are to live beyond fear, beyond desire, and rise above the unpredictable, external circumstances of Fortune.]

Quid, quod tam bonis quam malis voluptas inest nec   8.1
minus turpes dedecus suum quam honestos egregia delectant? Ideoque praeceperunt veteres optimam sequi vitam, non iucundissimam, ut rectae ac bonae voluntatis non dux sed comes sit voluptas. Natura enim duce utendum est; hanc ratio observat, hanc consulit. Idem est ergo beate   8.2
vivere et secundum naturam. Hoc quid sit iam aperiam: si corporis dotes et apta naturae conservarimus diligenter et impavide tamquam in diem data et fugacia, si non subierimus eorum servitutem nec nos aliena possederint, si corpori grata et adventicia eo nobis loco fuerint quo sunt in castris auxilia et armaturae leves—serviant ista, non imperent—ita demum utilia sunt menti. Incorruptus vir sit   8.3
externis et insuperabilis miratorque tantum sui,

 . . . fidens animo atque in utrumque paratus,

artifex vitae; fiducia eius non sine scientia sit, scientia non sine constantia; maneant illi semel placita nec ulla in decretis eius litura sit. Intellegitur, etiam si non adiecero, compositum ordinatumque fore talem virum et in iis quae aget cum comitate magnificum. Externa ratio quaerat sen-   8.4
sibus irritata et capiens inde principia—nec enim habet

aliud, unde conetur aut unde ad verum impetum capiat—,
at in se revertatur. Nam mundus quoque cuncta com-
plectens rectorque universi deus in exteriora quidem tendit,
sed tamen introsum undique in se redit. Idem nostra mens
faciat: cum secuta sensus suos per illos se ad externa por-
rexerit, et illorum et sui potens sit. Hoc modo una efficietur   8.5
vis ac potestas concors sibi et ratio illa certa nascetur,
non dissidens nec haesitans in opinionibus comprension-
ibusque nec in persuasione, quae cum se disposuit et partibus suis consensit et, ut ita dicam, concinuit, summum
bonum tetigit. Nihil enim pravi, nihil lubrici superest, nihil   8.6
in quo arietet aut labet; omnia faciet ex imperio suo
nihilque inopinatum accidet, sed quidquid agetur in bonum
exibit facile et parate et sine tergiversatione agentis; nam
pigritia et haesitatio pugnam et inconstantiam ostendit.
Quare audaciter licet profitearis summum bonum esse
animi concordiam; virtutes enim ibi esse debebunt ubi consensus atque unitas erit: dissident vitia.

*[S. continues by answering a series of imagined arguments
(which he identifies as false or misapplied Epicureanism)
that there is an intrinsic and necessary link between pleasure and the highest good, virtue. S. counters with the ortho-
dox Stoic position that, while virtue may bring pleasure, it
is a good to be pursued in and of itself, regardless of its
consequences, and it alone is sufficient for happiness.]*

Si quis itaque ex istis qui philosophiam conlatrant quod   17.1
solent dixerit: "Quare ergo tu fortius loqueris quam vivis?
Quare et superiori verba summittis et pecuniam necessarium tibi instrumentum existimas et damno moveris et
lacrimas audita coniugis aut amici morte demittis et respi-
cis famam et malignis sermonibus tangeris? Quare cultius   17.2
rus tibi est quam naturalis usus desiderat? Cur non ad praescriptum tuum cenas? Cur tibi nitidior supellex est? Cur

apud te vinum aetate tua vetustius bibitur? Cur aurum disponitur? Cur arbores nihil praeter umbram daturae conseruntur? Quare uxor tua locupletis domus censum auribus gerit? Quare paedagogium pretiosa veste succingitur? Quare ars est apud te ministrare nec temere et ut libet conlocatur argentum sed perite struitur et est aliquis scindendi obsonii magister?" Adice si vis: "Cur trans mare possides? Cur plura quam nosti? Cur turpiter aut tam neglegens es ut non noveris pauculos servos aut tam luxuriosus ut plures habeas quam quorum notitiae memoria sufficiat?" Adiu- 17.3
vabo postmodo convicia et plura mihi quam putas obiciam, nunc hoc respondeo tibi: non sum sapiens et, ut malivolentiam tuam pascam, nec ero. Exige itaque a me, non ut optimis par sim, sed ut malis melior: hoc mihi satis est, cotidie aliquid ex vitiis meis demere et errores meos obiurgare. Non perveni ad sanitatem, ne perveniam quidem; deleni- 17.4
menta magis quam remedia podagrae meae compono, contentus si rarius accedit et si minus verminatur; vestris quidem pedibus comparatus, debiles, cursor sum. Haec non pro me loquor—ego enim in alto vitiorum omnium sum— sed pro illo cui aliquid acti est.

[S. answers further accusations in the same vein, that philosophers do not practice what they preach. His arguments against these accusations take essentially these two forms: (1) one should not complain about the speck in one's neighbor's eye when there's a log in one's own (cf. S.'s reworking of this proverbial idea in 27.4, below), and (2) no one should fault a person for not perfectly meeting high, uncompromising standards; better that than to lower one's moral standards to match one's actual performance.]

"Quare ille philosophiae studiosus est et tam dives vitam 21.1
agit? Quare opes contemnendas dicit et habet, vitam contemnendam putat et tamen vivit, valetudinem contemnendam, et

tamen illam diligentissime tuetur atque optimam mavult? Et
exilium vanum nomen putat et ait 'quid enim est mali
mutare regiones?' et tamen, si licet, senescit in patria?
Et inter longius tempus et brevius nihil interesse iudicat,
tamen, si nihil prohibet, extendit aetatem et in multa senec-
tute placidus viret?' Ait ista debere contemni, non ne   21.2
habeat, sed ne sollicitus habeat; non abigit illa a se, sed abeuntia securus prosequitur. Divitias quidem ubi tutius fortuna
deponet quam ibi, unde sine querella reddentis receptura
est? M. Cato cum laudaret Curium et Coruncanium et illud   21.3
saeculum in quo censorium crimen erat paucae argenti
lamellae possidebat ipse quadragies sestertium, minus sine
dubio quam Crassus, plus quam censorius Cato. Maiore
spatio, si compararentur, proavum vicerat quam a Crasso
vinceretur, et, si maiores illi obvenissent opes, non sprevisset. Nec enim se sapiens indignum ullis muneribus fortuitis 21.4
putat. Non amat divitias sed mavult; non in animum illas
sed in domum recipit, nec respuit possessas, sed continet, et
maiorem virtuti suae materiam subministrari vult.

Quid autem dubii est quin haec maior materia sapienti   22.1
viro sit animum explicandi suum in divitiis quam in paupertate, cum in hac unum genus virtutis sit non inclinari
nec deprimi, in divitiis et temperantia et liberalitas et diligentia et dispositio et magnificentia campum habeat paten-
tem? Non contemnet se sapiens, etiam si fuerit minimae   22.2
staturae, esse tamen se procerum volet. Et exilis corpore
aut amisso oculo valebit, malet tamen sibi esse corporis
robur, et hoc ita ut sciat esse aliud in se valentius. Malam
valetudinem tolerabit, bonam optabit. Quaedam enim,   22.3
etiam si in summam rei parva sunt et subduci sine ruina
principalis boni possunt, adiciunt tamen aliquid ad perpet-
uam laetitiam et ex virtute nascentem. Sic illum adficiunt
divitiae et exhilarant ut navigantem secundus et ferens ventus, ut dies bonus et in bruma ac frigore apricus locus. Quis 22.4

porro sapientium—nostrorum dico, quibus unum est bonum virtus—negat etiam haec quae indifferentia vocamus habere aliquid in se pretii et alia aliis esse potiora? Quibusdam ex iis tribuitur aliquid honoris, quibusdam multum; ne erres itaque, inter potiora divitiae sunt. "Quid ergo," inquis, "me derides, cum eundem apud te locum habeant quem apud me?" Vis scire quam non eundem habeant locum? Mihi divitiae si effluxerint, nihil auferent nisi semet ipsas, tu stupebis et videberis tibi sine te relictus, si illae a te recesserint; apud me divitiae aliquem locum habent, apud te summum; ad postremum divitiae meae sunt, tu divitiarum es.

[S. elaborates here on some of the moral quandries involved in the acquiring and giving of money, then proceeds to deny that wealth is a good in and of itself, asserting, rather, that it is something the wise man or woman should regard with indifference.]

"Quid ergo inter me stultum et te sapientem interest, si   26.1
uterque habere volumus?" Plurimum: divitiae enim apud sapientem virum in servitute sunt, apud stultum in imperio; sapiens divitiis nihil permittit, vobis divitiae omnia; vos, tamquam aliquis vobis aeternam possessionem earum promiserit, adsuescitis illis et cohaeretis, sapiens tunc maxime paupertatem meditatur cum in mediis divitiis constitit. Numquam imperator ita paci credit ut non se prae-   26.2
paret bello quod, etiam si non geritur, indictum est: vos domus formosa, tamquam nec ardere nec ruere possit, insolentes, vos opes, tamquam periculum omne transcenderint maioresque sint vobis quam quibus consumendis satis virium habeat fortuna, obstupefaciunt. Otiosi divitiis luditis   26.3
nec providetis illarum periculum, sicut barbari plerumque inclusi et ignari machinarum segnes laborem obsidentium

spectant nec quo illa pertineant quae ex longinquo struun-
tur intellegunt. Idem vobis evenit: marcetis in vestris rebus
nec cogitatis quot casus undique immineant iam iamque
pretiosa spolia laturi. Sapientis quisquis abstulerit divitias,
omnia illi sua relinquet; vivit enim praesentibus laetus,
futuri securus.

*[S. now imagines what a Socrates would say in defense of
such charges of hypocrisy. A true philosopher, S. imagines
him to say, is not concerned with what other people think
about him but, rather, stays the course, true to the rational
pursuit of his or her convictions. Even the behavior of
Jupiter, S. argues, is slandered by poets. Why should it be
any different for the philosopher, who, like a god, rises
above the petty concerns of the world? If you have nothing
good to say, S. concludes, say nothing at all.]*

Vobis autem vacat aliena scrutari mala et sententias ferre   27.4
de quoquam? "Quare hic philosophus laxius habitat? Quare
hic lautius cenat?" Papulas observatis alienas, obsiti pluri-
mis ulceribus. Hoc tale est, quale si quis pucherrimorum
corporum naevos aut verrucas derideat, quem foeda scabies
depascitur.

Notes and Commentary

LETTER 60

SENECA . . . SALUTEM : Supply the verb *dicit*. This third-person greeting is a standard, formulaic salutation in Roman letters (the grammatical core of which is often abbreviated as *S. D.*).

LUCILIO SUO : All the letters collected in this volume are addressed to S.'s friend and philosophic protégé Lucilius, about whom we know rather little; for further details, see the notes on *provincia*, Letter 43.3, and *Eques Romanus*, Letter 44.2.

1 **Queror, litigo, irascor :** a good example of *asyndeton* (words juxtaposed without connectives; Lanham 25). *Litigo* suggests that the verbs, taken together, form something of a metaphor drawn from the law courts. S. is lightheartedly "pressing his case" against Lucilius and is upset at his friend's ready capitulation to the expectations and desires of others.

quod : not the conjunction "because," but, as often, the relative pronoun with antecedent suppressed (A&G 307c).

tua agrees grammatically with the closest noun, *nutrix*, but is to be understood with all three (A&G 287.1).

nutrix . . . paedagogus : the use of wet-nurses (usually household slaves) was common in upper-class Roman families; a *paedagogus* was a slave who escorted Roman children to and from school and who was in charge of them at home.

mali : partitive genitive with *quantum* (A&G 346a.3); lit. "how much *of* evil/trouble," translated idiomatically as "how much evil/trouble." S. does not say specifically why or how other people's wishes are harmful to us, but one may infer from what follows that it is because, if we are controlled by them, they make us prone to acquisitiveness (cf. *ambitio* below).

optaverint : perfect subjunctive in an indirect question, primary sequence of tenses (A&G 575).

nobis . . . nostrorum : S. uses the pronoun and adjective forms of the same word to contrast self-interest (*nobis*) with the interests foisted upon us by others (*nostrorum*). The repetition adds emphasis and

43

irony. The adjective *nostrorum*, "of our friends and family" (L&S *noster*, II.A), is used substantively (A&G 288).

eo . . . felicius : "Indeed, the more favorably [their prayers] have turned out, the more harmful they are." A similar pessimism stands behind our saying "Beware of what you ask for. You just might get it." S. does not so much *explain* this paradoxical statement as *illustrate* it by what follows: Human prayers that do not fall in line with the workings of Nature are ill-conceived and harmful to the soul. Animals do not pray for success—they know their place in the scheme of things and are content with it. On the Stoic concept of Nature, see under *natura*, §3 below.

eo . . . quo : "the . . . the." Two ablatives (ablatives of degree of difference)—one a demonstrative pronoun, the other a relative—are used correlatively with clauses that contain adjectives or adverbs in the comparative degree, here *inimiciora* and *felicius* (see A&G 414a).

cessēre = *cesserunt* < *cedo*, -ere, "to turn out/succeed." The *-ēre* ending for the third-person plural perfect indicative (a poeticism) is frequent in S. This form looks deceptively like an infinitive, but it can be readily distinguished from one by the verb stem. There is no second conjugation verb *cesseo -ēre*, or third conjugation *cesso, -ere* from which a form like *cessere* (without the macron) could come (cf. *amavere* vs. *amare*).

Iam non : *iam* + a negative means "no longer" (A&G 322).

a prima pueritia : When it refers to time, *primus* means not "first," but "the beginning of" (L&S *primus*, II.A).

execrationes : S. plays with the sense of this word, which can mean both "curses" directed against someone else and "fervent prayers" offered up on one's own or another's behalf. In the latter, more positive sense, a curse was invoked upon the praying person's head if he did not comply with the terms of the agreement offered to the deity in prayer. S. implies that prayers are in fact curses when they are not "according to Nature."

exaudiant : hortatory subjunctive (A&G 439)—a frequent construction in S. given the hortatory nature of the Letters.

di = *dei* < *deus*.

nostram . . . pro nobis : cf. *inimica nobis . . . nostrorum* above.

gratuitam : "free of charge," or "without interest," "spontaneous." The adjective is used predicatively and functions almost as an adverb governed by the verbal force latent in the noun *vocem* (see A&G 282b, 290): "let the gods hear our voice [which is offered up] freely."

2   **poscemus** : *posco* takes a double accusative (A&G 396).

ita quasi . . . : Sometimes called a conditional clause of comparison (A&G 524), this construction lies partway between a result clause (with *quasi* substituted for *ut*) and a contrary-to-fact condition (in which case the *quasi* clause represents the protasis, and the apodosis is implied in the *ita* clause).

ipsi . . . nos is emphatic. The problem with us, S. insists, is lack of self-sufficiency.

Quamdiu . . . Quamdiu . . . Quamdiu : The repetition of the same word or phrase at the beginning of successive clauses for rhetorical effect is called *anaphora* (Lanham 11).

sationibus : Rome depended on grain imported from Egypt.

campos : a *campus* is any flat, open expanse—in particular, a civic space reserved for public use (for example, the Campus Martius at Rome). But certainly, with *sationibus*, there is also a play on the word's primary denotation, thus "fields."

unius . . . multa . . . non ex uno : note the emphatic contrast between "one" and "many" in this and the following sentence.

iugerum : genitive, a syncopated/contracted form of *iuger[or]um*.

una silva elephantis pluribus : A clever sentence in which the adjectives (A) and nouns (B) are arranged *chiastically,* thus $A^1B^1B^2A^2$ (Lanham 33), the effect of which is to juxtapose the elephants and their habitat, while separating (and thus contrasting) "one" and "many."

3   **homo et terra et mari pascitur** : *pasco(r)* is used primarily of animals (cf. *taurus . . . pascuo* above), but it is often extended metaphorically to humans. Here the verb establishes a connection between human and animal, only to throw the difference between them into high relief: Where one forest is plenty for many elephants, the human animal requires many ships and estates to furnish a single meal. *Et terra et mari,* "on *both* land *and* sea," neatly sums up the territory covered in the preceding rhetorical questions.

Quid ergo? such inferential questions—often rhetorical expressions of shock or surprise at something just described—are common in S. Supply a verb appropriate to the context: "What, then [are we to say/do]?" or "What, then [are we to make of this situation]?"

Tam . . . vinceremus : *tam . . . ut* form a result clause (A&G 537); *cum* here introduces a concessive clause (A&G 549).

natura : An important word and concept for Stoicism, *natura* (Greek *physis*) is a shorthand term for the divine principle that animates the Stoic universe: "[Nature] sanctions a norm for particular things—the nature of plants, animals and men—by reference to which they can be said to attain or not to attain their individual ends. . . . The value of anything else in the world depends upon its relationship to Nature. Accordance with Nature denotes positive value and contrariness to Nature the opposite" (Long pp. 179–80).

modica : "small" or "of moderate size" (as compared with elephants and bulls), antithetical to *insatiabilem*.

vastissimorum edacissimorumque animalium aviditatem : The polysyllabic mouthful of a-, s-, and m-sounds in these plural superlatives makes good use of *alliteration, assonance,* and *homoioteleuton* (Lanham 7, 24, 83–85). Sound and sense combine to suggest the extent and degree of human rapacity.

Minime : "not in the least"; with this response (*minime* is the superlative adverb of *parvus*) and with the word *quantulum* (a diminutive of *quantus*) in the next sentence, S. indulges in another playful antithesis—that of big and small (continued with *parvo* and *magno* below).

naturae : here perhaps *our* nature, or "our place in the scheme of Nature," since for the Stoics it is all of a piece.

Parvo . . . dimittitur : "[Our nature] is kept at bay [like a creditor] with a small amount," that is, it does not take much to meet our needs. For the sense of *dimitto* here see L&S II.A.1. For the thought and idiom with *parvo*, cf. Horace *Carmina* 2.16.13–16: *vivitur parvo bene, cui paternum / splendet in mensa tenui salinum / nec levis somnos timor aut cupido / sordidus aufert* ("a man lives well on but a little if his family's / food stores shine like jewels at a humble meal / and if no fear or rotten greed steals his pleasant sleep away").

nobis . . . magno constat : "costs us a lot"; *magno* is an ablative of price (A&G 416); for the idiom, see L&S *consto*, II.B.6a.

ambitio : lit. "a going around [about town]," hence "showiness," "ostentation," or a desire to be noticed.

4   **ut ait Sallustius :** The historian Sallust (Gaius Sallustius Crispus) was a younger contemporary and political supporter of Julius Caesar. The quotation here is taken from the philosophical introduction to his monograph *Bellum Catilinae*, an account of the attempted coup at Rome by a disenfranchised senator in 63 B.C.E. The image of the grazing herd harks back to Plato (*Republic* 586a–b). Nietzsche uses it with great effect in the first section of his essay *On the Advantage and Disadvantage of History for Life*. The passage from Sallust is worth quoting here more fully since it suggests Seneca's train of thought: *omnes homines, qui sese student praestare* ceteris animalibus, *summa ope niti decet ne vitam silentio transeant veluti pecora, quae* natura *prona atque ventri oboedientia finxit. Sed nostra omnis vis in animo et corpore sita est. Animi imperio, corporis servitio magis* utimur (*BC* 1.1–2; "Everyone who is eager to stand out from the other animals ought to strive with all the means at his disposal to avoid passing his life in silence like the cattle whom nature has fixed face to the ground to serve their stomachs. The whole of *our* strength, by contrast, is situated in the mind and body. We use our minds more for governing, our bodies for service"). For *natura* cf. §3 above; for *ceteris animalibus, utimur,* and the moral obligation to be *utilis* to oneself and society, see below.

numeremus : hortatory subjunctive.

animalium . . . ne animalium quidem : a pun on the word *animal*. In the first instance it is used as a noun meaning properly "animal"; in the second it is a substantive adjective meaning "the living" (*animal, animalis < anima, -ae*) in contrast with *mortuorum*. Such, S. suggests, is the descent of man. For *ne . . . quidem* ("not . . . even"), see A&G 322f.

Vivit is qui . . . se utitur : a further contrast between "one" (the self) and "many" (others), with a play upon *utor*. This seems to be the moral of the letter: "Make use of yourself for the benefit of society. Only then are you truly human and truly alive." As often in S., the development of the thought is less linear and deductive than it is a free association of related ideas. Note, however, that the progression of thought moves us from looking outward ("Do not be bound by the desires/prayers of others"), to looking inward ("Rather, live a life of

moderation and self-sufficiency in accordance with Nature"), to looking outward again ("so that you can make use of yourself for the benefit of others").

Roman Stoics, following principles laid down by their founders
Zeno, Cleanthes, and Chrysippus, tended to see the pursuit of philosophy as compatible with political participation and social activism (cf.
Sandbach pp. 140–48), as S. implies is the case in his exhortation
here, though he expresses mixed feelings about this doctrine elsewhere (see heading to Letter 28 and the note on *Servitus una est*, 28.8).

multis . . . usui est : "exists *as* a help/benefit for many." *Usui* is dative
singular of the fourth declension noun *usus*, used here with *multis* (a
dative of advantage) and the verb "to be" to express purpose. On this
construction, often called a double dative, see A&G 376 and 382.1.

conditivo : a place where something is stashed away; here a "tomb."

licet : lit. "it is permitted," but *licet* + subjunctive (here *inscribas*) is
very idiomatic and has a wide range of connotations. It is often best
translated with "perhaps" or "although" (A&G 527b).

nomen : here, following S.'s burial metaphor, "epitaph."

MORTEM SUAM ANTECESSERUNT : This sentence stands in
apposition to *nomen* and represents the content of the imagined
inscription (hence my use of capital letters). For a picture of a Roman
house tomb of the type envisioned here, see Beard, North, and Price,
Religions of Rome (Cambridge: Cambridge University Press, 1998)
2:104.

LETTER 5

1   **Quod :** A clause that serves as the object of a verb is called a substantive (or noun) clause. For a classification of such clauses see A&G
560–90. *Quod* is frequently used with the indicative mood to form
such a clause, which is often the object of emotive verbs (A&G 572),
here *probo* and *gaudeo*. Substantive clauses with *quod* are usually best
translated with the phrase "[as to] the fact that" or sometimes "with a
view to" + an English gerund.

omnibus omissis : ablative absolute (A&G 419–20).

hoc unum . . . ut : the demonstrative *hoc*, the direct object of *agis*,
anticipates a substantive clause of result (introduced by *ut*), which

stands in apposition to it (A&G 570). This anticipatory use of the demonstrative is very common in inflected languages and is known generally as *prolepsis* (anticipation); see A&G 297e.

meliorem : agreeing of course with *te*; a good, straightforward example of an adjective used predicatively with a factitive verb (A&G 273 n.1; 285.2).

nec : "and not" is technically correct and often a more helpful translation of *nec* than "nor," which is archaic and often misleading.

ut perseveres : a substantive clause of purpose, also called indirect command (A&G 563).

illud . . . ne : *prolepsis,* the same construction as in *hoc . . . ut* above, except that it is negative (cf. also *id agamus, ut* and *illud quoque efficimus, ut* §3 below). The *ne* negates *facias*, not *more*.

aliqua is neuter accusative plural. For the form (this instead of the expected *aliquae*), see A&G 151e.

quae . . . sint is a relative clause of purpose, where *quae = ut ea* (A&G 537.2).

2   **et . . . et . . . et . . . et . . . et** : The exaggerated use of connectives for rhetorical effect—the opposite of *asyndeton* (cf. note on *queror*, Letter 60.1)—is called *polysyndeton* (Lanham 117).

humi is locative (A&G 427a).

ambitionem : see note on *ambitio*, Letter 60.3.

perversa via is ablative, either of manner = "paradoxically" (so Summers), or, given the personification involved in *via . . . sequitur*, with a more spatial sense = "on its crooked course." Be that as it may, it is clearly paradoxical to suggest that the neglect of one's appearance is a form of *ambitio*.

sequitur : lit. "follows," "follows from," or here perhaps "attends."

evita is imperative and is the main verb in this sentence.

invidiosum : not so much "full of envy" as "full of/prone to hostility," meaning that it causes hostility in others.

quid . . . excerpere? "What [hostility would arise]" or "What [would happen] if . . ."; *consuetudini* is a dative of separation (A&G 381).

Intus . . . frons : note the antithesis.

sint . . . conveniat, etc. : hortatory subjunctives.

3   **non splendeat . . . non habeamus . . . non putemus** : apparently also hortatory, though *non* here is idiosyncratic, *ne* being standard.

ne ... quidem : here "not . . . either" (A&G 322f).

caelatura : "an engraved decoration."

descenderit : "has been inlaid" (perfect subjunctive in a relative clause of characteristic; A&G 535).

indicium is predicate noun to *caruisse* in indirect statement with *esse* omitted. The force of the perfect tense in *caruisse* is probably "gnomic" (A&G 475), to indicate a general truth or a general state achieved in the past, the results of which persist into the present.

id . . . ut : prolepsis.

fugamus < *fugo, -are,* not *fugio, -ere.*

nostri : partitive genitive with *nihil.*

ne imitanda sint omnia : *imitanda* is a gerundive used to express necessity (A&G 500) in a substantive clause after a verb of fearing, in which case *ne* represents what *is* feared, not what is not (A&G 564).

4   **Hoc :** prolepsis; *sensum communem* (not "common sense," but "sentiments shared by all people") etc. stands in apposition.

A qua : Latin sentences that begin with a relative word—called connecting *qui* clauses—often continue the thought of the previous sentence (cf. A&G 308f). In such cases, the relative represents a connective word or conjunction like *et* or *ut* plus a demonstrative pronoun, thus here *a qua* [*professione*] = *et ab ea* (cf. note on *quae . . . sint,* §1 above).

ne . . . sint : substantive clause of purpose (A&G 563).

ista : the demonstrative *iste* points to the second person and means "that which is [somehow] of concern to you," or "that of which you speak" (A&G 297c).

secundum naturam vivere : see note on *natura,* Letter 60.3. For a Stoic, "living according to Nature" was the modus operandi and ultimate goal of a philosophic life, since through the principle of *natura/physis* Stoic ethics were bound closely to Stoic cosmology. Sandbach summarizes the connection as follows: "Literally [*physis*] means 'growth', then 'the way a thing grows', and by extension 'the way a thing acts and behaves'. By a further extension it came to mean 'the force that causes a thing to act and behave as it does'. For the Stoics this force was something material, a constituent of the body it controls; it was found both in plants and in animals. Each individual animal has its own *physis* or way of growing and behaving, and by this is to be understood the way normal for members of its species. . . . When [a human being] acquires reason, which happens spontaneously by the age of fourteen, he begins to modify . . . primitive impulses; since reason is a gift of nature, this modification is also natural. . . . It is this new rational constitution and all that goes with it that he now feels to belong to him. He now knows his affinity to morality and to wisdom" (Sandbach, pp. 31–34).

torquere . . . odisse . . . adpetere . . . uti : the infinitives all stand in apposition to *hoc* in prolepsis. This list complements the polysyndetic list in §2 above.

faciles : "requiring no special effort."

5   **desiderare delicatas res :** subject of *est.*

luxuriae . . . dementiae : When an infinitive is used as a noun, it is often limited by a genitive of possession in the predicate (A&G 343c); after *dementiae* (parallel to *luxuriae*) supply *est.*

magno : ablative of price (as in Letter 60.3), taken with *parabiles.*

Hic . . . modus . . . temperetur, etc. : more prolepsis.

non incompta : an instance of *litotes*, "an understatement that intensifies" (Lanham 95–96).

bonos mores et publicos : note how, for S., good mores and public mores are not necessarily equivalent.

agnoscant : "understand" or "recognize" the truth or correctness of the philosopher's way of life (so Summers).

6   **"Quid ergo?" etc. :** S. imagines Lucilius' objections. The technique of raising questions only to answer them is known as *hypophora* (Lanham 87) or *ratiocination* (Lanham 129).

sciat qui inspexerit : *sciat* is a hortatory subjunctive (cf. miretur below); *inspexerit* is probably a perfect subjunctive in a relative clause of characteristic (A&G 535) with the antecedent suppressed (same construction as *qui intraverit . . . miretur* below).

Magnus . . . nec minor : These two sentences say fundamentally the same thing in two different ways, a feature of S.'s style referred to as *copia*, "abundance" (Lanham 42), that came in for criticism by the rhetorician Quintilian and others. Its purpose is primarily rhetorical (note how the sentences are structurally identical except for the exchange of *nec minor* for *magnus* and the position of *argento* and *fictilibus*).

Infirmi animi : A noun and adjective in the genitive case often serve as the predicate of nominal sentence (a genitive of quality; A&G 345); for the construction, cf. note on *luxuriae* §5 above. This and the previous two sentences advocate indifference to the trappings of wealth, not an outright abnegation of them, a fact that perhaps explains S.'s own vast wealth and his ready surrender of it to Nero. On the Stoic concept of moral "indifferents," see note on *haec quae indifferentia vocamus*, in De vita beata, 22.4.

pati . . . divitias is an oxymoron (Lanham 106).

7   **Sed** : "Be that as it may." The transition to S.'s "thought for the day," a quotation from Hecato (see below), is somewhat abrupt and elliptical grammatically. The progression of thought, however, is as follows: the discussion of wealth at the end of §6 brings hope to mind (cf. *sperare*, *spem* below), the lack of wealth implies fear (cf. *timent, metus, timoris*).

lucellum : diminutive of *lucrum*, which means "gain" or "profit"; an apt metaphor, given the foregoing discussion of wealth. S. ends many of his letters with a quotation for Lucilius to consider (cf. Letters 28.9 and 18.14).

apud Hecatonem nostrum : a Greek philosopher from the island of Rhodes who lived in the latter half of the second century B.C.E., a pupil of the famous Stoic Panaetius. *Apud* is often used for citing an author; *nostrum* is a term of familiarity and endearment, here "our own, [i.e., a Stoic]."

proficere : construe with *ad . . . remedia*; subject is *finem*.

desieris : future perfect < *desino*; note the chiasm in S.'s translation of this sentence, which is probably original to Hecato's Greek. For the thought, compare the words of the Sibyl to Palinurus in the Underworld (*Aen.* 6.376): *Desine fata deum flecti sperare precando* ("Cease to hope that the gods' decrees will be changed by means of prayer").

cum : concessive (A&G 549); the implied subject of *videantur* is hope and fear, represented in the previous sentence by the infinitives *timere* and *sperare*, and below by the nouns *spes* and *metus*.

coniuncta sunt : hope and fear are connected in that both emotions are concerned with expectations of the future (cf. *pendentis animi . . . futuri exspectatione solliciti*, §8 below).

custodiam . . . etc. : *custodiam* here = "prisoner." Military analogies abound in S. The image here is vivid: Hope, like a soldier, is ostensi-

bly in control of the situation, and fear, like a prisoner, is forced to follow, but both are chained, and hence neither is free.

8   **sic :** "in the way I just mentioned."
    pendentis animi : genitive of quality (cf. *infirmi animi*, §6 above).
    futuri : used substantively, dependent upon *exspectatione*.
    solliciti agrees with *animi*.
    quod : as in §1 above.
    providentia, maximum bonum condicionis humanae : S. here
plays on the sense of *providentia*. Providence or "forethought" is "the
greatest good for the human condition," in a double sense. On the one
hand, this notion harks back to myths like that of Prometheus (whose
name means "Fore-thinker"), who, by stealing fire from the gods and
giving it to man, provided the essential tool of cultural progress (cf.
Aeschylus, *Prometheus Bound* 436–506; Plato, *Protagoras* 320d–322d).
On the other hand, the providential ordering of the universe by a benevolent deity is a central Stoic doctrine. For the Stoic, nothing happens in
the world that is not fated to happen, and all of it is for the ultimate good
(see Brennan ch. 14, and S.'s essay on this topic, included in this volume). The paradox that S. is underscoring here is that hope and fear—
emotional responses to our capacity for forethought (*providentia*)—
misdirect our attention away from the present moment (where we can
focus on making moral progress) toward future uncertainties that are out
of our control. Thus, "providence"—which in the larger scheme of things
is a divine, cosmic force for our good—becomes a bad and harmful thing
(*in malum versa est*).

9   **Ferae :** subject of both *vident* and *fugiunt*; for the contrast of human
and animal behavior, recall Letter 60.2ff.
    effugere : third-person plural; see note on *cessere*, Letter 60.1.
    venturo ... praeterito : both participles (ablatives of means) are used
substantively. Note how S. uses the future active participle (*venturo*,
lit. "that which is to come") to refer to the future and the perfect passive participle (*praeterito*, "that which has gone by") to refer to the
past—the meaning, in other words, is mirrored in the morphology.
    Multa bona nostra nobis nocent : note the staccato, alliterative
rhythm of this paradoxical sentence, each word containing only two
syllables. For the sound and sentiment, cf. *O quam inimica nobis sunt
vota nostrorum* (Letter 60.1).

memoria . . . **providentia** : an antithesis of nouns corresponding to
praeterito and *venturo* above.
reducit : in its literal sense, "brings back again"; contrast the pessimism (realism?) of S.'s view with the optimisim of Vergil's famous
line (*Aeneid* 1.203): *forsan et haec olim meminisse iuvabit* ("Perhaps
one day to remember these [sufferings] will make you glad").
Nemo tantum praesentibus miser est : a synthesis of the previous
antithesis, and the moral of the letter; *praesentibus* is used substantively and is probably an ablative of cause (A&G 404).

LETTER 43

1   **hoc** . . . **id** . . . **quod** all refer to an unspecified thing; while not actually stating what it is, S. is playfully waving Lucilius' "secret" in front
of his face. The nature of that secret is not important beyond the fact
that it provides the occasion for the present discussion.
pervenerit . . . **narraverit** : perfect subjunctives, each in an indirect
question, primary sequence of tenses (see note on *optaverit*, Letter
60.1).
rumor here is being personified. Vergil personifies *fama* (a synonym
of *rumor*) as a swift winged monster with multiple eyes, ears, and
tongues (*Aeneid* 4.173–87).
Non est quod + subjunctive verb (a favorite introductory idiom in S.)
= "it is not [necessary] that," i.e., "[you/he/they etc.] should not" (see
L&S *quod* [1], II).
ad : "with reference to," a common usage (L&S *ad*, D.1).
hunc locum : i.e., Rome.
istum : supply *locum*.
2   **modum** : "limit."
certum : "fixed," "absolute."
comparatio : i.e., comparison *with something else.*
illam : i.e., *magnitudo.*
Navis . . . **Gubernaculum, etc.** illustrates the point made with *magnitudo* . . . *comparatio, etc.*
3   **provincia** : Lucilius was one of thousands of civil servants in the
emperor's employ. At the time of this letter, he seems to have been
procurator of Sicily.

licet : "although"; see note on Letter 60.4.

quaeritur, scitur are both used impersonally here, as is often the case when a verb has a phrase or clause as its subject. For a list of impersonal verbs and a summary of the conditions under which regular verbs tend to be used impersonally, see A&G 208.

eo : ablative of degree of difference (with *diligentius*), though *eo* is often used idiomatically with a causal sense to mean "for that reason," "therefore" (see A&G 414 with n.).

vivendum est : a gerundive used impersonally (A&G 500.3); *tibi* is dative of agent with it (A&G 374).

Tunc refers to the future circumstances laid out in the *cum* clauses (note the future tenses).

circumdatos : supply *esse*.

nobis: compound verbs (here *circumdo*) often take the dative (A&G 370), but the use here is not far from a dative of advantage (A&G 376).

tutius vivamus . . . peccemus occultius : note the chiasm.

4   **ex :** "based on" (L&S *ex*, III.E).

Ianitores : the "house" implied in this metaphor is the Self. Wealthy Romans posted *ianitores* (probably large slaves) at the outer doors of their houses, who performed a function not unlike that of the modern bouncer. For the crowds of people who might congregate at an influential person's doorstep, see notes at Letter 84.12 and cf. *turbam* below.

conscientia nostra, non superbia : more personifications. *Conscientia* here means *bad* conscience, or "sense of shame," since it is contrasted with the *bona conscientia* (mentioned below), which throws its doors open to the crowd. Conversely, *superbia* means "pride" in a good sense (cf. L&S *superbus*, II).

opposuit is used absolutely: "stations"; *ob-* in verbal compounds means "in the way of" or "in front of" (L&S *ob*, III).

deprendi sit subito adspici : *deprendi* and *adspici* are passive infinitives; the adverb *subito* goes with *adspici*, and together they form the subject of a nominal sentence in a result clause (*deprendi* is the predicate).

mala : sc. *conscientia*.

5   **in solitudine anxia atque sollicita est :** note how the antithetical words *solitudine* and *anxia* are juxtaposed; note too the wordplay in *solitudine . . . sollicita*.

nii deco prodesse - I judge to be profitable

O te miserum : The accusative case is often used in exclamations (A&G 397d).

hunc testem : i.e., yourself; the implication being that you are your own best prosecutor.

LETTER 84

1   **mihi :** Dative of separation with a compound verb (A&G 381), but as with most datives, this could also be understood as a dative of advantage/disadvantage (here advantage; A&G 376); cf. note on *nobis*, Letter 43.3.

et . . . et joins *valitudini* and *studiis*. These two words serve to organize the next two sentences, where S. explains what he means with two *quare* clauses, the first of which addresses *valitudini* (cf. *valitudinem* below), the second *studiis* (cf. *studio*).

prodesse : infinitive of *prosum*, here in indirect statement with *iudico*.

Quare = *qua* + *re*; lit. "by which thing," or "the way in which," thus "how."

adiuvent : subjunctive in an indirect question introduced by *vides*, primary sequence of tenses (same construction in *quare . . . indicabo* below).

cum : *cum* + subjunctive here is either causal or concessive. Either way, S. is admitting to the facts about the state of his physical fitness.

neglegentem corporis litterarum amor : a clever, almost imperceptible chiasm consisting of accusative object + genitive/genitive + nominative subject, in which each element is antithetical to its correlate— conceptually, body versus mind; grammatically, patient versus agent.

aliena opera : ablative of means. *Alienus* means primarily "that which belongs to someone else." Summers (p. 284) suggests that it refers to the work of the slaves who carry S. around in a sedan chair.

studio quare prosint : prolepsis (see note on *hoc . . . unum*, Letter 5.1, and see A&G 576 where it is misleadingly called the accusative of anticipation. In fact, the anticipatory word will be in whatever case the syntax requires; here it is dative). Prolepsis is frequently found in indirect questions, as in the bibical verse "Consider the lilies, how they grow" (= "Consider how the lilies grow"). The subject of *prosint* here is *itinera*.

a lectionibus nihil recessi : this sentence answers the question posed by *quare*. *Nihil* has been added by modern editors (some supply *non*). The usage is Senecan, and if *nihil* is correct here, it is to be taken adverbially—"in no respect."

cum : temporal, answered by *tum*.

et de inventis indicem et cogitem de inveniendis : another clever chiasm that utilizes grammatical variation and *paromoiosis*, a type of sound parallelism between two clauses of approximately equal syllabic length (Lanham 109).

non sine : litotes (see note on *non incompta*, Letter 5.5); we often say "not without" in English, as in "That woman is not without a certain charm" (meaning that she has plenty of it). Here *non sine* serves to underscore the paradox that the same act of reading exhausts, yet also invigorates, the intellect.

2   **tantum** : adverbial = "only" (L&S *tantus*, II.B).

scribere tantum nec tantum legere : yet another chiasm.

hoc . . . illo : these ablatives, joined by the first *et*, go with *commeandum*; *hoc* answers to the infinitive *legere*, *illo* to *scribere*; *hoc* = "the latter"; *illo* = "the former" (A&G 297a–b).

commeandum . . . temperandum : gerundives expressing necessity or obligation (see note on *ne imitanda*, Letter 5.3); *commeandum* is used here impersonally with *hoc et illo* (lit. "there must be a going to and fro from the latter to the former"), *temperandum* (joined by *et* to its subject, *alterum*) is in the personal construction.

alterum altero : the juxtapositioning of the same word in different cases, a common figure of speech in inflected languages, is known as *polyptoton* (Lanham 117).

3   **Apes . . . debemus imitari** : the activity of bees provides an apt analogy for reading (*lectio*) for the primary meaning of *lego* is "to gather or collect."

quae : subject of both *vagantur* and *carpunt*.

ad mel faciendum : gerundive expressing purpose (A&G 506), dependent here on *idoneos*.

attulere : perfect, third-person plural (see note on *cessere*, Letter 60.1). Notice how this word is carefully juxtaposed with its antonym, *disponunt*.

Vergilius noster : By Seneca's time, Vergil was already considered Rome's national poet. This passage comes from a simile at *Aeneid*

1.432–33, where Vergil describes the new building projects underway in Dido's Carthage. For an explanation of the metrical pattern of this passage (dactylic hexameter), see A&G 615.

dulci agrees with *nectare*.

mella is accusative neuter plural (< *mel, mellis*).

4   **illis** refers to *apes*, which is also the unexpressed subject of the third-person plural verbs that follow.

non satis constat : *satis constat*, here negatived, is a common idiom meaning "it is well established" (L&S *consto*, II.B.2); it is used impersonally and construed with a subject accusative + infinitive.

utrum . . . an : alternative indirect question (A&G 335d), hence the subjunctives *ducant* and *mutent*.

sit = "becomes"; subjunctive in a relative clause of result (see note on *quae . . . sint*, Letter 5.1 above). But the subjunctive mood is also used in any clause that depends upon another subjunctive clause (here the indirect question) if that clause is considered to be an integral part of the one that contains it (A&G 593).

quae : here an indefinite pronoun (A&G 149), accusative neuter plural, object of both *collegerunt* and *mutent*.

mixtura : ablative (of means).

spiritus is genitive.

illis : dative of possession (A&G 373).

Aiunt : a common formula used to introduce material derived from secondary sources, i.e., from *lectio* (L&S *aio*, II.D). This and the next ostensibly digressive sentence in fact illustrates Seneca's own vast reading and his special interest in natural history, about which he himself wrote extensively in his *Quaestiones naturales*.

mel in harundinum foliis is probably sugar cane (Summers p. 286).

ros . . . umor : note the chiasm.

illius : pointing away from Italy toward India—"the sky or climate *there.*"

gignat : transitive, object is *quod*; subjunctive in a subordinate clause in indirect statement (A&G 580).

poni : passive infinitive in continued indirect statement; supply *aiunt*.

animal huic rei genitum : the "creature born for this purpose" is a scientific-sounding periphrasis for the bee.

verti : passive infinitive in indirect statement (cf. *poni* above), here construed with *existimant*; the subject accusative is expressed in the relative clause, *quae . . . decerpserint.*

quae : impersonal pronoun, as above (cf. *quaecumque* below).

tenerrimis virentium florentiumque : the genitives are partitive, as is often the case with genitives dependent upon superlatives (A&G 346.2); these adjectives/participles are used substantively, in which case one needs to supply an appropriate noun, here perhaps "plants" (A&G 288).

decerpserint : the subject is still *apes*.

non sine . . . fermento : note the parallelism with *non sine studio* above; this verbal echo anticipates S.'s point, elaborated in the culinary and digestion metaphors below, that the processes involved in *studium* are, as it were, a kind of *fermentum*.

ut ita dicam : "so to speak" (L&S *ut*, II.C.5.c), qualifying the author's use of a word or phrase (here *fermento*).

5   **ne . . . abducar** : either a hortatory subjunctive or a negative purpose clause with some introductory sentence implied like "Let me return to my point now" (equivalent to *ut . . . communicem*, Letter 5.7).

de quo agitur : as often, the demonstrative one expects after *quam* is suppressed. For the impersonal use of *agitur*, see L&S *ago*, II.D.9d.

congessimus, separare : an echo of the antithesis *attulere, disponunt* above.

melius enim distincta servantur : *melius* is the comparative adverb/adjective of *bene /bonus*; here possibly a pun on *mel*. The idea that things are better remembered when compartmentalized in the mind derives from ancient mnemonic techniques.

in unum saporem : cf. *in hunc saporem* above.

libamenta : lit. preparatory offerings of food or wine to the gods; here simply, "foretastes," or "samples," without any religious overtones.

confundere : like *imitari*, dependent upong *debemus*.

ut etiam si apparuerit . . . appareat : note the elaborate chiastic structure of this sentence with its semantic repetition and the syntactical variation of verbal tense and mood (*apparuerit . . . sumptum sit . . . sumptum est . . . appareat*). For a similar semantic chiasm involving antithesis compare *omnia quibus est adiutus abscondat, ipsum tantum ostendat quod effecit* (§7 below).

Quod . . . videmus : *quod* here is a relative pronoun (with antecedent suppressed) that is answered by the demonstrative *idem* in §6 (see note on *idem* below).

sine ulla opera nostra : contrast *aliena opera* above and *ne aliena sint* below.

naturam : see note on *natura*, Letter 60.3.

6   **solida innatant :** the adjective is used predicatively (cf. *pigrum*, §1 above).

quod erant : this *quod* is a predicate nominative (for the singular with a plural verb, a "construction according to sense," see A&G 280a, 286b); the subject is *alimenta*.

idem : this demonstrative, the object of *praestemus*, harks back (after two parenthetical sentences) to the activity described in the clause *quod . . . videmus facere naturam*.

praestemus : hortatory subjunctive.

ut . . . non : a substantive (noun) clause of result in apposition to *idem* (cf. A&G 570); this sentence is a restatement of the previous point *melius enim distincta servantur*.

ne aliena sint : contrast *aliena opera* above.

7   **Concoquamus . . . adsentiamur . . . faciamus :** hortatory subjunctives.

alioqui : "otherwise."

in memoriam ibunt, non in ingenium : While it is true that you only know what you can recall, it is also the case that one must make knowledge one's own by internalizing it.

nostra : accusative, used predicatively.

cum . . . comprendit : for the indicative, see A&G 549a.

Hoc : used proleptically; the sentence beginning with *omnia* stands in apposition to it.

omnia quibus est adiutus abscondat : the fourth-century author Macrobius seems to have taken S.'s advice to heart, excerpting large portions of this letter without acknowledgment in the preface to his *Saturnalia*.

8   **si cuius :** *cuius* here is genitive of the indefinite pronoun *aliquis* (A&G 151e); the *ali-* prefix falls out after *si, nisi, num,* and *ne* (A&G 310a).

comparebit < *compareo*, not *comparo*.

quem : antecedent is *cuius*.

non quomodo imaginem : *imagines* were the wax death masks or busts of deceased ancestors that Romans kept in their household shrines. Hence S.'s statement *Imago res mortua est.*

ne intellegi quidem : the phrase *ne . . . quidem* ("not . . . indeed, not . . . even") emphatically negates whatever word it encloses, thus serving almost as typographic italics (A&G 322f). The Latin literally says "I think that it can not even/indeed be perceived [whose speech, etc.]." But since *intellegi* is answering in the negative to *intellegetur*, the main verb of the original question, we should translate more idiomatically, "No, sometimes I think it can*not* be perceived," etc.

imago : an extension of the use above; here perhaps simply "copy," or "representation."

haec = *vera imago.*

quo : indefinite pronoun (for *aliquo*).

9 **vocibus :** ablative with *constet.*

aliqua : here used as an adjective; supply *vox* (note the anaphora).

illic : in the chorus.

10 **De choro dico . . . :** if S. means the classical Greek philosophers and the dramas performed in the Theater of Dionysus (cf. *theatris*), the mention of women is odd, as they did not take part in the performances. However, nontheatrical female choruses were common.

commissionibus : "celebrations."

vias : here = "aisles."

cavea . . . pulpito : the *cavea* is where the spectators sit (perhaps "venue," or "arena"), the *pulpitum* is the stage.

multae . . . multa . . . multarum : note the anaphora, with polyptoton; supply the appropriate form of the verb "to be" in these sentences.

11 **si nihil :** this is a second answer to the imagined question *"Quomodo hoc effici poterit?"* Answer: "[We will be able to do this] *if . . . "* etc.

hanc = *ratio*, which is also also subject of *dicet*; note how *ratio* is personified in what follows (so too *ambitum* below).

iamdudum : construe with *discurritur* (which is used impersonally).

vana, ventosa : note the asyndeton.

tam . . . quam are used correlatively here.

ne . . . videat . . . ne . . . : fear clauses dependent on *sollicita est* (see note on *ne imitanda sint*, Letter 5.3); for *quem*, cf. note on *si cuius*, §8 above.

se : reflexive pronoun referring to *ambitum* as a *tumida res*.

invidia : ablative (with *duplici*); the implied subject of *laborat* is *ambitus* (= *res*).

autem : "in fact" or "indeed"; *autem* here is not concessive or adversative but simply confirms and emphasizes points made in the previous sentences, especially the words *videat* (cf. *vides*) and *invidia* (cf. *invidetur, invident* below). See L&S *autem*, B.II.

is cui invidetur et invidet : this clever phrase explains under what circumstances *invidia* is *duplex*; *invidetur* is used impersonally ("there is envy").

12   **domos** is feminine.

rixa is ablative.

salutantium refers to the patron-client system that structured Roman society, in which clients from various walks of life paid daily visits to the homes of the patrons in order to offer a greeting (*salutatio*), wish them well, and receive a gift of food or some other favor, like advocacy in court. The clients would "pay" for such favors with their political support.

habent : subject is *limina* or *domus*.

plus : supply *contumeliarum*.

Praeteri : imperative.

praerupto . . . lubrico : both used substantively; supply an appropriate noun.

eius : "her" referring to *sapientia* personified.

13   **humillimorum** : objective genitive with *comparatione* (A&G 348–49); the adjective is being used substantively.

adeuntur : the indefinite *quaecumque* is the subject.

in fastigium dignitatis : the prepositional phrase modifies *via*; *confragosa* is the predicate nominative.

cui : the antecedent is *hunc verticem*.

pro : "as"; for this idiom with *habeo* (= "consider"), see L&S *habeo*, II.D.1.

LETTER 56

1   **in studia** : *studia* is accusative because of the motion implied in *seposito*.

seposito is dative, perfect passive participle of *sepono*; construe with *necessarium* and supply either *alicui* or *mihi*.

balneum : Roman baths were large public buildings that also included exercise facilities.

cum : This and the following *cum* clauses are temporal-circumstantial.

manus plumbo graves iactant : "throw about their hands, [which are] weighted down with lead"; *plumbo* refers to exercise dumbbells and is an ablative of means (A&G 409a) describing how and why their hands are heavy.

laborantem imitantur is a joke at the expense of those who only pretend to be working out, yet S. himself is pretending too in that he is imitating their grunts and groans linguistically (see next note).

quotiens . . . respirationes : note the alliteration of -t- and -s- sounds, which represent phonetically the meaning of the words, an example of *onomatopoeia* (Lanham 105). *Respirationes* is joined with *gemitus* by *et*, and both are objects of *audio*.

hac plebeia unctione : "a cheap massage," one that a plebeian could afford; *hac* here means something like "you know the kind I mean" (cf. L&S *hic*, I.G).

manus is genitive singular and is being modified by *inlisae*.

quae : antecedent is *manus*.

pervenit : "reaches its destination" (i.e., someone's back and shoulders).

pilicrepus < *pila* + *crepo*; a *pilicrepus* was a ball-game official who kept score by calling out the number of balls dropped and caught (cf. *numerare . . . pilas*). In Petronius' *Satyricon*, the lowbrow millionaire Trimalchio plays a similar game before having his bath, where a eunuch *numerabat pilas* (27–28).

supervenit : "comes upon the scene."

actum est : "it's all over," i.e., "I'm done for."

2   **Adice :** "throw into the mix"; continuing the construction begun with *propone,* etc. above.

scordalum : this rare Latin word, borrowed from the Greek, means "cocky"—after the garlic Greek game-cocks were fed before a fight (Costa p. 172).

deprensum : "caught in the act."

cui vox sua in balineo placet : a universal phenomenon then, as now, of which Horace and others often complain. Cf. Horace: *sunt multi quique lavantes* [recitent]: / *suave locus voci resonat conclusus* (*Satires* 1.4.75–76). In defense of shower singers, however, it must be said that the acoustics in Roman vaulted baths must have been phenomenal. Today, concerts are still held in the ruins of the baths of Caracalla.

piscinam : any artificial pool or basin for swimming, not necessarily with fish in it.

ingenti impulsae aquae sono : note how *ingenti* . . . *sono* frames *impulsae aquae.*

rectae : "trained" or simply "good."

alipilum : a slave who depilated bathers' bodies.

cogita : cf. *puta*, Letter 44.6.

tenuem et stridulam vocem stands in apposition to *alipilum* (a "partitive" apposition; A&G 282a). "Imagine the depilator, his tinny and grating voice. . . ."

quo sit notabilior : The ablative *quo* (= *ut eo*) is used as a conjunction in purpose clauses that contain a comparative word (A&G 531.2a).

vellit < *vello, -ere*, not *volo, velle.*

alas : "armpits."

pro se : "instead of himself," "in his place."

libari : genitive singular < *libarius, -ii*, "pastry cook."

botularium . . . crustularium : "Sausage seller" and "baker," respectively; these words are found only in this passage.

sua quadam et insignita modulatione : "each with his own distinctive pitch"; ablative of manner (A&G 412).

vendentis is accusative plural; the -*īs* ending is common in third-declension i-stems and in poetry (A&G 74c, 77).

3   **"O te . . . ferreum aut surdum . . . " :** for the accusative in exclamations, see note on *O te miserum*, Letter 43.5. The tone here is that of mock epic.

Chrysippum . . . salutatio : Chrysippus was an important Stoic sage (see the Philosophy section in the Introduction); though some editors propose reading *Crispus*, one of S.'s friends, as the noisy *salutatio* was a Roman, not a Greek, custom (see notes on *salutantium*, Letter 84.12, and *ianitores*, Letter 43.4).

fluctum ... deictum are nouns.

audiam, subjunctive with *quamvis* (A&G 527a), is introducing an indirect statement with *fuisse*.

cuidam genti ... non potuit : S. tells this story elsewhere in his *Quaestiones naturales* (4.2.5). The people in question are not named, but Pliny the Elder says that they moved because the noise of the waterfalls at the source of the Nile caused them to go deaf (*Natural History* 6.181). Cf. S.'s *migrabo*, §15 below.

4   **vox ... crepitus :** The distinction between *vox* and *crepitus* lies in the fact that only the former distracts the *animum*. The next few sentences elaborate on this.

Illa ... hic : referring to *vox* and *crepitus*, respectively.

In his : antecedent of *quae* and referring with a generalizing neuter plural to various forms of *crepitus*.

essedas : The *esseda* was a two-wheeled chariot of Celtic origin. Here the word probably refers—again, with mock epic exaggeration—to workmen's carts (cf. *fabrum* and *serrarium* below).

fabrum ... vicinum : "the welder next door and his neighbor, the lumberjack" captures the connotations and sounds implied in these professsions. A *faber* is a forger or joiner; a *serrarius* (< *serra*, *-ae*) is a man who sharpens saws. *Inquilinus* (< *in* + *colo*, *-ere*) refers to someone who lives in a place not his own, either a "tenant," or possibly here, "immigrant." As today, Roman shops were located at street level, with apartments above.

Metam Sudantem : The "Sweating Pyramid" is a fountain shaped like a turning post for chariots (= *meta*). Though he himself appears to be staying near Baiae at a friend's country estate at the time of writing (cf. Letters 55 and 57), S. may be referring here to a fountain at Rome located near the Circus, the remains of which can still be seen near the Colosseum. In any event, given its name (*Meta*), his mention of this landmark picks up the metaphor latent in *essedas* above (cf. too *verberat*).

tubulas ... exclamat : *Tubulas* and *tibias* in this passage are thought to refer to pipes through which water trickled down the side of the fountain (hence the epithet "sweating"). *Tubulas*, however, is a modern emendation of the undecipherable *tabulas* found in the manuscripts, so the text is somewhat uncertain. The passage seems to describe either the fountain repairman singing while he works (with a pun on *tubulas* and *tibias*, "horns" and "flutes"), or an instrument vender, hawking his wares, whose stall is located near the Sweating Pyramid.

5   **sonus . . . continuatur** reiterates the distinction between *vox* and *crepitus*, *animum* and *aures* above.

pausarium : "coxswain"; "barker."

possim : subjunctive in a result clause.

modos dantem : "calling out the time"; "establishing the rhythm [of the stroke]."

externa . . . intus : for the thought, cf. Letter 5.2; see too *speciosa*, §11, and *introrsus . . . intus*, §12 below.

dum + subjunctive (a proviso clause) = "provided that" (A&G 528).

tumultus is genitive with *nihil* (see note on *mali*, Letter 60.1).

non is irregular; normal usage is *ne*; see note on *non* Letter 5.3.

adfectus : "state[s] of mind."

6   **Omnia . . . quiete :** The citation is from a minor Latin poet's adaptation of Apollonius of Rhodes' Greek epic on Jason and the Argonauts. *Composta* is a syncopated, poetic form of *composita*.

falsum est : the subject of this sentence is the whole of the previous quotation.

nisi quam ratio composuit : Note how S. uses the same verb used in the quotation. For *ratio* personified, cf. Letter 84.11.

explicatur : In poetry, night or sleep is often said to "embrace" or "enfold" (*complectitur*) a person's body. So, e.g., Vergil: *sopor fessos complectitur artus* (*Aen.* 2.253). *Explicatur*, its opposite, means "to unwind." It is probably significant that S. uses it here of the *animus*, not the body, as this is precisely the contrast he develops below (cf. *corpus*, §8).

7   **cui :** a dative of advantage; or, alternatively, a dative of agent (a poetic use; see A&G 375a).

laxae domus go together and are dependent upon *silentio*. *Laxus* can mean both "spacious" and "relaxed." Given the context, both senses may be intended here—i.e., everyone in the spacious house has all gone to bed except the slaves who are scurrying about, performing their various tasks.

cuius aures ne quis agitet sonus : prolepsis (see note on *studio quare prosint*, Letter 84.1).

suspensum . . . vestigium : "a hovering footstep" = "tiptoe"; *accedentium* is a genitive plural participle, modified by *proprius*.

8   **Quae non audit audisse se queritur :** Even when he hears nothing, in his psychologically turbulent state he thinks he does. This same contrast between reality and perception or appearance is repeated in §11: *Otiosi videmur, et non sumus* (cf. too *sanitate simulata*, §10).

in causa esse, "to be the cause of," is idiomatic.

seditio : a loaded word, given the mention of slaves above. Although S. does not say so explicitly here, the fear of a slave rebellion was every Roman master's nightmare. Pliny the Younger tells a story of a master murdered by his slaves while taking a bath (*Letters* 3.14). Long before S., Plato used the metaphor of a slave rebellion to describe the state of injustice in the soul of the tyrannical man, whose "waking life is like a nightmare" (cf. *Republic* 578d–79e).

non est quod : see note on *Non est quod*, Letter 43.1.

quies inquieta : note the oxymoron.

ac joins the two participles *excitandi* and *occupandi* with *sumus* to form a passive periphrastic construction.

bonarum artium : those pursuits that cultivate good character.

male habet, "treats us poorly," is an idiomatic construction influenced perhaps by Greek idiom (L&S *habeo*, II.C.5).

sui : "of itself" (i.e., *inertia*); *patiens* takes the genitive.

9   **male parere** is parallel to *male habet* above; *parere < pareo*, "to obey"—a further illustration of *seditio* developed into a military metaphor over the next few sentences.

compescunt : cf. *compescenda est* above.

vacat is impersonal.

districtis : "engaged," with either *labore* or *expeditionibus* (*distringo* in fact, as a military term, is a synonym for *detineo*, used above; cf. L&S *distringo*, II.1).

discuti : for the word, cf. Letter 28.1. *Otii vitia negotio discuti* was apparently a proverb. Curtius Rufus (7.1.4) uses the same phrase to describe the commandeering techniques of Alexander the Great.

taedio rerum civilium : for the thought cf. Letter 28.6–7.

paenitentia, like *taedio*, is an ablative of cause; the genitive *stationis* (another military word) and the two adjectives *infelicis* and *ingratae* are dependent upon it; *ingratae* = "thankless."

latebra . . . recrudescit : both words have military connotations.

ambitio : for the personification cf. Letters 5.1 and 84.11.

desit < *desino, -ere*; as subject supply *ambitio*, with which *excisa* agrees.

sibi refers to *ambitio*.

10   **cessisse :** cf. *cedentibus* above.

professos is used substantively: "those who have professed [frugality]."

voluptates non damnatas, sed relictas continues the military metaphor. Like an imprudent general who does not prosecute a rebellious enemy to the fullest extent, we are more prone to spare our pleasures than to exterminate them.

eo . . . quo : see note on *eo . . . quo,* Letter 60.1.

in aperto : "on the surface," or "when they're out in the open," contrasted with *ex abdito* below (with which cf. *latebra,* §9 above).

tunc is answered by the *cum* clause, explaining under what conditions the statement of the main sentence is true (same construction in the application of the analogy below—*tunc perniciosissima . . . cum . . . subsidunt*—and in §14).

ad sanitatem inclinant . . . : S. means that symptoms are a sign that a disease is near the tail end of its period of activity, which is true enough of the common cold and of, say, chicken pox.

scias is a potential subjunctive.

simulata sanitate : ablative absolute. The idea is that moral *vitia*, like physical *vitia*, do more damage to a person when they are latent. Someone may appear healthy, but just under the surface a disease is at work. Conversely, someone may look sick but is in fact on the road to health.

11   **bona fide :** "[in a state of] good faith," i.e., "really," "truly."

receptui cecinimus : lit. "to have sung for the retreat," i.e., "to have sounded the retreat"; *receptui* is dative of purpose in this fixed military idiom (A&G 382.2).

ut paulo ante dicebam : namely, in §4.

iam : i.e., once the conditions of the three *si* clauses have been met.

12   **ad :** "at."

accidentia : as Summers suggests (p. 239), "those things that meet [the ears]."

erigitur : "is startled."

curiosum : not "curious," but "full of cares."

Vergilius noster . . . : These words are spoken by Aeneas as he flees from the city of Troy at the very moment the Greeks are sacking it (*Aen.* 2.726–29).

me is the object of *movebant*.

ulla iniecta . . . tela go together.

adverso glomerati ex agmine Grai : *adverso* agrees with *agmine*, *glomerati* with *Grai*. The disjunctive word order (called *hyperbaton*; Lanham 86) is typical of Latin poetry. Translate: "The Greeks who have amassed themselves in a battle line against me . . ."

suspensum et . . . timentem agree with *me*.

comitique onerique : the *comes* is Aeneas' son Ascanius; the *onus* is his aged father Anchises, whom he is carrying on his shoulders.

13 **Prior ille . . . Hic alter :** This distinction hinges on *dudum . . . nunc* in the Vergil passage. According to S., the Aeneas who was formerly unperturbed by the din of battle is *sapiens*, the Aeneas who gives in to fear is *imperitus*.

crepitum . . . vox : an echo of §4 above.

pro : "as if it were"; "instead of"; cf. *pro*, §1 above.

sarcinae : referring to the *onus* that is Anchises, but more generally of Aeneas' larger poltical task in the *Aeneid* of founding the city of Rome. For the metaphor, cf. *sarcinas*, Letter 44.7, and *onus animi*, Letter 28.2.

14 **istis felicibus :** "those people you consider fortunate"; for the meaning of *istis*, see note on *ista*, Letter 5.4.

scito is future imperative (A&G 163b.2–3).

clamor : an echo of §1.

tibi : see note on *mihi*, Letter 84.1.

inani sono vana : with *vana* supply *vox*; note the use of two different words for "empty." In addition to intelligible threats and flattery, this third type of distracting *vox* is meaningless—as it were, "sound and fury signifying nothing."

15 **Itaque . . . migrabo :** A humorous, self-effacing anticlimax to S.'s moralizing.

Experiri et exercere me volui : On the surface, this statement is in conflict with the belief expressed in Letter 28.7 that it is not a good idea to put oneself in harm's way, but S. here is neither perfectly serious, nor is he always consistent with himself.

diutius : "any longer."

Ulixes . . . Sirenas : At *Odyssey* 12.177ff., Odysseus (= *Ulixes*) orders his men to put wax in their ears and row speedily past the Sirens. Odysseus himself, however, listens to their enchanting song, strapped to the mast in order to prevent himself from jumping overboard. This Homeric passage was the subject of much philosophical moralizing in antiquity.

LETTER 28

1   **rem novam** stands in apposition to *hoc*, which is proleptic with *quod*.
discussisti < *discutio, -ere.* The prefix *dis-* signifies separation.
Animum . . . caelum : for *caelum*, "climate," "weather," cf. 84.4. For the sentiment, cf. Horace *Epistles* 1.11.27: *caelum non animum mutant qui trans mare currunt.*
Licet : see note on *licet*, Letter 60.4.
Vergilius noster : see note on Letter 84.3. This passage (*Aen.* 3.72) comes from the book of Aeneas' "Odyssean" wanderings en route to Italy. S. changes the indicative of the original (*recedunt*) to subjunctive to fit his syntax with *licet*.

2   **Hoc idem querenti cuidam Socrates ait** : "To someone [who was] complaining of this very thing Socrates said." Often in Latin the distinct actions of two parties can be conveyed in one simple sentence instead of two, the action of one expressed by the main verb, the other by a participle in an oblique case (here *querenti cuidam*). Another example of this pervasive feature of Latin style appears below (see note on *vatis*, §3). The source of this saying attributed to Socrates is unknown.
Quid : here "why," but below "what."
nihil : adverbial.
cum : causal (A&G 549).
Premit te eadem causa, quae expulit : The *causa* is the Self, which drives one away like an exile and continues to harrass one while

abroad. There is perhaps a double entendre with *premit*, which can also mean "keep close to shore" (L&S *premo*, I.B.1).

cognitio urbium aut locorum : a Latin echo of the opening lines of the *Odyssey* (cf. *Od.* 1.3)

In inritum cedit . . . iactatio : the phrase *in inritum cadere* (to result in no effect) is a common idiom. However, the citation from *Aeneid* book 3, coupled with the *Odyssey* allusion above, makes this sentence a metaphor for a sea voyage and gives both *cedit* and *iactatio* a more literal sense.

Tecum fugis : a restatement of *cum te circumferas* above.

Onus animi : cf. *sarcinas*, Letter 44.7 and Letter 56.12.

3   **tuum** is predicative.

vatis is genitive of possession dependent upon *qualem* (supply *habitum*); *concitatae*, *instigatae*, and *habentis* are modifying it. The passage describes the Sibyl, a prophetess whom Aeneas consults at the outset of his journey to the underworld (*Aen.* 6.78).

inducit : "brings in [to his narrative]."

multum, direct object of the participle *habentis*, goes with *spiritus* (which is genitive) in a partitive construction (see note on *mali*, Letter 60.1).

Bacchatur : "Raves like a devotee of Bacchus." Bacchus (Dionysus) was the god of wine and ecstasy.

si . . . possit : In poetry, *si* is often followed by the subjunctive to express a wish (A&G 442a). The construction is not too far removed from a purpose clause (cf. S.'s use of *ut* below when he applies the analogy). "She raves like a devotee of Bacchus *with the hope that* [= *si*] she could. . . ."

excussisse : cf. *discussisti* above and *concutis* below.

magnum . . . deum : Apollo, the god who inspires the Sibyl's prophecy.

Vadis : possibly a pun on *vatis*, especially with the word *excutias* (cf. *excussisse*) in the same sentence.

insidens is neuter agreeing with *pondus*.

ipsa : "precisely that [*iactatione*]"; cf. *ipso motu* below

onera : cf. *onus* (*animi*) above. In this analogy Lucilius himself is compared to a ship loaded with cargo, which tends to list to one side or the other when the load is not well tied down or is unequally distributed in the hold (cf. *inaequaliter*).

eam partem is the direct object of *demergunt*.

incubuere is third-person plural, perfect (see note on *cessere*, Letter 60.1); subject is *onera*.

aegrum : "[a man who is] sick"—"seasick" might even be an apt translation, given the extended metaphor, but the sickness is of course a psychic malady.

4   **cum :** temporal (A&G 547); note the future perfect, *exemeris*: the terms of the *cum* clause must be met before the main sentence can be true. Note that S. is not opposed to travel per se, but he decries the notion that travel can provide any lasting relief from one's problems.

expellaris : cf. *expulit, §2* above. S. himself spent eleven years in exile (see Introduction). Exile was a reality that many practicing philosophers faced under the Roman emperors.

quolibet . . . qualiscumque : These indefinite adjectives emphasize the indifference one will feel toward place once one's mind is at peace.

Magis quis veneris quam quo interest : a very compressed statement in which *quis* and *quo* ("who" and "where") are contrasted: "It is more a question of who you are than where you're going." *Veneris* is perfect subjunctive in an indirect question. The Stoic poet Persius puts many of these same ideas a different way (*Satires* 4.51–52): *respue quod non es, tollat sua munera cerdo / tecum habita: noris quam sit tibi curta suppellex* ("spit out what is not you, let the handyman do his own repairs; / cohabit with yourself, and know how small your furniture is").

addicere : "attach" or "apply."

vivendum est : impersonal use (see note at Letter 43.3).

patria mea totus hic mundus est : a commonplace in Hellenistic philosophy, beginning with the Cynics (see the Philosophy section in the Introduction).

5   **Quod si liqueret tibi . . . :** "And if that were clear to you, you would not . . ." *Quod* is a connecting relative (see note on *a qua*, Letter 5.4) used proleptically. *Liqueret* is imperfect subjunctive in the protasis of present contrary-to-fact condition (A&G 517).

nil : adverbial; see note on *a lectionibus nihil*, Letter 84.1.

priorum taedio : "Out of boredom with your previous [settings]." *Priorum* is an objective genitive (supply *regionum*); *taedio* is an ablative of cause (A&G 404).

Prima : Supply *regio.*

si omnem tuam crederes : *tuam* is predicative (cf. *tuum* above), with which supply *esse*. For the idea, cf. 1 Corinthians 3:22: "Whether Paul, or Apollos, or Cephas, or the world, or things present, or things to come; all are yours."

cum : concessive.

bene vivere stands in apposition to *illud*; this is the topic of S.'s essay *De vita beata* (included in this volume).

6   **turbidum :** to continue S.'s nautical metaphor, "stormy."

disponere se : "to station oneself."

fugiam is present subjunctive in the apodosis of a future less-vivid condition (A&G 514 B.2.a).

ut : correlative with *ita.*

aliqua : supply *loca.*

parum : the adverb modifies *salubria*, creating a litotes (see note on *non incompta*, Letter 5.5).

7   **qui ... conluctantur :** S. is speaking metaphorically here of people who argue that putting oneself in difficult, morally risky positions—specifically public life (cf. *forum* above)—builds character. The wise man, S. says in the next sentence, will endure public duties, but he will not choose them.

multum is adverbial.

alienis : supply *vitiis*; on the meaning of *alienus*, see note on Letter 84.1. S. here is essentially advocating quietism. The idea is not unlike the biblical "Sufficient unto the day is the evil thereof" (Matthew 6:34).

8   **inquit :** Summers (p. 196) suggests that the subject is some imaginary member of the *hi qui* camp mentioned above. The historical reference is to the time in 404 B.C.E. when Athens was ruled by thirty oligarchs, afterward remembered as "tyrants" for the reign of terror they presided over. Socrates and four others were commanded by these leaders to fetch an innocent man for his summary execution, an illegal order that Socrates refused to carry out, though he risked his life to do so. Plato has Socrates give an account of his behavior on this occasion

in the *Apology* (32c). Socrates' bravery made a deep impression on Plato, convincing him also that he should never enter politics (*Seventh Letter* 324d8). S.'s distaste for public life stems from this tradition.

Servitus una est : "Servitude is singular." Given the context of this passage, S. is not far from claiming here that public service is a form of slavery, a bold statement for a Roman citizen to make, and atypical of classical Stoicism (see note on *Vivit is . . . utitur*, Letter 60.4).

turba dominantium : something of an *oxymoron* (Lanham 106).

9   **Tempus est desinere . . .** is an apt transition from the main theme of the letter to S.'s "thought of the day" for Lucilius (see note on *lucellum*, 5.7). The *portorium* was a tax paid by traveling merchants for the right to sell goods in a country. At least once in literary Latin it means the fare paid to a ferryboat captain and this sense may have been common in colloquial idiom (cf. L&S *portorium*, II). S. has, as it were, arrived at his intended destination (the end of the letter) and is "paying his fare."

sed si prius : "but not before."

Egregie : "outstandingly."

Epicurus : Epicurus (341–270 B.C.E.) was the founder of a school of philosophy that offered a materialistic explanation of the world as a random confluence of atoms. The school was informal and was referred to as The Garden, after the original spot where Epicurus and his disciples met and lived. Like the Stoics and Cynics, the Epicureans were primarily concerned with achieving an unperturbed state of mind in an unpredictable world, and believed in the fundamental equality of all people on the path to wisdom. Epicurus wrote extensively on physics and moral philosophy and his cardinal ethical doctrines were anthologized at an early date. Although as a Stoic S. would have disagreed with Epicurus on key points, he quotes him more than any other single author, the rationale being, as S. says elsewhere in the Letters (16.7), *quicquid bene dictum est ab ullo meum est.*

10   **qui :** The antecedent is logically *quidam . . . gloriantur*, but grammatically it is unexpressed; supply *illos* as subject of *cogitare* in this indirect statement.

virtutum loco : "in the place of virtues," i.e., as if they were virtues (L&S *locus*, II.F).

te ipse coargue, inquire in te : Note the chiasm. As Summers notes (p. 197), this is a paraphrase of the famous Greek injunction to "Know Thyself" cast in Roman legalese.

partibus : the word is used in both legal and dramatic contexts.

fungere is imperative < *fungor.*

LETTER 44

1   **malignius :** comparative adverb; take with *egisse*, which is an infinitive in an indirect statement, with *naturam . . . fortunam* its subjects.

tecum egisse : "has treated you."

cum is concessive.

eximere . . . vulgo et ad felicitatem . . . emergere : note the chiasm (so too above in the structure of the previous sentence organized around *facis et dicis*).

Si quid : see note on *si cuius*, Letter 84.8.

aliud . . . boni : see note on *mali*, Letter 60.1.

stemma = a family "tree," lit. a "garland," referring to the genealogical wreaths painted on the walls of the room where the Roman family's ancestral busts were kept (see note on *non quomodo imaginem*, Letter 84.8).

2   **Eques Romanus :** *Equites*, as the name suggests, were originally a census class of citizens who could provide their own horse on military campaigns. By the late republic and early imperial period, they were the "businessmen" of the state and manned most of the administrative posts in the Roman civil service. *Equites* comprised an aristocratic order second only to the senatorial class. By S.'s time, membership in the order was determined purely by financial holdings (like a modern tax bracket). As a class, there were many more *equites* than senators, and their numbers and influence greatly increased as Roman citizenship was extended to the provinces. Lucilius, S. informs us here and elsewhere, was a "self-made" *eques* (cf. *industria* below).

quattuordecim : As one of several social distinctions conferred on *equites* (including special togas and finger rings), fourteen rows of seats were reserved for them in the theater.

curia : The senate house at Rome, and hence, by *metonymy* (Lanham 102), the Senate itself.

quos : antecedent is unexpressed (see note on *quod*, Letter 60.1).

recipiant : subjunctive in a relative clause of characteristic (A&G 535).

legunt : "choose," the primary meaning of this word (L&S *lego* I.B.1); the grammatical subject is *castra*, but logically, the subject is the *recruiters* for the army.

ad hoc : *hoc* refers to *bona mens*; on *ad*, see note at Letter 43.1.

nobiles : The word means "known" or "noteworthy," but it had a more technical meaning for Romans. To be *nobilis*, one had to be descended from someone who once held the consulship, the highest office of state. In S.'s time the word probably still carried this connotation.

lucet seems to have been chosen for its sound as much as its sense (*eligit—lucet*). "It shines its light on all" is not an obvious alternative to *nec reicit* or *nec eligit* unless perhaps we are to imagine a building or enclosure as the point of reference (i.e., one is either "in" or "out"). Philosophy, by contrast, like the sun, shines equally on all in the open air. For the sentiment, compare Petronius, *Satyricon* 100: *Sol omnibus lucet*; and Matthew 5:45: "for he maketh his sun to rise on the evil and on the good."

3   **Patricius Socrates non fuit :** Socrates was not an aristocrat, but (traditionally) the son of a stoneworker and a midwife. He eschewed a political career in the traditional sense, preferring instead to spend his time discussing ideas in the public square in Athens. The patricians at Rome tended to control the highest offices of state, including priesthoods. Unlike the equestrian class, they were aristocratic purely by birth.

Cleanthes : an important Stoic sage whose majestic philosophical hymn to Zeus survives; see the Philosophy section of the Introduction.

rigando horto : gerundive; the dative expresses purpose (A&G 505, 382).

locavit manus : *manus* is accusative; *locavit manus* is a variation on the idiom *se locare*, "to hire oneself out." Cleanthes was, as it were, a "hired hand."

Platonem . . . fecit is in the literal sense untrue. Plato came from a very high-born and aristocratic family, though S. is clarifying here what he means by *nobilem*: for the philosohper it is not a political term (Plato, like Socrates, eschewed politics), but an ethical one.

Quid est quare : "What is [the reason] why . . ."

maiores : "ancestors."

nobilitate : ablative of specification (A&G 418).

4 **Omnibus nobis :** dative of possession (A&G 373).

nullius non : the first of several double negatives in the following paragraphs, which cancel each other out (rhetorically, a form of litotes; see note on *non incompta*, 5.5). Note too the alliteration and assonance in *omnibus nobis . . . ante nos sunt nullius non*, etc.

Platon ait . . . : a paraphrase of the thought at *Theaetetus* 174e–75a.

sursum deorsum : note the jingle created by the juxtaposition of these adverbs. The image is of the Wheel of Fortune, a commonplace in Latin elegiac poetry (cf., e.g., Tibullus 1.5.70: *versatur celeri Fors levis orbe rotae* ["Fortune spins blithely with her swift circling wheel"; where *Fors = Fortuna*]), and is used by Cicero to drive a point home in the law courts (*Against Piso* 10.22). In later art, the goddess Fortuna was depicted next to a large wheel (not unlike a Ferris wheel) to which men and women were affixed. She spun them round and round over a large pit. S. himself uses the image elsewhere in his tragedy *Agamemnon* (71–72), where the opening chorus declares that it is Fortune who turns the fate of kings upside down (*praecipites regum casus / Fortuna rotat*—cf. *regem . . . regibus* above).

5 **generosus :** "wellborn."

compositus : "disposed" or "fitted out"; this is an answer to the preceeding question; supply *ille qui est*.

Hoc : not proleptic here, but pointing back to the thought of the previous sentences, namely, that a person be *bene compositus ad virtutem*.

vetera is being used substantively.

nemo non inde est, ante quod nihil est : a torturously clever sentence; *nemo non* = "everybody." The idea seems to be that if we were to go back to the world's most primitive state, before the dawn of culture and social stratification, everyone would be on an equal footing. Essentially the same thought is expressed in *omnes, si ad originem primam revocantur, a dis sunt*, §1 above.

ex splendidis sordidisque : note the juxtaposition of opposites.

alternata series : Another implicit metaphor for the spinning of Fortune's Wheel; compare *ista longa varietas* above.

nobilem : supply *aliquem*.

fumosis imaginibus : This phrase is S.'s adaptation to Roman idiom of the honorific epithet "smoky" applied to palaces in Homer, which were oriented around a central hearth, with the roof above being open to the sky. At Rome, the *imagines* of ancestors were kept in the atrium of one's home, a rectangular, columned entryway, also open to the air. Indeed, the hearth of the Roman house once stood in the atrium (*atrium < ater*, "black"). Hence, by a double metonymy, comes *fumosis imaginibus*.

in : "with a regard to."

nec quod ante nos fuit nostrum est : note the heavy alliteration.

supra fortunam : All the Hellenistic schools of philosophy were concerned with the individual's attitude toward events that he or she could not control. The Stoics believed in a deterministic universe in which every effect has a cause. Thus, from the perspective of universal Nature, nothing happens by chance. Things only seem to be fortuitous from the limited human point of view. The goal for the Stoic was not to try to escape the inescapable, but to accept what one cannot change, and take comfort in the fact that everything is part of the larger, benevolent design of Nature. To "rise above fortune," then, is a psychological state in which one ceases to derive one's identity from one's external, mutable circumstances. Take, for example, the resignation expressed by Marcus Aurelius: "I am part of a Whole which is governed by Nature . . . nothing which benefits the Whole is injurious to the part" (*Meditations* 10.6; trans. Farquharson).

6   **Puta :** "imagine."

libertinum : "Freedmen" in Rome were manumitted slaves. Upon being granted freedom by their masters, they were eligible for citizenship. In the imperial period, many *libertini* achieved considerable economic success and political power. In the eyes of freeborn Romans, however, they were viewed as social inferiors. Here S. suggests that, even in this hypothetical scenario, Lucilius could still be truly free (i.e., wise—see next note).

solus . . . liber inter ingenuos : One of the cardinal teachings of the Stoics was the paradox that only the wise man is free (*ingenuus* = "of free birth").

Si . . . distinxeris : this is an answer to the imagined question with the apodosis suppressed (see note on *quid . . . excerpere*, Letter 5.2).

non populo auctore : ablative absolute. Since there is no present active participle of *esse* in classical Latin, a noun and adjective or two nouns can stand alone in this construction when the verb "to be" is understood (A&G 419a).

veniant . . . eant : the subject is unexpressed but is probably "things" (cf. *mala bonaque* above). The idea of looking at the end, goal, or purpose of particular things (teleology) is a concern of most philosophies.

vitam beatam : the subject of S.'s essay *De vita beata* (selections from which are included in this volume).

suo iure : "in its own right," in contrast to *populo auctore.*

7   **non potest :** subject is *bonum.*

erratur : The passive of intransitive verbs is often used impersonally (A&G 208d).

Quod : "because," in answer to the hypothetical question.

instrumenta eius pro ipsa habent : *ipsa* and *eius* refer back to *beatam vitam*; for the idiom *habeo pro*, see note on *pro*, Letter 84.13.

illam = *beatam vitam.*

cum : concessive (A&G 549).

summa : here a noun = "the chief goal" or "the end" (in the sense described above, §6).

per insidiosum iter : the military march is a common image in S., an emblem primarily of drudgery.

sarcinas = the baggage of a soldier on the march, which could weigh over one hundred pounds (cf. *sarcinae* in Letter 56.13); the metaphor is anticipated by *colligunt.*

effectu : "the result"; the ablative is one of separation.

quo plus . . . hoc . . . magis : See note on *eo . . . felicius*, Letter 60.1.

Quod : see note on *A qua*, Letter 5.4.

labyrintho : a shift of image, from a straight Roman road to a complex maze.

LETTER 47

1   **Libenter** modifies *cognovi*; *familiariter* modifies *vivere.*

"Servi sunt." Immo homines . . . : The anaphoric repetition is very effective rhetorically. The imagined speakers of the refrain "Servi sunt" are the *istos* whom S. mocks below. Note how each *immo* retort in the series gradually increases in syllabic length, grammatical complexity, and semantic force.

contubernales : "messmates" (i.e., metaphorically, on life's tedious campaign), a military term that anticipates *cum servo* . . . *cenare*, §2 below, and immediately puts slave and master (from S.'s point of view) on the same footing.

conservi : for the thought, cf. Letter 28.8.

tantundem governs *fortunae*; for the grammar see note on *mali*, Letter 60.1; on *fortuna* see notes on *supra fortunam*, Letter 44.5 and *sursum deorsum*, Letter 44.4; cf. *fortuna depressit*, §10 below.

2   **turpe** is a neuter adjectve; supply *esse* (in indirect statement).

Quare, nisi quia . . . **:** an elliptical expression: "Why [would they say or think this] except for the haughty custom [which] stations a crowd of standing slaves around the master as he dines?" For the construction of *cenanti domino*, see note on *hoc idem* . . . , Letter 28.2.

Est ille plus quam capit : lit. "He eats more than he has room for," i.e., he is already too large for his frame; *est < edo, edere*, not *sum, esse*.

distentum : predicative, "until it is stretched tight."

desuetum modifies *ventrem*; *officio* is dependent upon it.

ut : "with the result that."

egerat < *egero, -ere*, not *ago, -ere*.

3   **at :** strongly adversative: "by contrast . . ."

in hoc : proleptic, answered by the *ut* clause; not only can the slaves not eat, they are not allowed to talk either.

tussis, sternumenta, singultus all stand in apposition to *fortuita*.

Magno malo (an ablative of means) goes with *luitur* (*malo* = "punishment"); *ulla voce* goes with *interpellatum*.

4   **de . . . coram . . . cum . . . pro :** note how the prepositions organize the contrasts S. develops in this section with respect to masters.

illi : "those slaves of yore," as indicated by the imperfect tenses.

consuebatur < *consuo*, not *consuesco*.

porrigere cervicem : the infinitive is dependent upon *parati*.

imminens modifies *periculum*.

in caput suum avertere is in asyndeton, or simply apposition, with *porrigere cervicem*.

in conviviis loquebantur, sed in tormentis tacebant : It was thought that information derived from slaves was unreliable unless it was extracted by torture.

5   **totidem hostes esse quot servos :** this stands in apposition to *proverbium*; in translation supply "namely that" and translate the infinitive with a finite form of the verb, and the accusatives with nominatives.

praetereo . . . : This is a textbook case of *praeteritio* (also called *occultatio*), the disingenuous "passing over" of details only to emphasize them (Lanham 104). In fact, S. enumerates quite a few examples of how masters abuse slaves in what follows.

Cum ad cenandum discubuimus . . . : Many of the slave tasks listed in §§6–8 are vividly portrayed in Petronius' description of a Roman dinner party at the house of Trimalchio (*Satyricon* 26–79), and in Frederico Fellini's 1969 film interpretation of Petronius, *Fellini Satyricon*.

discubuimus : *dis-* here means "in our respective locations"; Romans dined facing one another on couches arranged rectilinearly in a horseshoe shape around the dining room.

alius . . . : the anaphoric repetition of this word in the following sentences gives a sense both of the quantity of slaves in a wealthy household and of the almost mechanical drudgery of the extraordinary tasks they were forced to perform.

sputa : either "spittle" or (more probably) "vomit."

reliquias : scraps of food—bones, pits, rinds, etc.

subditus : "hidden away under [the couch or table]"; the idea is that the slave is on his hands and knees picking up the revellers' mess.

6   **certis ductibus :** "with precise motions."

frusta, "chunks" or "slices," is object of *excutit*, and *eruditam manum* is object of *circumferens*.

voluptatis causa refers both to the pleasure the slave instructor takes in teaching the fine but meaningless art of carving meat and to the master's pleasure for whose sake the task is performed. Morally speaking, S. suggests, either of them is more wretched than the poor apprentice slave who must acquire this skill *necessitatis causa*.

7   **vini minister . . . luctatur :** an effeminate, post-pubescent male slave whom his master is trying to keep pretty (cf. *retritis pilis aut penitus evulsis*) in order to continue using him as a sexual toy. The mythic pro-

totype is Ganymede, whom Zeus snatched up to Olympus to be his cupbearer.

militari habitu : "in military garb" is a more natural translation of this phrase than (for example) "though he now has a soldier's bearing" (Costa p. 31), which somewhat glosses over the sexual role-playing the passage suggests; cf. *pervigilat*, a military word, which continues the metaphor.

retritis pilis : "with his hair scraped off"; *retritus* is the perfect passive participle of *retero, -ere* (to rub off/away), and refers to the scraping off of body hair, probably with a strigil.

tota nocte : The use of the ablative, as opposed to the accusative, to express duration of time is non-standard, but admissable (A&G 424b).

in cubiculo vir, in convivio puer est : meaning perhaps that he takes the dominant role in the bedroom, though he cultivates a boyish demeanor at dinner parties.

8   **convivarum censura** is humorously ironic. The *censura* was a real public office at Rome. The person who held it was responsible for public morals and tax assessment. Here S. uses it comically of the slave whose job it is to monitor the guests' behavior—to ensure that it is sufficiently outrageous to be invited back to dinner again.

quos . . . revocet : relative clause of characteristic (A&G 535) with the antecedent of *quos* suppressed.

adulatio et intemperantia aut gulae aut linguae : a very clever chiastic arrangement of words. *Adulatio* refers to the parasite who fawns on his host and goes logically with *linguae*; *intemperantia*, with *gulae*, refers to the gourmand. But the jumbled succession of words gives the impression that these activities are all of a piece, which of course for S. they are.

notitia : "knowledge [of]" or "familiarity [with]."

cuius . . . cuius . . . cuius : In this lengthy indirect question, each *cuius* is an adjective agreeing with *rei* (expressed only once). Note how S. varies the construction over the course of the sentence: the first two *cuius* phrases are dependent upon nominatives (*sapor, aspectus*), the third on the ablative *novitate*; the two final questions in the list are introduced by the interrogative pronoun *quid*. The very structure of the sentence thus conveys both the mind-boggling *notitia* required of the household slaves who do the shopping and, at the same time, the complexity of the master's decadent taste.

erigi, "to be aroused," was apparently a standard term for overeating to the point of nausea (so Summers p. 212).

Di melius! "The gods [would want] better!" With this sentence S. comments on the absurdity of any such master as described above refusing to eat with his slaves. Who, S. asks, is the real slave here? The thought is more fully developed in §17 below.

9 **habet :** the unexpressed subject is the master; the point of the statement "How many masters from among those [slaves] does he have?" is illustrated in the next sentences.

Callisti dominum : Callistus, whose original master is unknown, was subsequently sold to and manumitted by the imperial household. He was one of an increasing number of freedmen under the empire who acquired considerable wealth and influence at court under the emperors Caligula and Claudius.

titulum : a "For Sale" sign with the slave's name, price, and provenance affixed.

reicula : "rejects," "castoffs"; some editors prefer *ridicula* instead of *reicula.*

produxerat : "put him up for sale."

aliis intrantibus : an ablative absolute with concessive force.

in primam decuriam : a *decuria* is any lot of ten items; the first *decuria* was apparently where *ridicula* (or *reicula*) *mancipia* were sold.

praeco = the slave auctioneer; Callistus was sold with the bargain merchandise while the auctioneer was still warming up, before the event even started in earnest.

ipse is Callistus.

apologavit : not "apologized" but "rejected" (a Greek word and idiom).

domino quam multa Callistus! "how much has Callistus [cost] his master" (i.e., in the end).

10 **Vis** (< *volo, velle*) here is idiomatic = "please, if you would," in which case translate *cogitare* as an imperative.

isdem . . . eodem . . . aeque : note the variation of construction to express the same basic idea. For S.'s view of human equality, cf. Letter 44.

ingenuum : see note on *solus . . . inter ingenuous*, Letter 44.6.

Variana clade refers to the decimation of three entire legions (approximately fifteen thousand men) under the command of Varus by German tribes in 9 C.E. Varus' military debacle was the Romans' Pearl Harbor, a symbol of utter misfortune. In our extant sources, no one is reported to have survived this disaster, so either S. had access to other versions or the ablative *Variana clade* is more temporal than one of source or origin (though *depressit* suggests the latter). Be that as it may, S. is clearly using the event as an instance of the unpredictability of Fortune (cf. *sursum deorsum*, Letter 44.4).

senatorium per militiam auspicantes gradum : in one sense, the career path to the Senate was always *per militiam*, as all entry offices of state were connected to the military. In S.'s time, however, induction into the Senate was normally restricted to the sons of senators in a way it was not in the late republic and early empire.

contemne nunc : the tone is sarcastic.

eius fortunae : a genitive of quality depending on *hominem* (A&G 345); cf. *sordidioris operae*, §15 below.

11   **Nolo . . . immittere . . . disputare . . . :** Another textbook case of *praeteritio* (see note on *praetereo*, §5 above). S. has given us plenty of detail in the previous sections on how Roman masters are *superbissimi, crudelissimi,* and *contumeliosissimi.*

locum : not a physical place, but a "topic."

summa : see note on *summa*, Letter 44.7.

sic cum inferiore vivas quemadmodum tecum superiorem velis vivere : a Stoic version of the Golden Rule, reiterated in the correlative expression *quantum . . . tantundem* below. For the thought that power and prestige is relative, not absolute, cf. Letter 43.2.

12   **Bona aetas est** : "You're young yet" (Summers p. 214), as opposed to the persons in the examples cited below.

Hecuba . . . Croesus . . . Darei mater . . . Platon . . . Diogenes : The list of characters moves from an example from myth to two from history and closes with two (very close to home) from philosophy. Hecuba was the Queen of Troy, familiar from Homer's *Iliad*. Her capture and reduction to slavery is the theme of Euripides' *Hecuba*. Croesus was the wealthy king of Sardis, whose hybris led to his capture by

Cyrus (Herodotus, *Histories* 1.25–93). The Persian King Darius' mother was Sisigambis, whom Alexander captured after his victory at Issus. Plato is said to have been captured by pirates and ransomed by his friends on his way back from a research trip to Sicily (Diogenes Laertius 3.19–20). Diogenes the Cynic was also captured by pirates and sold as a slave to a Corinthian master. The story goes that on the auction block Diogenes was asked what he could do and replied "Rule over people." He then pointed to a rich passerby and said, "That man needs a master." For his wit, Diogenes was purchased by the man and became tutor to his children. He lived so contentedly in his master's house that he refused to be ransomed (Diogenes Laertius 6.74).

13   **consilium :** "the decision-making process."

Hoc loco : "On this point," referring to the bold statement S. has just made.

delicatorum is used substantively.

Hos ... eosdem : i.e., the masters who say *nihil turpius*, etc.

alienorum servorum osculantes manum : in an attempt to ingratiate themselves with the slaves' master, these forlorn masters must stoop to ingratiating themselves with the master's slaves.

14   **quam :** "how."

invidiam ... contumeliam : "Ill will" (felt by slaves) and "abuse" (inflicted by masters) are what the *maiores* kept at bay from both parties, knowing that one breeds the other. For the contrast between current and past practices in slaveholding, cf. note on *illi*, §4.

patrem familiae ... familiares : cf. *familiariter*, §1 above. S. seeks an etymological validation of his claims about the slave-owning principles of the *maiores*. The *paterfamilias* (= *pater* + an old genitive form of *familia*) was an important legal term and concept at Rome. The appellation *familiares* for slaves, contrary to what S. implies here, was not limited to the mimes in S.'s day.

diem festum : the Saturnalia, the topic of Letter 18 (included in this volume).

utique : "in particular". Masters, according to S., are entitled to eat with their slaves on any day they please, though he notes with interest that during the Saturnalia a special day was reserved for that practice.

honores : not "honors," but "offices."

ius dicere : "to pronounce verdicts."

15   **sordidioris operae :** a genitive of quality depending on *quosdam* (cf. *eius fortunae*, §10 above).

ut puta : "as/take for example, . . ."; for the use of *puta*, cf. Letter 44.6.

Sibi quisque dat mores, ministeria casus adsignat : this statement explains *non ministeriis . . . sed moribus* above. The philosopher Heraclitus once said that a man's fate is his character.

quia digni sunt . . . ut sint : i.e., in either case, good company breeds good character.

ex : see note at Letter 43.4; same construction with *ex* below, §16.

16   **Non est . . . quod :** see note on *non est quod*, Letter 43.1.

et here is adverbial.

cessat : "is useless."

experire : not an active, fourth-conjugation infinitive but the second-person singular, present imperative form of a deponent verb.

equum . . . : a positive analogy that picks up on *iumenta* above (§5); the horse is an example of *bona materia*, literally without trappings (cf. *sine artifice*).

vestis modo : "in the manner of clothing"; *vestis* is genitive, *modo* ablative. S. here qualifies his metaphor slightly, telling us how our *condicio = vestis*.

17   **"Servus est" :** a rhetorical reprise of the opening sentences.

alius . . . alius . . . alius . . . : note how the point of reference for the *alius* has changed: in §1 it was the slave; here it is the would-be master. In the following examples, S. mocks the slavish addiction of respectable free citizens of high standing to the goods and services typically provided by slaves. The point is summed up by *nulla servitus turpior est quam voluntaria* below.

aniculae . . . ancillulae : a tongue-twisting pun.

mancipia pantomimorum : either supply *esse* in indirect statement with *ostendam* or take in apposition to *iuvenes*.

Quare : not "why" here but "wherefore" in a connecting *Qui* clause (*quare = et ea re*; see note on *a qua*, Letter 60.4).

non est quod : see note at Letter 43.1.

quo minus (= *ut eo minus*), lit. "whereby the less," is used in result clauses that are introduced by a main verb of hindering or preventing (A&G 558b).

superbe superiorem : more wordplay.

18 **vocare ad pilleum servos et dominos de fastigio suo deicere :** note the chiasm, framed as an antithesis. *Vocare ad pilleum*, "to manumit," refers to the felt skullcap (*pilleum*) that freed Roman slaves wore as a sign of their new status. See note on *libertinum*, Letter 44.6.

clientes . . . salutatores : see notes on *ianitores*, Letter 43.4, and *salutantium*, Letter 84.12.

quod deo sat est : the verb *colo, -ere*, which has religious connotations, is what prompts this unfavorable comparison of masters to gods.

non potest amor cum timore misceri : In the context of gods and punishment, cf. 1 John 4:18: "There is no fear in love, but perfect love casts out all fear. For fear has to do with punishment."

19 **verborum . . . verberibus :** note the wordplay; for the thought, cf. §3 above.

et : not "and," but "also" (*non* here negates *laedit*).

20 **Regum nobis induimus animos :** "We have adopted the attitude or temperament of kings," not in a good sense, but in the haughty way described in the previous and subsequent sentences.

obliti < *obliviscor* takes the genitive case.

sic . . . sic is answered by *quasi*.

a cuius rei periculo : ablative of separation in a connecting *qui* clause; see note on *a qua*, Letter 60.4.

nocendi . . . querendo : S. underscores the absurdity of equating mere complaint with actual injury by expressing both with the same part of speech—a gerund—yet using it differently: the genitive *nocendi* depends on *occasionem*, *querendo* is an ablative of cause or means.

acceperunt iniuriam ut facerent : with *facerent* supply *iniuriam*. Does *ut* introduce a purpose clause or a result clause? Do kings look for an excuse to harm others by claiming to be harmed (= purpose clause), or do they do so as a result of taking minor irritants (cf. *offendit*, §19) too seriously? The linguistic ambiguity here seems to mirror the motivational ambiguity.

21 **non est enim tibi exhortatione opus :** This statement could well apply to all of S.'s letters to Lucilius. On this occasion S. has already expressed confidence in his friend's fair treatment of his slaves (cf. *prudentiam tuam . . . eruditiam*, §1 above).

placent sibi : i.e., good character is its own reward.

LETTER 62

1   **studia liberalia** are essentially the same as the "liberal arts," as understood today (see Costa, *17 Letters*, pp. 190–91). They are "free" because only free men with free time on their hands could pursue them; for *ad*, see note on *ad*, Letter 43.1.

videri is dependent upon *volunt*, the infinitive *obstare* upon *videri*, which is used impersonally; the subject of *obstare* is *turbam negotiorum*.

simulant . . . augent : People invent excuses (*occupationes*; cf. *causas* below) to avoid intellectual pursuits.

ipsi se occupant : note how S. uses the verb form derived from the noun. *Ipsi se* is emphatic (cf. *ipsi . . . nos*, Letter 60.2). This whole sentence puts the blame where it belongs—on the individual person, not her circumstances.

Vaco : "I am *un*occupied."

ubicumque sum, ibi meus sum : Self-sufficiency (in Greek, *autárkeia*) was the chief aim of Hellenistic philosophy, a concept that harks back to the Socratic ideal of "being stronger than oneself," i.e., of allowing reason to govern one's appetites and the emotions.

non trado, sed commodo : terms of commerce that make it clear what S. means by *occupationes*. S. does not sell, but only lends, himself out (cf. *meus sum*, "I belong to myself").

consector is an "intensive" or "iterative" form of *consequor, -sequi*. Such verbs add *-to, -ito*, or *-so* to the supine stem and denote repeated or intensive action (A&G 263.2). *Tracto* (< *traho, -ere*) and *converso* (< *converto, -ere*) below are also iteratives. In using them here S. is emphasizing lifestyles, that is, habituated behavior.

perdendi temporis : gerundive (A&G 504).

salutare : not the infinitive of *saluto, -are*, but neuter singular of the adjective *salutaris, -e*, modifying *aliquid*.

2   **cum** : the first *cum* in this sentence is a conjunction, the second a preposition.

non tamen mihi abduco : cf. *non trado sed commodo* above; for the dative see note on *mihi*, Letter 84.1; for the thought, cf. Letter 28.

quibus : the dative is dependent upon *congregavit*.

tempus : "occasion."

cum optimo quoque : "with whoever is best."

in quocumque saeculo fuerunt : S.'s intellectual companions are not limited to a particular time or place.

3   **Demetrium** : A Cynic philosopher from Greece, who lived and preached at Rome during the reigns of Caligula, Claudius, and Nero. S. holds Demetrius up as a model of virtue in several of his writings. He is said to have been exiled by Nero sometime after S.'s death.

conchyliatis = "men dressed in purple," so called after the composted mussel shells that provided the dye for the togas of high-ranking Romans. The adjective is used substantively here and forms an ablative absolute with *relictis*.

seminudo : The Cynics prided themselves on their disregard for appearances; cf. Letter 5.2.

nihil ei deesse : see note on *ubicumque . . . sum*, §1 above.

Brevissima ad divitias per contemptum divitiarum via est : the paradox hinges on the fact that *ad divitias* is figurative, *divitiarum* literal. With the meaning of the sentence in mind, note how far away *brevissima* is from its noun, *via*.

aliis habenda permiserit : with *habenda* supply *omnia*. S. seems to mean that Demetrius was not, so to speak, a Cynic without a cause, who simply denounced *omnia*, but rather that he was self-sufficient and engaged in self-abnegation in order to "enrich" others' lives. *Permiserit* picks up on *commodo*, §1 above.

LETTER 18

1   **December . . . sudat** : an obvious oxymoron; the city "sweats" in the cold month of December owing to the bustling spirit of holiday cheer. However, *civitas sudat* may also be a distant echo of Plato's famous description of the "feverish city" (*Republic* 372e), which can only be cured by philosophy (cf. *sanitatis*, §15 below).

Ius = the legal "right" to indulge in a pubic display of luxury. In all periods of Roman history, there was some form of luxury tax or morality legislation. During the Saturnalia, such laws were curtailed.

sonant omnia : Pliny the Younger complains bitterly of Saturnalian noise (*Letters* 2.17.24).

tamquam : "as if."

dies is accusative plural, joined by *et* with *Saturalia*; both are objects of the preposition *inter*.

Adeo . . . ut non forms a result clause. S.'s point here comes as a surprise. One expects S. to say that there is, or should be, no real difference between holidays and business days because a day is a day, and that we should go on conducting our business on holidays (a thought he in fact entertains in §2). But instead of making a normative statement to that effect here, he ironically concedes that there is no difference between the two (*nihil interest*) because the populace at large treats the whole year as if it were a holiday. Officially the Saturnalia ran through December 17–23. Many of its traditions have been incorporated into the Christmas and New Year's holiday.

errasse = *erravisse*.

2 **haberem . . . conferrem** : imperfect subjunctives in a present contrary-to-fact condition.

existimares is subjunctive in an indirect question.

ne dissidere videremur cum publicis moribus : *videremur* is subjunctive in a negative purpose clause; for the sentiment, cf. Letter 5.2.

hilarius is a comparative adverb modifying *cenandum*, which is a gerundive being used impersonally (supply *esse*).

togam is accusative, continuing the indirect statement set up by *existimares*. During the Saturnalia, Roman men would "shed their togas" and don a flimsy dressing gown called a *synthesis*, which they wore to dinner parties.

quod : see note on *quod*, Letter 60.1.

nisi here = "except."

civitatis : objective genitive.

vestem mutavimus : *vestem mutare* is a fixed idiom meaning "to go into mourning" (L&S *vestis*, I.2.a). The Roman state would do this only in times of national crisis, thus S. is adding an ironic twist to the phrase here by applying it to a different set of circumstances—the gaiety of the Saturnalia.

3 **partibus** : see note on Letter 28.10; the ablative is dependent upon *functus*.

per omnia : "altogether"; "in everything."

pilleatae turbae : see note on *vocare ad pilleum*, Letter 47.18.

voluisses : pluperfect subjunctive in the apodosis of a "mixed" contrary-to-fact condition, whose protasis contains the perfect indicative, novi (see A&G 523).

animo is the object of *impero*, which is used here impersonally; *ut* introduces a substantive clause of purpose (A&G 563).

solus : supply *animus*.

illas : i.e., *voluptates*.

tunc is answered by *cum*.

procubuit is used here both figuratively and literally since the Romans dined on couches.

capit : the subject is *animus*.

nec it nec abducitur covers both active and passive tendencies to luxury.

4   **Hoc . . . illud** : both demonstratives are proleptic; the infinitives that follow stand in apposition to them.

     eadem, sed non eodem modo, facere : the polyptoton emphasizes the contrast between the end result of an action (*eadem . . . facere*) and the motivation behind it (*non eodem modo*).

5   **Ceterum** : essentially an accusative of respect (lit. "with respect to the rest"), *ceterum* can be used idiomatically with restrictive force to mean "but" (L&S *ceterum*, II.4).

     praecepto . . . praecipiam : Note the chiastic structure of this sentence, which juxtaposes the source of S.'s instruction and its destination: Lucilius, too (*tibi quoque*), is to be the beneficiary of what S. has learned *ex praecepto magnorum virorum* (namely, Epicurus and his circle; see §9 below).

     interponas : "set aside"; hortatory subjunctive (so too *dicas*, below). S. here is proposing days of fasting as an antidote to days of feasting.

     quibus is ablative of time (A&G 423).

6   **Hoc** = the *vilissimus cibus . . . dura atque horrida vestis* of the previous section.

     In ipsa securitate . . . firmetur : another instance of rhetorical redundancy, or copia (see note on *magnus . . . nec minor*, Letter 5.6); *securitate* (< *sine cura*) = "the condition of being free from cares"; for *ipsa*, see note at Letter 28.3.

     decurrit : "performs maneuvers" (Summers p. 183).

supervacuo labore : "hard work that has no immediate purpose"; a large part of the soldier's job, then as now, involved training and construction projects.

necessario : in contrast with *supervacuo*, though here it is dative (dependent on *sufficere*; supply *labori*).

Quem . . . nolueris . . . exerceas forms a future condition introduced by a relative pronoun (where *quem* = *si [ali] quem*; see A&G 519).

Hoc : used proleptically with *ne . . . expavescerent*.

quod is the object of *expavescerent* (subjunctive in a purpose clause); the demonstrative *illud* is unexpressed.

7   **Non est . . . quod** : see note on Letter 43.1.

dicere : "mean."

Timoneas cenas : Timon of Athens—from whose name the adjective *Timoneus* is formed (and after whom Shakespeare's play is named)— was a misanthrope who dropped out of society and lived in a cave. Summers (p. 183) suggests that *Timonea cena* may have been a colloquial phrase for a meal taken out of doors, i.e., a picnic. Similarly, *pauperum cellae* were rooms in the homes of the rich decorated in a rustic fashion to which they could retire occasionally from their day-to-day opulence.

divitiarum taedio ludit : Roman imperial excess in a nutshell.

verus : as opposed to a make-believe one (cf. *ludit* above, *lusus* below). S. is clarifying here what he meant by *paupertatem imitati*, §6 above.

. . . et sagum et panis durus ac sordidus : None of the adjectives actually agrees with *sagum* (cloak), which is neuter, but *verus*, *durus*, and *sordidus* are meant to be taken closely with all three nouns— *grabatus*, *sagum*, and *panis*. (The same effect as in *adulatio . . . linguae*, Letter 47.8).

ut non is a result clause with a point: i.e., this is the way to guarantee that one is not just playing games.

ad : "with a view to"; see note on Letter 43.1.

fortuna is ablative with *opus esse*.

debet is used absolutely: "owes" or "is bound to provide" (Summers p. 183).

irata has a concessive force here: "though she [*Fortuna*] is angry about it."

8   **Non est . . . quare :** "There is [no reason] why you should . . ."; cf. *Quid est quare*, Letter 44.3

tibi . . . videaris : the idiom *videor mihi* means "I think" (A&G 375b).

Facies . . . faciunt : this sentence is a remarkable expression of S.'s awareness of and compassion for human suffering.

illo nomine te suspice, quod : "admire yourself on that account, namely" (see L&S *nomen*, I.B.2); *illo* is proleptic.

non coactus : To actively choose any state of affairs makes one psychologically impervious to the twists and turns of fortune. Cf. *hoc est praeoccupare tela fortunae*, §11 below.

pati semper quam aliquando experiri : the contrast is between both "always" and "sometimes" and "suffering" and "experience" (cf. *experimentum*, §7 above).

palum : a stake planted in the ground at which Roman soldiers practiced combat techniques.

Securius divites erimus, si scierimus . . . : note the alliteration, assonance, internal rhyme, and paradox (*divites . . . pauperes*) of this sentence; take the adverb *securius* with *divites*.

9   **ille magister voluptatis Epicurus :** see note at Letter 28.9. Epicurus taught that pleasure was the goal and object of human life, but that a self-sufficient individual will forgo pleasure if it leads in any way to pain. Thus, although a hedonist, Epicurus was also an ascetic and was famous in antiquity for his austere lifestyle.

quibus : same as *quibus*, §5 above.

maligne : "sparingly"; "grudgingly."

visurus expresses purpose (A&G 499.2).

dignum : supply *esset* in indirect question (cf. *deesset . . . deesset*).

quod . . . pensaret : this *quod* clause (a kind of relative clause of characteristic; A&G 535f) depends on *dignum*.

quis for *aliquis*.

magno labore : ablative of price (A&G 416).

Charino magistratu : an ablative absolute expressing time. The Greek cities officially recorded dates by stating who held the archonship (= *magistratu*) in that year. Charinus was archon at Athens in 290–289 B.C.E.

Polyaenum : one of Epicurus' original disciples.

non negates *toto*.

Metrodorum : another original Epicurean, often mentioned in Epicurus' letters.

tantum profecerit : *tantum* may be understood either as an accusative of extent of space ("he had not yet made progress to such an extent/degree") or an internal accusative ("he had not yet made so much progress"). See A&G 390c with n. 2. Given *non toto asse,* the use of *tantus* is somewhat ironic.

10   **hoc :** "this *kind* [of]"; cf. *illa* below, "that kind [of]."

Et : i.e., in addition to being *saturitas.*

subinde : "continually."

hordeacei panis : "barley bread."

ad id : "to that point/place/condition"; answered by *quod* (same construction in §11 below).

11   **qui occisurus est :** i.e., the executioner.

descendere is the predicate to *quanta . . . est magnitudo.*

sua sponte : cf. *non coactus,* §8 above.

ad extrema . . . decretis : "those who have been sentenced to death."

12   **minimoque :** cf. *parvo . . . dimittitur,* Letter 60.3.

paupertate . . . commercium : another effective oxymoron, complementary to *divites . . . pauperes,* §8 above.

aude . . . deo : the quotation is from Vergil, *Aeneid* 8.364–65. King Evander is speaking to Aeneas, urging him to follow the precedent set by Heracles, who did not despise Evander's humble accommodations. Heracles was a mythological paradigm for Stoic self-sufficiency.

13   **deo** = Heracles, but by extension "God," the animating force of the Stoic universe. Note how S. echoes the language of the quotation.

Quarum : Connecting *qui* clause; antecedent is *opes.*

efficere . . . ut : a substantive clause after a verb of effort (A&G 563.e).

quod : another connecting *qui* clause comprising the apodosis of a condition; the antecedent is the whole of the previous sentence.

illis . . . illas : the referent is still *opes.*

exituras : "on their way out the door."

14   **complicare :** "fold up," both literally (referring to the wax tablet or piece of papyrus on which S. would have written the original form of his letter) and figuratively.

"redde quod debes" : see notes on *lucellum*, Letter 5.7 (cf. 28.9).

Delegabo : *delego, -are* = "to transfer or reassign a debt."

numeratio : continuing the monetary metaphor, "tally."

Hoc, quam verum sit, necesse est scias : note the multiple prolepses; *quam*, "how," introduces an indirect question.

cum : causal.

15 **affectus** : "emotion/state of mind."

ex amore . . . ex odio : Cf. Catullus' well-worn epigram (85): *odi et amo. quare id faciam, fortasse, requiris? / nescio, sed fieri sentio et excrucior* ("I hate and I love. Why do I do that, perhaps you will ask? / I'm not sure, but I certainly feel it when it happens and it's like torture").

non minus inter seria quam inter lusus et iocos : here S. ties the saying of Epicurus into his larger theme.

nec . . . ex quam magna. . . sed in qualem : for the thought, cf. Letter 28.4.

quam is adverbial, "how," with *magna.*

ignis : the analogy follows from *exardescit* above.

quo : supply *loco.*

maximum : supply *ignem.*

solida : like *arida* and *facilia* below, a neuter generalizing plural adjective used substantively; see note on *tenerrimis*, Letter 84.4.

receperunt : the perfect tense is "gnomic," indicating a general truth (A&G 475).

rursus : "conversely."

corripi facilia : lit. "things easy to be ignited," i.e., easily flammable; *facilis* is one of several adjectives denoting fitness or quality that can take an infinitive to complete its meaning (A&G 461).

DE PROVIDENTIA

1.1 **Lucili** : the same Lucilius of the Letters (see note on *LUCILIO SUO*, Letter 60.1).

ita : not the correlative that one often finds in the apodosis of a condition (A&G 512b), but idiomatically with *quid* expressing surprise or reproach (L&S *ita*, I.D.a): "How/Why then?" Since the apodosis is

cast as a question (see note on *regeretur* below), there is obviously
some doubt about the truth of the protasis in the speaker's mind (i.e.,
that the world is in fact ruled by Providence; otherwise there would be
no need for this treatise). About the apodosis (that bad things happen
to good people), there is no doubt. Translate: "Why, then, if [as you,
Seneca, suggest] the world is ruled by Providence, do bad things happen to good persons?"

providentia : On the Stoic conception of Providence, see note on
providentia, Letter 5.8.

regeretur . . . acciderent : *regeretur* (= imperfect subjunctive in a
dependent clause in an indirect question introduced by *quaesisti*) represents what would probably have been a present indicative in the
original question. *Acciderent*, the main verb of the indirect question
(and apodosis of the condition), is imperfect subjunctive following the
rule of secondary sequence of tenses (A&G 575).

commodius : comparative adverb.

operis : a written work or treatise.

redderetur < *reddo, reddere* (< *re* + *dare*), lit. "to give back"; here "to
answer" or "address." The subjunctive has a potential force ("would"
or "might"; see A&G 445); the imperfect tense "denotes a future act
transferred to the point of view of past time" (A&G 511 n.1); in this
way it is not unlike the apodosis of a present contrary-to-fact condition (see A&G 517 n.1 and 447.3 note).

cum . . . probaremus : circumstantial *cum* with imperfect subjunctive
(see A&G 546); this clause represents the circumstances under which
the sentence with *redderetur* would be true (or would have been true
if carried out). The whole sentence might be translated as follows:
"This would be better addressed in the course of a treatise when/where
we would show that providence presides over all things and that God
has our interests at heart."

contradictionem : "opposing argument."

manente lite integra : ablative absolute; the *lis* is the whole imaginary lawsuit of which S.'s defense forms a part.

rem non difficilem : perhaps the matter is "not difficult" because the
gods—paradoxically, the defendants in this case—are on S.'s side.

causam deorum agam : note the legal metaphor (see L&S *causa*,
II.E; cf. *lis* and *contradictio* above).

1.5   **adversus :** a preposition governing *optimos* (cf. *adversus*, 2.6, 4.5, and 6.6 below). *Adversus* can simply mean "toward" or "with respect to," but given the argument that follows, there seems also to be a double entendre here that announces the paradoxical theme of the essay: The gods are "best toward the best men," but they sometimes are so by setting adversity in their paths.

optimis : agrees with *diis*; translate as a relative clause: "with the gods [who are] best toward the best men."

natura : for the importance of *natura* in Stoic philosophy, see note at *natura,* Letter 60.3.

ut . . . noceant : A substantive clause of either purpose (A&G 563) or, arguably, result (A&G 568).

bona bonis : S. moves from the particular and personal (*optimos optimis*) to the abstract (*bona* and *bonis* are neuter plural), keeping the terms similarly juxtaposed.

conciliante virtute : ablative absolute; virtue is what good men and the gods have in common.

dico : not so much "say" as "mean" (cf. *dicere,* Letter 18.7).

Immo etiam : this combination of words can contradict a preceding statement or simply qualify it. Here S. clarifies what he means by the surprising statement that there exists a friendship among men and gods: "Do I mean friendship? Yes, but what I mean by that is . . ."; or "Do I [really] mean friendship? Well, not quite that, but . . ."

necessitudo : "a close connection," "relationship," or "bond" (L&S *necessitudo,* II).

bonus : an adjective used substantively (A&G 288).

tempore : they differ in time (*tempore* is an ablative of specification; A&G 418) because gods are immortal, men are not.

tantum : the limiting adverb "only."

discipulus . . . aemulator . . . progenies : these nominatives stand in apposition to *bonus.* Note the balanced phrasing of this sentence: there are three terms of description each for man and god.

educat is indicative < *educo, educare,* not *educo, educere.*

2.5   **quanto :** ablative of degree of difference with *aliter* (A&G 414); *indulgeant* is subjunctive in indirect question.

ad studia obeunda : gerundive with *ad* expressing purpose (A&G 506).

mature is an adverb.

feriatis : perfect participle from the deponent verb *ferior*, "to rest from work, observe a holiday, be idle."

illis refers to *liberos*; it is a dative of separation with the compound verb *excutiunt* (A&G 381).

2.6 **Patrium** : adjective with *animum*, in an emphatic position.

fortiter amat : cf. the English expression "tough love."

operibus . . . doloribus, damnis : note the asyndeton (see note on *queror*, Letter 60.1).

exagitentur : a hortatory or "jussive" subjunctive (A&G 439).

saginata : neuter plural perfect passive participle used substantively (< *sagino, saginare*, "to fatten").

nec labore tantum sed motu : just to move around is a chore for fat things; for *tantum*, see note 5 above.

ipso . . . onere : like *labore* and *motu*, an ablative of cause (A&G 404).

sui : either a possessive genitive (A&G 343), "of themselves" or "their own" (i.e., the *saginata*), or a genitive of material (A&G 344), "[consisting] of themselves."

Non fert ullum ictum inlaesa felicitas : a clever *sententia* rounds off the thought and provides a transition to the next point. Note S.'s pairing of the semantically related words *ictum* and *inlaesa* (the noun *ictum*, "blow" < *icio, icere*, "to strike"; the adjective *inlaesa* < *in* (= "not") + *laedo, laedere*, "to harm, hurt, injure"). The staccato rhythm and alliteration of this sentence add to its effect. The idea that too much happiness or prosperity is a dangerous thing—it was thought that it provoked the gods to jealousy (though this is not S.'s own point here)—is very old. Cf. the story of King Croesus (Herodotus, *Hist.* 1.29–92).

cui : dative of possession (A&G 373), or better, a paradoxical dative of advantage (A&G 376).

fuit : "has been."

suis : "his own," reflexive possessive adjective harking back to *cui*.

callum . . . duxit : *callum, -i* is hardened or tough skin; *duco, ducere* here means "produced," "acquired," or "created" (L&S *duco*, I.B. 6–7); for the subject of *duxit* supply the demonstrative *is* (answering to *cui*).

cedit . . . cecidit : note the wordplay. The good man does not yield (*cedo, cedere*) to anything bad, but even if he falls (*cecidit* < *cado, cadere*), he still fights from his knees.

2.7 **quam** : *quam* + a superlative (here *optimos*) = "as . . . as possible" (A&G 291c).

impetum capiunt : "feel moved" (lit. "take [in] an impression"); supply "the gods" as subject.

spectandi : a gerund, dependent on *impetum* (translate "at observing"); *magnos viros conluctantis* is its object.

conluctantis : accusative plural (A&G 77). Note the athletic metaphor here and, with *exerceantur* above, continued below with the depiction of Cato's suicidal heroism as a *spectaculum*.

2.9 **vir** stands in apposition to *spectaculum*.

fortis cum fortuna : note the wordplay, which emphasizes the struggle of the brave man with fortune.

compositus : agrees with *vir*; *compono* + *cum* is an idiom used especially of gladiators being "matched" for combat (L&S *compono*, I.B.1). With the words *spectaculum, par* ("a match"; cf. L&S par, II.B), *ecce . . . ecce*, and *provocavit* (see note below), S. is clearly trying to conjure up an image of a gladiatorial contest at which he is playing the part of *magister ludorum*. But the adjective *compositus* can also mean "calm," "unperturbed." Perhaps both meanings are to be felt here.

utique : "especially."

provocavit : "to egg on," "call forth [to fight]," "challenge" (L&S *provoco*, I.B.1), as any crowd-pleasing gladiator would do.

eo : *eo* is added by a modern editor; if correct it means "to the matter," or "in that direction" (i.e., toward earth).

quam : "than" with the comparative *pulchrius* above.

ut spectet : a substantive clause of purpose (A&G 563d).

Catonem : Marcus Porcius Cato, the Younger (95–46 B.C.E.), great grandson of Cato the Censor (234–149 B.C.E.), a Stoic "saint" and revered Roman statesman.

iam partibus non semel fractis : ablative absolute; *partibus* = "political party or faction" (L&S *pars*, II.A). In the last days of the republic, Cato had joined the side of Pompey and his supporters against Caesar during the civil war. The Pompeians were defeated at the Battle of Pharsalus (48 B.C.E.) and finally overthrown in North Africa at Thapsus (46 B.C.E.).

inter ruinas . . . rectum : Cato was "upright" in both the physical and moral senses: "standing erect" (in the midst of ruin), and "just" (in the midst of civic upheaval).

2.10   **Licet** : see note on *licet*, Letter 60.4.

in : here = "to."

unius : the one man is Julius Caesar.

qua exeat : *qua* is ablative; supply *viam* as an antecedent; *exeat* is subjunctive in a relative clause of purpose (A&G 537.2; and see note on *quae . . . sint*, Letter 5.1).

latam < the adjective *latus, -a, -um*.

purum et innoxium : i.e., the sword was not used to carry out massacres, assassinations, or proscriptions during the civil war.

libertatem : cf. *libertati* above; not political freedom but moral, psychological freedom. Paradoxically, Cato, like Martin Luther King Jr., will be "free at last" in death.

patriae non potuit : Supply *dare*.

Aggredere : imperative < the deponent verb *aggredior, aggredi*.

diu modifies *meditatum*.

alter alterius manu caesi : "each slain by the hand of the other"; the singular forms *alter alterius* denote reciprocity of action by two persons (A&G 315a) and thus can agree with the plurals *iacent* and *caesi* (cf. A&G 317d, e). Juba and Petreius, both supporters of Pompey, intentionally killed each other in a duel in order to avoid capture (and ignominious pardon) by Caesar.

fortis . . . conventio : supply *fuit*.

fati conventio : a "coming together of Fate," perhaps in two senses: the actual duel fought to the death by Juba and Petreius and, metaphorically, the culmination of their respective fates on a more cosmic scale.

nostram : Cato is still speaking to his *animus*, or simply using the "royal we," a common practice in Latin.

tam turpe est . . . : what Cato means is that he does not need a fellow soldier to kill him, as Juba and Petreius did, to avoid being captured alive and being tempted to beg for his life; he will commit suicide instead.

tam is correlative with *quam*, "as . . . as."

2.11   **spectasse** is perfect infinitive, a contraction for *spectavisse* (A&G 181a) in an indirect statement after *liquet*.

dum . . . dum . . . dum . . . dum : the anaphora gives a vivid sense of what the gods see, as the dramatic events of Cato's suicide unfold.

sui vindex : something of a paradox, since by definition an avenger is someone other than the one from whom revenge is exacted. Cato is mentally fierce and resolute enough (*acerrimus*) to be his own avenger (i.e., he does not need, nor will he wait for, an enemy to take vengence on him).

alienae saluti : referring to *discedentium* below. For the meaning of the adjective *alienus*, see note on *aliena opera*, Letter 84.1.

discedentium : i.e., the soldiers and entourage accompanying Cato in retreat from Caesar.

studia etiam nocte ultima tractat : a true philosopher, Cato spends the evening of his demise in study; cf. Seneca's own suicide, where, according to Tacitus, he spent his last moments dictating to secretaries (*Annals* 15.63).

indignamque quae . . . contaminaretur : *quae* introduces either a relative clause of characteristic (A&G 535f) or, arguably, a relative clause of result (A&G 537.2): Cato's soul was so holy that it was incapable of being sullied by the sword. According to Plutarch (*Cato the Younger* 70), the wound Cato inflicted upon himself did not kill him at first; death came only when he tore open the wound that his doctor had begun to˜stitch back up.

2.12 **Inde** : "for this or that reason," proleptic with *non fuit . . . semel* below (for prolepsis, see note on *hoc unum . . . ut*, Letter 5.1).

crediderim : potential subjunctive (A&G 447).

non fuit . . . semel : this sentence answers to *inde*. Plutarch says the wound was not decisive because Cato had previously injured his sword hand by slapping a disobedient slave.

parte : "role" (a metaphor from the theater). Like a winning actor, Cato's virtue comes back for an encore performance.

se ostenderet : the subject is *virtus*; *ostenderet* is subjunctive in a purpose clause.

non enim tam magno animo mors initur quam repetitur : lit. "for not with as great a soul is death encountered as it is sought a second time," meaning that it takes a greater soul to seek death twice than to encounter it once.

Quidni : "How or why not . . . ?"

spectarent is a potential subjunctive (see note on *redderetur*, 1.1 above).

mors illos consecrat quorum exitum et qui timent laudant : lit. "Death deifies [or 'immortalizes'; see L&S *consecro*, I.B.1, II.C] those whose method of death [see L&S *exitus*, II.A.3] even [those] who fear [that method of] praise." In other words, in spite of being too cowardly to commit suicide themselves, people praise the courage it takes to do it, and it is the suicide's death that makes him immortal or godlike in people's eyes.

4.4 **Avida est . . . virtus :** another paradox (i.e., how can virtue be greedy?).

periculi : objective genitive (A&G 348–49).

quo : "whither," or "[the direction] in which."

quid . . . quod : both are direct objects of the deponent verb *patior*.

laeti : an adjective that agrees with the subject or object of the verb often has the force of an adverb (A&G 290).

meliori casu : probably an ablative of cause (A&G 404); the event or [mis]fortune (= *casus*) is "better" or "quite lucky" (*meliori*), because the wound was not deadly and to be wounded—especially on the front of the body—brings glory.

idem . . . fecerint : "done the same," that is, "done their part," "done their job" (i.e., "fought"); for the subjunctive, see note on *licet*, Letter 60.4.

4.5 **consulit :** *consulo, consulere* + dat. (L&S I.A.2) = "to take care for," "have regard for," "to act or consult in the interest of."

aliquid : direct object of the gerund *faciendi*.

ad quam rem : referring both to *animose fortiterque faciendi* and *esse quam honestissimos*.

intellegas : potential subjunctive (A&G 445).

tibi : dative of possession.

animi : partitive genitive with *quantum*, as is *constantiae* below.

diffluis : "languish," "be weakened by," or "be awash in" (L&S *diffluo*, II).

Unde possum scire . . . : the second of three rhetorical questions with anaphora to illustrate the point.

populare is an adjective with *odium*, not an infinitive.

inexpugnabilis : the favor is "irresistible" (lit. "incapable of being fought off") from the point of view of the person who loves praise and admiration.

pronus : "bending, inclining toward," with *favor* (which makes *inclinatione* slightly redundant).

sequitur : with *favor,* a mild personification.

sustulisti : < *tollo, -ere,* "raised," "reared" (L&S *tollo,* I.A.2a), an etymological play on words with *laturus sis* above.

cum : "[on occasions] when." The use of the subjunctive with *cum* in a temporal clause does not refer to definite time but "describes the circumstances that accompanied the action of the main verb" (A&G 546).

tunc : proleptic with the *si* clause.

conspexissem . . . vetuisses : pluperfect subjunctives in a past contrary-to-fact condition (A&G 517).

conspexissem : "then I might have understood [or been impressed] . . ." (L&S *conspicio,* I.B).

4.6　**quis** : for *aliquis,* "someone."

qui : the antecedent is *illos.*

nimia felicitate : cf. *felicitas inlaesa* above.

torpescunt . . . velut in mari lento : cf. *diffluis* above.

novum : a predicate adjective: "will come as a new [or strange] thing." See note on *meliorem,* Letter 5.1.

4.7　**saeva inexpertos** : both adjectives are used substantively.

suspicionem : "hint," or "mere thought" of a wound.

tiro < *tiro, tironis,* "rookie," "new recruit."

vicisse : the perfect infinitive represents the confidence and past experience of the veteran who knows that once blood has been spilled, victory is not far-off.

quos probat, quos amat, indurat, recognoscit, exercet : note the asyndeton.

venturis malis : the dative phrase is to be taken closely with the adjective *molles* to denote "that to which the given quality is directed" (A&G 383).

4.14　**Romana pax** : the so-called *pax Romana* (*pax* = "empire" or "dominion," and the cultural influences that went along with it) that was imposed upon much of Europe by Roman conquests under the emperors.

desinit < *desino, desinere,* "not be present [among]," "be lacking."

Germanos . . . quicquid circa Histrum : cf. Caesar's description of the enlightened land management of the nomadic Germani (*De bello gallico* 6.21–23); the *Hister* is the Danube River.

dico : "mean," as at 2.5 above.

tristis : "unpleasant."

solum < *solum, -i,* "ground," "soil," not *sol, solis.*

defendunt : "ward off "; the object is *imbrem.*

super durata glacie persultant : cf. Ovid's description of indigenous peoples in the Black Sea region skating on frozen rivers and lakes (*Tristia* 3.10).

in alimentum : *in* here means "for" or "as" food.

4.15   **in naturam . . . consuetudo** : an interesting view of the relationship between Nature and Nurture. That "custom" or "habits" should be in accordance with nature is a recurring Stoic theme. S. here boldy implies that the Germans live this way instinctively, to the shame of a Roman high culture addicted to *luxuria.*

paulatim . . . coeperunt : S. of course cannot know how happy people living under such conditions really are (and he ignores the obvious shortcomings of a subsistence lifestyle), but he is impressed with what he imagines to be their simple self-sufficiency and contentment.

voluptati = the second dative of a "double dative" construction (see note on *multis . . . usui,* Letter 60.4), with a dative demonstrative like *illis* supressed (cf. *illis* immediately below).

lassitudo : "exhaustion," somewhat personified.

in diem : "each day" (L&S *dies,* I.A.b).

vilis . . . victus, horrenda iniquitas . . . intecta corpora : supply the appropriate forms of the verb "to be."

et hic . . . : supply *est* twice in this sentence, once with *vilis . . . victus,* then with the gerundive *hic . . . quaerendus:* "their food is vile, and even this [i.e., what food they are able to scrounge] must be sought by hand."

hoc quod tibi calamitas videtur tot gentium vita est : in a sense, this observation is as true today as ever. By comparing the Romans' and Germans' standards of living, S. wishes to underscore his ongoing point that what we often consider to be misfortune is really a necessary and important part of living a noble life.

6.6   **"At multa . . . toleratu"** : This is an imagined retort to the god (or God) whom S. is now impersonating.

toleratu : the supine in *-u* is used with an adjective that describes any effect on the senses, especially ones that denote ease or difficulty (here *dura*; A&G 510).

non poteram : the god is unable because even the gods are subject to fate.

istis : ablative of separation without the preposition (A&G 401).

ferte fortiter : note the wordplay (cf. *fortis cum fortuna*, 2.9 above).

Hoc : neuter singular demonstrative pronoun used proleptically and pointing to the clause beginning with *ille*.

quo : "[a way] in which."

deum antecedatis . . . : a bold statement (put on the lips of God himself) reinforced by the contrast between *extra* used of gods and *supra* of men.

nemo tam pauper vivit quam natus est : the idea is that, since we come into the world as babies (naked, with no property or possessions), no adult can be as poor as when he or she was born.

aut solvetur aut solvet : supply *dolor* as subject. The idea is that pain should be of no real concern to the wise man; either it will "pass" (*solvetur*) or it will cause the sufferer to "pass away" (*solvet*) and thus be gone forever. A similar play of thought in *mortem . . .* below.

illi : dative; the referent is *fortunam*.

feriret < *ferio, ferire*, "to strike"; subjunctive in a relative clause of purpose.

6.7   **patet exitus . . . licet fugere :** "to flee" or "escape" is a euphemism here for suicide; cf. the use of *exitus* in the example of Cato above. The Stoics believed that under certain conditions (so long as the act was not an avoidance of making moral progress in virtue), suicide was an acceptable method of death. While S. seems to hold contradictory opinions on the topic, conditions under which he says suicide is justified include insanity, incurable illness, and tyrannical rule (see Motto, *Guide to the Thought of Lucius Annaeus Seneca*, pp. 206–7 for specific passages). In Letter 78, Seneca tells us that he himself once considered suicide, in his midthirties, but decided against it on account of his family responsibilities. *Aliquando enim et vivere fortiter facere est*, he concludes about that experience: "Even to live is sometimes an act of bravery."

mori : the infinitive, a verbal noun (A&G 451), is used here in a comparative construction with *quam* after *nihil . . . facilius.*

Prono . . . loco : "in a steep place," or "on an incline"; ablative of place where, without a preposition (A&G 429.1).

trahitur : supply *anima* as subject, but the meaning of *traho* here is perplexing. Some editors have conjectured *traditur.*

ad libertatem : again, cf. the example of Cato, §2.10.

Non tam longas in exitu vobis quam intrantibus moras posui : another contrast between the processes of death and birth; cf. *si homo tam tarde moreretur quam nascitur* below; with *intrantibus* supply *vobis.*

alioqui : "otherwise."

magnum in vos regnum fortuna tenuisset . . . : the pluperfect subjunctive forms the apodosis of a mixed contrary-to-fact condition. S.'s point seems to be that a person has no control over his birth (that is part of the *regnum fortunae*), but he does, by God's permission, have control over the hour of his death (by suicide), and that comes quickly if self-inflicted.

in vos : *in* = "with regard to," or "over."

6.8   **doceat :** hortatory subjunctive (A&G 439).

quam facile sit renuntiare naturae et munus illi suum impingere : on the surface, a difficult thought to reconcile with the Stoic ideal of living according to nature. Nature's own gift (*munus . . . suum*) in this context is the gift of life, so to "renounce" Nature (L&S *renuntio*, II) or to "report back" (L&S *renuntio*, I) and "throw her gift in her face" (L&S *impingo*, II) is to take death into one's own hands by committing suicide.

inter ipsa altaria et sollemnes sacrificantium ritus . . . : The religious ritual of animal sacrifice serves to illustrate the point that the moment of death is short.

sacrificantium : genitive plural participle used substantively.

ritus is accusative plural.

dum optatur vita, mortem condiscite : The chiastic word order reinforces the stunning irony of this passage. The god invites Lucilius to consider how swiftly death comes to humans by considering the quick fate of the sacrificial animal about to be slaughtered in order to give the worshipper nourishment, life, and an answer to his prayers.

Note the contrasts between large and small, human and animal, in what follows.

tenui : not < *teneo*, but *tenuis, -e.*

committit : "connects."

6.9   **Non in alto latet spiritus . . . in proximo mors est :** Note the *pleonasm* (Lanham 116, and see the note on *magnus   nec minor,* Letter 5.6). The point is that the life (*spiritus*) of a man or animal lies close to the surface and will flit away like a breath, so it does not take a deep, gory wound with a blade (*ferro*) to accomplish the task.

quacumque : "in whatever way."

vis < *volo, velle.*

pervium is probably a neuter noun (as opposed to an adjective): "way" or "passage."

mori : an infinitive used as a noun; cf. the note on *mori* §7 above.

ut . . . possit : a substantive *ut-* clause (A&G 561) used in place of a noun in a comparative construction after *quam.*

fauces : "throat."

elisit : "strangled" (L&S, *elido*, II).

in caput lapsos subiacentis soli duritia comminuit : "the hardness of the ground underneath has shattered those who have slipped [and fallen] headfirst."

subiacentis : genitive singular participle < *sub-iaceo, -ēre* used as an adjective with *soli.*

haustus ignis : either an "inhalation [or draught] of fire" (*haustus* as nominative < *haustus, -ūs, ignis* as genitive), or "fire that has been inhaled" (*ignis* nominative and *haustus* perfect passive participle < *haurio, haurīre*). Either way, the circumstances under which one might actually inhale fire, either on purpose or by accident, are not entirely clear. Hurst and Whiting (p. 218) suggest the reference is to the intentional inhalation of carbonic-acid gas from a charcoal fire (a "frequent means of self-destruction among the Romans"). Portia, wife of the Brutus who killed Julius Caesar, is said to have swallowed hot coals upon learning of her husband's death at the Battle of Philippi.

animae : "breath."

remeantis : genitive singular participle < *remeo, remeare,* "to return."

interscidit : < *interscindo, -ere,* "cut off/interrupt."

ecquid : "perchance."

erubescitis? : *erubesco, -ere* means to blush or feel shame, but perhaps also S. is imagining the reader growing embarrassed or squeamish at the vivid descriptions of violent death that bring the essay to a close. Note particularly how, in these last examples, death comes by means of natural elements—earth (*solum*), air (*haustus* . . . *anima*), fire (*ignis*), water (*aqua*). The Stoics accepted the traditional notion that the natural world was composed of these four elements but added to it the belief that these elements are periodically consumed by fire and the world is repeatedly reborn anew, as it were, from the ashes, an idea that S. may be evoking here with his imagery; cf. note on *cuncta conplectens*, in *De vita beata* 8.4).

DE VITA BEATA

1.1 **Gallio frater** : see "Life" in the Introduction.

ad : "with respect to"; for the construction with the gerundive *pervidendum*, see note on *ad studia obeunda*, in *De providentia* 2.5.

caligant : "to be in the dark [*caligant*] with respect to perceiving clearly [*pervidendum*]" is a calculated *oxymoron* (Lanham 106).

adeoque . . . ut : result clause (A&G 537).

eo . . . quo : see note on *eo . . . quo*, Letter 60.1.

via is ablative.

quae . . . ducit : the antecedent of *quae* is *via* with which it forms a connecting *qui* clause (see note on *a qua*, Letter 5.4) to explain why it is that, "if one slips from the path," the faster one is traveling, the more quickly the destination (i.e., the good life) will recede—(viz., because the slip might send one in the exact opposite direction (*in contrarium*); *ubi* here means "when."

ipsa velocitas : for *ipsa*, see note on *ipsa*, Letter 28.3; *velocitas* picks up *concitatius* above.

qua . . . possimus : *qua* (ablative, supply *via*), introduces an indirect question (A&G 574–75).

contendere illo : antecedent for *illo* is *quod*; *contendere* + dat. here means "strive for," "reach."

intellecturi : subject of *possimus*.

rectum : supply *iter*.

profligetur is highly metaphorical: the path "is brought to an end," or "is finished off" as if it were an adversary.

quantoque : ablative of degree of difference with *propius* (A&G 414).

propius ab eo : note how Latin can say "nearer from" (i.e., from the vantage point of the destination), where English says "nearer to" (see L&S *propius*, A.1.4).

1.2   **Quam** : "so long as."

in diversa : "every which way"; the phrase modifies the verbal action of *vocantium* (a participle used substantively).

errores : literally "wanderings," and only secondarily "mistakes." S. continues the wayfaring metaphor here: note *via, itinere,* and *passim vagamur* above, and the language of travel and tourism in the next several sentences (*quo tendamus . . . explorata . . . procedimus . . . peregrinationibus . . . limes . . . incolae . . . errare . . . via,* etc.).

brevis : nominative singular, modifies *vita*; the clause beginning with *etiam si* in turn modifies it.

bonae menti : a dative of end or purpose (A&G 382).

Decernatur : hortatory subjunctive, used impersonally.

et . . . et : "both . . . and."

quo : "in which [direction]."

qua : "the [way] in which," or "how"; like *quo,* with *tendamus.* The clause beginning with *non sine . . .* stands loosely in apposition to *qua* (or just as loosely with a repeated *tendamus* understood) and explains it.

cui : a dative of agent (A&G 375) and/or of reference with *explorata sint* indicating the vantage point from which something is considered (A&G 378.2).

hic : the adverb "here"; given the travel metaphor, virtually "on this road/path/journey"; so too with *hic* below.

in illis : supply *peregrinationibus.*

comprensus . . . interrogati : The verb *comprehendo* can be used in a both physical and intellectual sense. A *comprensus limes,* then, is a path that has been "taken up," or "traveled," by many persons in the past and so is "obvious" or "recognizable."

tritissima . . . decipit : a paradox, the force of which is as strong as the harmful prayers of loved ones mentioned in Letter 60.

celeberrima : most "crowded," or "frequented."

1.3   **quam** : with *magis*.

ne . . . **sequamur** : a substantive clause of purpose (A&G 563) introduced by a verb of urging (here *praesto* in the gerundive construction): literally, "Nothing is to be pointed out more than that we not . . ." (i.e., "We must emphasize this more than anything else, that we not . . .").

pecorum ritu : for the thought, see note on *ut ait Sallustius*, Letter 60.4; *ritu* is simply "in the manner [of]."

antecedentium : the participle is used substantively; cf. *vocantium*, §2 above.

pergentes : the participle agrees with the subject of *sequamur*.

non quo eundum est sed quo itur : the contrast, of course, is between the direction we should be going (expressed by the gerundive) and where we are in fact going (*itur* is used impersonally here; see A&G 208d); for *quo*, see note on *quo*, 1.2 above.

implicat : "ensnares."

quod : "the fact that"; see note on *quod*, Letter 5.1.

rumorem : "hearsay," i.e., secondhand information.

componimur has a middle sense here: "we connect ourselves."

rati : nominative plural participle from the deponent verb *reor*; *ea* is its object; *optima* is a predicate adjective (with *esse* omitted).

magno adsensu : ablative of manner (A&G 412).

quodque : *quod*, as above; the *-que* links the verbs *componimur* and *sunt*, each in a *quod* clause; *nec* negates *vivimus* = "and/but/yet [we do] not . . ."

similitudinem : given the context here, "conformity."

1.4   **Inde** : "from this source." This is a nominal sentence with the verb omitted; supply "is/comes/arises."

aliorum super alios ruentium : note how the trampled persons (*alios*) are sandwiched between *aliorum* and *ruentium*; *ruentium* is used substantively.

Quod : "[that] which" (the demonstrative is suppressed; A&G 307c); used proleptically with *hoc* below.

nemo ita cadit ut non et alium in se adtrahat : a result clause and a convincing description of the "domino effect" at work in a tangled mob.

exitio with *sequentibus* forms a "double dative" construction (see note on *multis* . . . *usui*, Letter 60.4).

Nemo sibi . . . errat, sed alieni erroris . . . auctor est : the point of the analagy is here summarized and underscored with this sententia.

nocet : used impersonally (it is harmful [to] . . .); *antecedentibus* depends on *applicari*.

unusquisque mavult credere quam iudicare : a succinct statement of the herd mentality: intellectually, people would rather follow (*credere*) than lead (*iudicare*).

iudicatur . . . creditur : used impersonally (A&G 208d).

versatque . . . praecipitat . . . error : With *versat, praecipitat,* and *error,* S. returns to his original metaphor of traveling (cf. note on *errores,* above).

traditus agrees with *error.*

per manus : "from hand to hand."

Alienis perimus exemplis : contrast the sentiment in Horace that one learns well—by observation—from others' mistakes (*Satires* 1.4.105–6); for the meaning of *alienus,* see note on *aliena opera,* Letter 84.1.

si is added by some modern editors; without it, there would need to be punctuation after *sanabimur,* and *separemur* would then be an independent (hortatory) subjunctive.

1.5 **in comitiis** : as in the street, so in the political arena. The word *comitia* (neuter plural of the noun *comitium,* a place of meeting at the foot of the Capitoline Hill) denotes any of several various assemblies of the Roman people for the purpose of voting candidates into political office.

eos factos esse praetores idem qui fecere mirantur : i.e., the very people who elect the leaders are afterward left scratching their heads over the choices they have made because they act *contra rationem* and are affected by *mobilis* ("fickle," "subject to change") *favor.*

praetores : praetors were elected officials at Rome, who presided over criminal courts, public games, and other matters of state.

fecere : perfect tense, third-person plural (see note on *cessere,* Letter 60.1).

eadem probamus, eadem reprehendimus : the voters' lack of discrimination is emphasized by the repeated *eadem* in clauses that contain antonymic verbs.

exitus : "outcome," "result."

omnis : genitive with *iudicii.*

datur : supply either *exitus* or *iudicium* as subject.

2.1   **agetur :** *ago* used impersonally in the passive voice with *de* means "[the topic/argument at hand] concerns," or "it is a question of " (L&S *ago*, II.D.9.d).

non est quod : see note on *Non est quod*, Letter 43.1.

illud is proleptic (see note on *hoc unum*, Letter 5.1), pointing forward to the content of the imagined response "*haec . . . videtur.*"

discessionum : literal "separations" or "splits" over an issue in the Roman Senate, where senators would walk over to the side whose position they favored and take their seats there.

peior : a syllabically truncated pun perhaps on *pars maior*.

agitur : *ago* used impersonally in the passive voice with *bene* is idiomatic for "it goes well" (L&S *ago*, II.D.8.b); note the wordplay in this result clause with *tam bene* and *meliora* ("it does not go so well that better things . . . ").

argumentum : "proof."

pessimi : the adjective is used substantively.

8.1   **Quid, quod :** supply *dicam de eo* after *quid*: "what is [the reason] that" or "what [should I say about] the fact that."

nec minus turpes dedecus suum quam honestos egregia delectant : *delectant* is used with two subjects here, *dedecus suum* (the object of which clause is *turpes*) and *egregia* (which is used substantively = "notable deeds"; the object is *honestos*). The reflexive possessive adjective *suum*, "their," agrees with *dedecus* but refers to the object *turpes* (supply the reflexive with *egregia* as well, referring to *honestos*). The point in this imagininary objection (which is simply a pleonastic restatement of the previous clause) is that, regardless of whether noble accomplishments please honorable persons or shameful deeds please rogues, both good and bad persons are deriving pleasure nonetheless. S. answers the charge in the next few sentences, suggesting that the difference between good and bad persons in regard to pleasure is that thinking persons see it as a desirable, but quite unnecessary by-product of virtuous living, whereas the unenlightened pursue it for its own sake—and, because they do so unphilosophically, what they think is pleasure is actually harmful to their souls.

voluntatis : "will," or "desire."

non dux sed comes sit voluptas . . . Natura enim duce . . . : for *natura*, see note on *natura*, Letter 60.3; for the image of leaders and companions (as if on a journey), see notes on *errores*, §1.2 and *versatque* . . . , §1.4, above.

8.2 **Idem est ergo beate vivere et secundum naturam :** *et* joins the adverb *beate* and the adverbial phrase *secundum naturam*. Note how the grammar and syntax of this elegant little sentence (the infinitive *vivere* used only once in a sentence where the neuter, nominative, singular *idem*, "same," is the predicate) reinforce its meaning: "To live happily and [to live] according to Nature is one and the same thing." This single sentence, in fact, captures the whole thrust of Stoic philosophy (see note on *secundum naturam vivere*, Letter 5.4).

Hoc quid sit : *hoc* is used proleptically with *quid* in an indirect question. See note on *illud*, 2.1 above.

corporis dotes et apta naturae : note the chiastic placement of words that belong in the same semantic register (*corporis-naturae*, *dotes-apta*); *dotes* are "endowments"; *apta* (< *apo*, *apere*, "to fit/join") are things "suited" to nature (*naturae* is dative).

conservarimus : a syncopated form of the future perfect *conservaverimus* (see A&G 181a), used here in the protasis of a future condition to indicate that the action of the protasis must be complete for the apodosis to be true (cf. A&G 516c).

in diem : perhaps literally here "given for a day and fleeting"; else "each day" (L&S *dies*, I.A.b).

eorum : referring to *corporis dotes* and *apta naturae*, which are to be regarded as *data in diem* and *fugacia*.

grata et adventicia : both adjectives are used substantively; *adventicius* can mean either "coming from abroad/foreign," thus *corpori grata et adventicia* = "things pleasing to the body, yet [considered by the philosopher] to be strange or foreign," which makes it almost a synonym for *aliena* in the sentence above; or (2) "things that happen to the body from the outside," and thus a synonym for *externis* . . . *externa*, used in §§ 3–4 below). Meaning (1) would anticipate the analogy to light-armed troops (*auxilia*), which were usually made up of non-citizens; meaning (2) would anticipate the discussion of externals that immediately follows, while echoing a common Senecan theme. Perhaps both meanings are in play.

nobis : dative of interest (or "reference"; A&G 378).

loco : "place," in the sense of "category."

serviant ista, non imperent : these are parenthetical potential subjectives (A&G 447) inserted into the protasis with asyndeton (see note on *Queror*, Letter 60.1).

ita demum : after three long protases with the future perfect, "finally" (*demum*) we reach the apodosis where the conditions are such that the things described in the protases can be considered useful to the mind.

8.3 **sit :** hortatory subjunctive.

miratorque tantum sui : the wise man will be "an admirer of himself only," not out of vanity or self-satisfaction, but rather, indifferent to the kinds of external things that one typically regards with wonder, he will focus his attention on the inner Self.

fidens animo . . . : a quotation from Vergil, *Aeneid* 2.61, with *animo* for *animi*.

in utrumque : "for whatever [may come his way]"; the phrase is modeled on the idiom in *utramque partem* (L&S *uterque*, I.A.1b).

artifex vitae : a bold metaphor that uses *artifex* (which can be either a noun or an adjective) in several senses: A wise person is the "builder/architect/master of his or her own life" (L&S *artifex*, I.A [with the noun phrase standing in apposition to *vir*]), and "skillful at living" (L&S II.A; cf. *paratus in utrumque* above). But the word *artifex* is also used metaphorically of God and Nature (L&S I.B), and in appropriating this language for the philosopher, S. anticipates his discussion immediately below (§§4 and 5), where he explicitly compares the wise man's relationship to the external world to God's. Thus, S. is playing here also on the meaning of *vitae*: Whereas God is the "author of life," the creator of living things (L&S *vita*, II.E), the philosopher is the author of his own way of life (L&S II.B).

fiducia eius non sine scientia sit, scientia non sine constantia : note the heavy alliteration with the letters *s* and *c*; each *non* here negates *sine* and forms a litotes (for which, see note on *non incompta*, Letter 5.5).

maneant illi semel placita : *maneant* is a hortatory subjunctive; *illi* is dative singular; *placita* is used substantively ("things that have been deemed pleasing" is a circumlocution for "decisions"); *semel* modifies *placita*. Rhetorically, this terse four-word sentence covers a lot of territory: it exhorts the wise man, whenever a decision is called for, to make up his mind once thend for all (*semel*) and, once the decision is made, not to waver in his judgment. The meaning, thus, is reflected in the choice of words.

litura : "smearing" (< *lino, -ere,* "to rub"), hence "[need for] correction," an image drawn from the way wax tablets were erased with the blunt end of the stylus.

Intellegitur is used impersonally here.

etiam si non adiecero : an example of *praeteritio,* or *occultatio* (Lanham 104), a rhetorical device in which a speaker adds emphasis by saying there is no need to mention things that he then proceeds to enumerate (here the adjectives *compositum, ordinatum,* and *magnificum*); cf. Letter 47.11.

compositum, ordinatumque . . . magnificum : these words and phrases form a *tricolon crescens* (Lanham 154), where each descriptive unit, or colon, increases in the number of syllables: first, the simple adjective *compositum,* then *ordinatumque,* which opens up into the syntactical core of the sentence (*fore talem virum*); the third element, *magnificum,* is further expanded by *cum comitate* and another prepositional phrase (*in iis*) that contains a relative clause (*quae aget*).

fore = the future infinitive *futurum esse* (A&G 170a) in indirect statement introduced by *intellegitur.*

talem virum : i.e., the kind of person idealized in the sentences above.

8.4   **Externa ratio quaerat . . . revertatur :** This difficult sentence introduces a difficult, but rewarding passage, which is abstract in its expression, technical in its terminology, but almost mystical in tone. S. explains here the relationship between a philosophic person's inner life and the external world, articulating Stoic views on how the mind takes in impressions through the senses. Translate: "Let our rational element, which is stimulated by the senses, inquire about things outside it, and, taking from that source [i.e., the external world] its first principles—for our rational element does not have any other source from which to attempt anything or any other source for making an assault on the truth—let it return to itself."

Externa : accusative plural, object of *quaerat.*

irritata agrees with *ratio*; not "irritated" in the sense of "annoyed," but simply "stimulated"; *sensibus* is ablative of means.

inde : see note on *inde*, 1.4 above.

principia : a techinical philosophical term in Latin for the "first principles" or "givens" in a logical argument or philosophical system (L&S *principium*, II.A).

nec enim habet aliud, unde . . . capiat : these two sentences are parenthetical to the thought and syntax of the main sentence.

impetum : object of *capiat*.

at : this word has been added by a modern editor by analogy with *sed* in the next sentence (which serves to illustrate this one). *At* may indeed have been inadvertantly omitted by an ancient scribe, who, having copied the last two letters in the preceding word, *capiat*, failed to copy the same two letters again for the word *at* (haplography). However, the sentence makes sense without it, in which case *et* would simply join the two hortatory subjunctives *quaerat* and *revertatur*. On the other hand, if we accept the restored reading, *et* would join the two participles *irritata* and *capiens* and the adversative *at* would connect—or rather disjoin—the two verbs.

mundus . . . deus : in Stoicism, the universe and the deity were regarded as one and the same thing.

cuncta conplectens . . . introsum undique : The Stoics pictured the divine, animating principle of the cosmos as a kind of elemental fire, from which all matter emerged by a process of mutation and into which all matter is periodically resolved in a cosmic conflagration (see Long and Sedley, 1:274–79 and cf. the note on *erubescitis*, in *De providentia* 6.9.

exteriora . . . redit : note the parallelism with the preceding sentence: *exteriora* corresponds to *externa*, *tendit* to *quaerat*, and *redit* to *revertatur*.

Idem nostra mens faciat . . . : The sentiment expressed here about the mind's relationship to external stimuli is not unlike S.'s view about the relationship of good reading to writing in Letter 84 (see notes there).

secuta sensus suos per illos : this phrase corresponds to *sensibus irritata* above; grammatically, *secuta* agrees with *mens*; *suos* agrees with *sensus*, not *illos*.

illorum : i.e., the *externa*; the genitive is dependent upon *potens*.

sui : i.e., *mens*.

8.5   **Hoc modo . . . tetigit** : The abundance of words with *con-* (and *dis-*) prefixes in this sentence serves to underscore the fundamental unity and operational harmony of an orderly mind: *concors . . . non dissidens . . . comprensionibus . . . disposuit . . . consensit . . . concinuit.*

nec haesitans in opinionibus : cf. *maneant illi semel placita*, §3 above.

se disposuit et partibus suis consensit : an interesting, verbally paradoxical pleonasm in which S. uses two verbs, one with the prefix *dis-* and the other with its antonym *con-*, to express essentially the same idea twice. *Disposuit se* means "stationed itself," or "put itself in order"; *partibus suis consensit* means "come to an agreement with its parts."

quae : a connecting relative (see note on *a qua*, Letter 5.4; its antecedent is *ratio*) in a circumstantial *cum* clause.

concinuit : < *cum + cano, -ere.*

summum bonum : to understand and attain "the highest good" for humankind was a chief goal of ancient philosophy.

8.6   **pravi . . . lubrici** : both objective genitives with *nihil* (A&G 348–49); note how S. varies the construction of the third *nihil* in this sentence with a relative clause, and how this forms something of a *tricolon crescens* (see note on *compositum*, 8.3 above).

arietet : "stumbles." This verb is formed from the noun *aries* and refers to "battering rams" used in military assaults. With *imperio, tergiversatione, haesitatio*, and *pugnam* below, it introduces a military metaphor.

in bonum : *in* here means "for."

facile et parate are adverbs.

agentis is used substantively.

summum bonum esse animi concordiam . . . : a summary statement of the foregoing argument.

17.1   **conlatrant** : "bark at."

quod solent : with *solent* understand the infinitive *dicere.*

"Quare ergo tu fortius loqueris quam vivis? . . . " : this is the first in a long series of charges by an imaginary interlocutor that philosophers do not practice what they preach. The rest of the essay is taken up with S.'s point-by-point rebuttals. Note the emphatic, anaphoric repetition of *quare* and *cur* in the flurry of questions that follows (on anaphora, see note on *Quamdiu*, Letter 60.2).

Quare . . . summittis . . . tangeris? : the extensive use of short words containing *m* and *s* sounds suggests perhaps the snarling of a dog (cf. *conlatrat* above).

verba summittis : "speak fawningly," in a way contradictory to the Stoic belief in moral equality and self-sufficiency.

damno : "loss."

lacrimas : object of *demittis*.

audita : agrees with *morte*, with which it forms an ablative absolute.

17.2 **cultius rus . . . quam naturalis usus desiderat?** : This probably refers to large estates or *latifundia* owned by wealthy absentee landlords. The objection here is perhaps that this land is being grazed or cultivated to excess for mere profit and pleasure, or that these country properties are "fancier" (*cultius*) than they ought to be.

ad : see note on *ad*, §1 above.

cenas is a verb.

nitidior : i.e., the furniture is "more splendid" than it ought to be for a philosopher.

apud te : "at your table"; rhetorically, a variation on the dative *tibi* used in the preceding sentences.

vinum aetate tua vetustius : possibly a reference to prized wine, *vinum Opianum*, so-called after its vintage year of 121 B.C.E. when L. Opimius was consul (so Hurst and Whiting, p. 298).

aurum : some editors conjecture the word *aviarium* here. For fowl as haute cuisine, see notes at Letter 47.6.

nihil is the object of the participle *daturae*.

uxor tua locupletis domus censum auribus gerit : i.e., she wears earrings that cost as much as the total value (*censum*) of a wealthy household.

paedagogium : "servant boys"; the word is neuter and singular, after the place where such boys received their training but here refers by synecdoche (Lanham 148) to persons.

ars est . . . ministrare : cf. the description of the slaves' tasks at Letter 47.6–8.

ut here, followed by the indicative, means "as."

argentum : silver ware.

perite is an adverb.

struitur is a conjecture; other editors prefer the reading *servitur* here.

scindendi obsonii magister : again, cf. Letter 47.6; *scindendi obsonii* is a gerundive expression (A&G 504).

possides is used absolutely: "have possessions."

plura : understand *plura* as the object of *possides* in the previous sentence.

nosti : a syncopated form of *novisti* < *nosco, -ere* (A&G 181a).

Cur : this *cur* has been added by a modern editor by analogy with the others.

noveris : subjunctive in a result clause; the perfect tense of *nosco* has a present meaning (A&G 205b, n.2).

plures . . . quam quorum notitiae memoria sufficiat : lit. "more than [your] memory is sufficient for the recognition of which"; the rich master has so many slaves that he cannot keep track of their names. Note the double indictment expressed here by the two *aut* clauses: masters with very few (*pauculos*) slaves do not know them by face or name because they are negligent (one should easily, in other words, be able to keep track of only a few), while those with too many slaves (*plures*) are guilty of the same by reason of an indifference spawned (presumably) by hybristic excess.

17.3 **postmodo :** "later," "in a moment."

non sum sapiens : "I am not a wise man," meaning that S. is not perfect in the morality that his philosophy requires of him.

pascam : as one might feed a dog? (cf. *conlatrat* above).

Exige : imperative < *ex + ago, -ere,* "require."

17.4 **delenimenta :** "relief" of symptoms, rather than a complete cure (*remedia*).

podagrae : a Greek word meaning "foot disease" or "gout."

verminatur : a picturesque verb formed from the noun *vermis,* "worm," that means "ache"—to ache in a manner as if caused by worms (e.g., a bellyache).

debilis agrees with *cursor* and has a concessive force: "[even though I am] impaired." The idea is that, compared with the persons who are leveling such accusations against philosophers, the gout-ridden S.

considers himself a moral sprinter. Other editors conjecture the form *debiles* (vocative plural), in which case S. would be addressing the naysayers directly.

Haec non pro me loquor . . . : S. is saying that the arguments he is offering in defense are not to be construed as self-serving. But it is hard not to see his responses to the charges of 21.1 below—especially *Quare ille philosophiae studiosus est et tam dives vitam agit* ("Why is that man so eager for philosophy yet he leads such a rich lifestyle?")—as not in some way self-referential (S. was notorious for his immense wealth; see the "Life" section of the Introduction.

acti : partitive genitive with *aliquid* = "some accomplishment."

21.1   **opes . . . vitam . . . exilium . . . tempus, etc. :** a litany of Senecan (Stoic) commonplaces. For references in the Senecan corpus, see passages listed under the relevant topic headings in Motto, *A Guide to the Thought of Lucius Annaeus Seneca*. This passage shows that S.—here in the guise of the imaginary interlocutor—was well aware of the sorts of charges that could be, and certainly were, leveled against him and his school. These objections are, in other words, very close to home, in spite of the distancing effect of *ille*.

21.2   **Ait :** subject is *ille*. Here begins S.'s reply.

contemni : passive infinitive.

non ne habeat, sed ne sollicitus habeat : an important distinction. S. is saying that the point of despising the things mentioned above (*opes, vita, valetudo*) is not necessarily to condemn those things out of hand, but is rather a way to prevent a person from being psychologically tied to them.

illa : neuter plural, referring to *opes*, *vita*, and *valetudo* (so too *abeuntia*).

abeuntia . . . prosequitur : the wise man "follows them [like guests] to the door as they leave, unconcerned," a pleasant personification.

securus : the antonym of *sollicitus* above. One should not be preoccupied with getting and keeping the good things in life, nor anxious about losing them.

fortuna, the subject of the sentence, is being slightly personified in this metaphor: fortuna only gives riches out on loan, as it were.

reddentis : genitive singular participle used substantively, dependent upon *querella*.

21.3 **M. Cato :** the Younger; see notes at *De providentia* 2.9.

  cum : concessive (A&G 549).

  Curium et Coruncanium : Manius Curius Dentatus and Tiberius
  Coruncanius were men of plebeian birth, who nonetheless rose to
  serve Rome as consul (Curius several times) in the third century B.C.E.
  Cato praised their frugality and staunch Republican values in his
  speeches.

  censorium crimen = a crime subject to the jurisdiction of the censors
  (of which there were two at Rome). The censors were charged with
  guarding public morals and had the authority to limit the civic participation of any citizen whose behavior they deemed reprehensible.

  erat agrees in number with the predicate *crimen*, though the subject is
  plural (*paucae lamellae*); see A&G 316b.

  argenti lamellae : "silver plate" = unminted sheets of raw silver. A
  senator named Cornelius Rufinus was said to have been ejected from
  the Senate by the censors in 275 B.C.E. for possessing too much silver
  plate.

  quadragies sestertium = 4 million sesterces. The sestertium was not
  a coin but a sum of money. It was worth one thousand sesterces. In
  Latin idiom, whenever *sestertium* is combined with a numerical
  adverb (here *quadragies*), the phrase *centena milia* ("hundreds of
  thousands") is to be supplied (see A&G 634).

  Crassus : Marcus Licinius Crassus (c. 112–53 B.C.E.) was fabulously,
  almost proverbially wealthy, having become so by confiscating the
  property of the well-to-do during Sulla's proscriptions in the early
  eighties B.C.E. With Caesar and Pompey he formed the first triumvirate
  and thus was Cato's political (as well as moral) antithesis.

  Censorius Cato : the Elder, Cato's great-grandfather.

  Maiore spatio . . . quam a Crasso vinceretur : S.'s point is slightly
  ironic: though in moral values the younger Cato was closer to his
  great-grandfather, in net worth he was closer to the rich Crassus.

  illi : object of *obvenissent.*

  obvenissent . . . sprevisset : Note the pluperfect subjunctives in a contrary-to-fact condition, reinforcing the purely hypothetical nature of
  this exemplum (cf., too, *si compararentur*); *sprevisset < sperno, -ere.*

21.4 **non in animum illas sed in domum recipit :** riches are external to
  one's self, not intrinsic to it.

possessas : perfect passive participle of *possideo*; supply *divitias*.

maiorem virtuti suae materiam : An interesting use of chiastic word order (see note on *una silva*, Letter 60.2) in which the intrinsic, moral quality that is to be cultivated (*virtuti suae*) is sandwiched between the external, subsidiary impetus that serves it (*maiorem . . . materiam*).

22.1 **quin . . . sit :** After negatived expressions of doubt, *quin* (but that) introduces a clause with a subjunctive (A&G 558a). The negatived doubt here is implied, couched in the form of a rhetorical question (What doubt is there?) that expects a negative answer (There is none).

explicandi is a gerund, dependent upon *materia* (*animum suum* is its object).

in hac : "in the former" (A&G 297a), that is, *paupertate*.

non inclinari nec deprimi : these infinitives stand in apposition to *unum genus*.

et . . . et . . . et . . . et . . . et : note how the polysyndeton (see note on *et*, Letter 60.2) reinforces the sense. Whereas poverty involves only one kind of virtue (expressed with two synonymous, negatived infinitives in the passive voice), the virtues required of the wealthy cover a wide range (*campum patentum*) of human endeavor.

22.2 **minimae staturae :** when it is modified by an adjective, a genitive of quality or characteristic can be used (in place of an adjective) as the predicate of a nominal sentence (A&G 345).

procerum : "tall."

exilis : "feeble," "weak."

hoc refers to the content of the clause *malet . . . robur*: "He will prefer to have strength of body, and this [he will prefer] in such a way [i.e., not with complaints or regret] that he knows he has something stronger inside himself [i.e., virtue]."

22.3 **in :** "with respect to" (L&S in, II.c).

summam rei : partitive genitive. The gender of *summam* in this construction is taken from the whole entity (*res, rei*), of which it forms a part (see A&G 346a.2).

subduci . . . principalis boni : Some things "can be taken away without the ruin of their principal Good," meaning that such attributes or benefits are not essential to the fundamental goodness of a thing (see notes about the Stoic concept of *indifferentia* at *Infirmi animi*, Letter 5.6, and at *haec quae indifferentia vocamus*, 22.4 below).

nascentem : with *laetitiam*; translate this participle as a relative clause; *ex virtute* goes closely with it.

ut : "as," used correlatively with *sic*.

apricus : "sunny."

22.4   **nostrorum** : i.e., Stoics. For the meaning of *dico* in this sentence, see note on *dico*, *De providentia* 2.5.

unum est bonum virtus : the hallmark of Stoic teaching.

haec quae indifferentia vocamus : *indifferentia*, the Latin translation of the Greek *adiáphora*, are things or qualities that intrinsically are morally neither good nor bad. Stoics ranked indifferents as "preferred" (those that are beneficial or useful to one's existence and livelihood, such as health, wealth, skill, etc.) and "non-preferred" (those that are harmful or interfere with it, such as sickness, poverty, ignorance, etc.). However, for a Stoic, only what is necessary for progress in virtue—that which is morally good—is truly good and worth the investment of one's intellectual, emotional, and psychological energy, and only things or situations that thwart such progress are truly bad. Thus, for example, death, sickness, or pain are not in themselves bad, nor wealth, health, or beauty good.

aliquid . . . pretii : partitive genitive (so, too, *aliquid honoris* below).

potiora : "preferable"; *aliis* is ablative of comparison.

Quibusdam ex iis : i.e., the *indifferentia* that have some value and are better to have than not (among which S. counts riches).

" . . . eundem apud te locum . . . quem apud me?" : The imaginary interlocutor is objecting here that S.'s position on riches is not so very different from that of the average man in the street. Both think it is better to have wealth than not have it. S. answers this objection immediately below by emphasizing that the philosopher, unlike the average person, will be utterly detached psychologically from wealth.

Mihi . . . tu . . . tibi sine te . . . a te . . . apud me . . . apud te . . . meae . . . tu : S. draws the sharpest possible contrast by the emphatic repetition of personal pronouns and adjectives.

Mihi : either a dative of separation with the compound verb *effluxerint* (A&G 381), or, more loosely, a dative of reference (A&G 376).

semet ipsas : *-met* is an ending added to the reflexive pronoun—here *se* (like *nihil*, the object of *auferent*)—to make it emphatic (A&G

143d); because *se* refers to *divitiae*, it is modified by the feminine accusative plural form of the intensive adjective, *ipsas*.

videberis tibi sine te relictus : "you will think [lit. 'seem to yourself'] that you have been abandoned [so as to be] without yourself." The idiom *videor mihi* and the juxtaposing of *tibi* and *sine te* in this sentence verbally reflect his opponent's solipsistic infatuation with riches.

divitiae meae sunt, tu divitiarum es : a fine sententia to drive the point home, nicely turned by the Loeb translator (Basore, 1932) as "I own my riches, yours own you."

26.1. **uterque :** "[we] both."

in imperio : the military analogies that follow in §2 (cf. *imperator*, below) expand on this metaphor.

tamquam : "as though," or "as if," introduces here a conditional clause of comparison (A&G 524).

earum : i.e., *divitiarum*, an objective genitive (*divitiarum* is also the referent for *illis* below).

tunc ... cum ... : *tunc* refers to the time expressed in the *cum*- clause. The sentiment is similar to the idea that life should be lived as a rehearsal for death.

26.2 **geritur :** the subject is *bellum*; the present tense is particularly important to the sense: "a war, which, even if one is not being waged [at the moment], has been declared."

tamquam : as above.

insolentes : agreeing with the first *vos* in the sentence and forming one of two objects for the verb *obstupefaciunt*.

vos opes : same emphatic collocation as *vos domus: vos* is the object, *opes* is the subject.

transcenderint : subject is *opes*; with *sint* it is one of two verbs in the *tamquam* clause.

maioresque ... quam ... habeat fortuna : this sentence is difficult to translate literally into English: *vobis* is a dative of possession; *quam* forms a comparison with *maiores* (supply *opes*); *quibus consumendis* is a dative gerundive dependent upon the notion of fitness or suitability (A&G 505a) expressed by *satis virium* (which forms a partitive genitive). Translate: "and [as though] you had greater [riches] than fortune had power to consume."

obstupefaciunt : a mild form of *zeugma* (Lanham 159–61), in which one verb is used with two different subject-object combinations, even though it is proper only to one of them. Here, the first *vos* of the sentence is modified by the predicate adjective *insolentes*, with which we would expect a simple *faciunt*, not *obstupefaciunt*, which is appropriate mainly for the second *vos* (which has no predicate adjective).

26.3 **plerumque** is an adverb: "often," "frequently."

segnes : an adjective used here with adverbial force (A&G 290) modifying *barbari*.

quo : "to what" (with *pertineant* introducing an indirect question).

illa : "those [activities]."

ex longinquo : "way off in the distance," "from afar."

marcetis : < *marceo*, *marcēre*, "to be languid," "enervated," "lazy."

casus is nominative plural.

iam iamque : the repeated *iam* (cf. L&S, *jam* I.A.1.b.a) vivifies the impending disaster.

laturi agrees with *casus*.

Sapientis : the genitive is dependent upon *divitias*.

omnia illi sua relinquet : a pleasant paradox: Should some invader steal all a philosopher's wealth, he nonetheless leaves him (*illi*) with everything that is truly his own (*sua*), namely his inner life of thought, reflection, and progress in virtuous living.

27.4 **sententias ferre de :** "pass judgement on."

Papulas . . . ulceribus . . . verrucas . . . scabies : two proverbial variants of the well-known (biblical) saying about the speck and the log (Matthew 7:3–5).

obsiti : perfect passive participle of *obsero, -ere* ("to be covered," "sown") agrees with the subject of *observatis*.

naevos aut verrucas : "moles, warts."

scabies : "scabies" (in animals, "mange") or some such unsightly skin disorder that causes severe itching.

A Note on the Vocabulary

This vocabulary is included primarily for the convenience of the reader. It is meant to be used in conjunction with the lexical and grammatical notes provided in the Commentary and, ideally, in tandem with a real lexicon. (See further "How to Use this Edition.") Or, to put it another way: neither the glosses provided in the notes nor this vocabulary should be approached as a "clipboard" from which to "cut and paste" a meaningful translation. Students will still need to parse sentences carefully before embarking on a translation. They will also need to draw on their knowledge of Latin morphology. Adverbs, for example, are not listed separately from the adjectives on which they are formed, unless that formation is irregular, or unless I thought there might be undue cause for confusion. The comparative and superlative degrees of adjectives and adverbs are generally not listed as separate entries either. Nor are gerundives and other forms of the participle. The forms of the personal pronouns are also omitted. The entries for verbs give principal parts and basic meanings, but not the various constructions or idiomatic uses. (Such things are, however, explained in the notes.) On this point, it may be helpful to review the differences between transitive and intransitive verbs (A&G 273, 274), and to be reminded that deponent verbs necessarily lack a perfect active form (see A&G 156). The entries for nouns follow the standard practice of giving the necessary information: nominative, genitive (stem), and gender. Adjectives also appear in the usual way. The quantity of vowels in words is only indicated where it is relevant to the identification of a form: for example, second-conjugation infinitives are listed as -*ēre* to help students distinguish them from third-conjugation verbs in -*ere*. I have chosen not to identify every single word by its part of speech (though this will be apparent enough from a word's definition). I have done this for my own convenience, but also because many a Latin word can function as a different part of speech depending on the use to which it is put. Neuter adjectives in the accusative or ablative case, for example, even though they often function as adverbs do not for that reason cease to be adjectives. Relative pronouns and adjectives can function as interrogatives and vice versa. Demonstratives can be used as either pronouns or adjectives, and so on. Although the notes offer plenty of help in this regard, students should be encouraged to analyze and determine for themselves the grammatical function of words in Seneca's sentences. For those interested in the linguistic development and conceptual origin of Latin morphology, grammar, and syntax, I heartily recommend E. C. Woodcock's *A New Latin Syntax* (Bristol Classical Press, 1987). One tip here, however, in advance: Seneca is particularly fond of using adjectives and participles substantively, that is, as nouns. I flag many such instances in the notes, but readers should be on the lookout for this stylistic habit.

Vocabulary

A

a, ab: prep. w/abl., from, by
abditus, -a, -um: hidden, concealed, secret
abduco, -ere, -duxi, -ductum: lead off, entice away, withdraw
abeo, -ire, -ii, -turum: go away, go forth, depart
abigo, -ere, -egi, -actum: drive away, drive off
abrumpo, -ere, -rupi, -ruptum: break, break off, separate
abscedo, -ere, -cessi, -cessum: withdraw, retire, depart, give way to
abscondo, -ere, -condi, -conditum: hide, conceal
abstineo, -ēre, -tinui, -tentum: keep back, keep off, hold back from
abutor, -uti, -usus sum: use up, consume, abuse
ac, atque: and; (with comparisons) than
accedo, -ere, -cessi, -cessurum: to approach, draw near, enter
accido, -ere, -cidi: reach; befall, happen
accipio, -cipere, -cepi, -ceptum: receive, accept; hear
accusator, -oris, m.: accusor, prosecutor, plaintiff
acer, acris, acre: sharp, bitter, vehement
acerbus, -a, -um: harsh, bitter, severe
acies, aciei, f.: a sharp edge, point; keenness of sight, eye
acutus, -a, -um: sharp, pointed, shrill, high-pitched
ad: prep. w/acc., to, toward, at, with respect to
adclamo, -are, -avi, -atum: shout at, call to, exclaim
addico, -ere, -dixi, -dictum: give assent, adjudge, assign
adduco, -ere, -duxi, -ductum: bring to, lead on, draw forth
adeo, -ire, -ivi, -itum: approach, go to, visit
adeo: adv., to this extent, to such a point, thus far, so far
adficio, -ere, -feci, -fectum: treat, manage, handle, affect, influence

adgestus, -ūs, m.: a bringing in, a collecting, throng

adhibeo, -ēre, -hibui, -hibitum: apply, add to, furnish, treat

adhuc: adv., until now, up to this point, yet, still

adicio, -ere, -ieci, -iectum: throw to, fling at, add, direct (the mind)

adiuvo, -are, -iuvi, -tum: to help, aid, assist

admiratio, -tionis, f.: admiration, wonder, respect, surprise

admiror, -ari, -atus sum: be amazed, wonder at, admire

admitto, -ere, -misi, missum: admit, give access, consult, permit

admoneo, -ēre, -ui, -itum: warn, advise

admoveo, -movēre, -movi, -motum: approach, move toward

adpeto, -ere, -ivi or -ii, -itum: seek, strive for, reach after

adsensus, -ūs, m.: an agreement, assent, approval

adsentior, -iri, -sensum: give assent, agree with, approve, admit

adsiduus, -a, -um: diligent, continual, careful

adsigno, -are, -avi, -atum: allot, assign, ascribe, entrust

adspicio, -ere, -spexi, -spectum: look at, behold, notice, examine

adsuesco, -ere, -evi, -etum: accustom, habituate; intrans., be accustomed to

adtendo, -ere, -tendi, -tentum: stretch toward, give heed, consider

adtraho, -ere, -traxi, tractum: drag forth, carry along

adulatio, -ionis, f.: fawning, flattery, adulation

adventicius, -a, -um: foreign, strange, accidental

adversus, -a, -um: facing, in front of, opposing

adversus: adv. and prep. w/acc., against, with respect to

advoco, -are, -avi, -atum: call forth, summon, invite

aeger, -gra, -grum: sick

aegritudo, -tudinis, f.: sickness, grief

aemulator, -oris, m.: an imitator, emulator

aenator, -oris, m.: a trumpet player

aeque: adv., equally, in like manner, just as

aestimo, -are, -avi, -atum: estimate, judge the value of, esteem

aetas, -tatis, f.: life, time of life, age

aeternus, -a, -um: lasting, enduring, permanent

affectus, -ūs, m.: disposition, mood, state of mind

afferro, -ferre, -tuli, -latum: bring, fetch, carry, convey

aggredior, -i, -gressum: approach, draw near

agito, -are, -avi, -atum: to impel, drive onward, excite

agmen, agminis, n.: band, throng, army troops

agnosco, -ere, -novi, -nitum: recognize, identify, acknowledge, understand

ago, -ere, egi, actum: lead, drive, conduct, handle; pass., be a matter of, concern

aio (ait, aiunt): defect. verb, say, say yes, assert

ala, -ae, f.: wing; armpit

alienus, -a, -um: belonging to someone else, foreign

alimentum, -i, n.: food, nourishment

alioqui (alioquin): adv., otherwise, in other respects, in general

alipilus, -i, m.: a depilator of armpits

aliquando: adv., at some time, sometimes, ever, occasionally

aliqui, aliqua, aliquod: some, any

aliquis, aliquid: pron. and adj., some, any

aliquo: adv., at some place, somewhere

aliquot: indef. num., some, several, a few

alius, alia, aliud: another, other, different

alo, -ere, alui, altum: nourish, cause to grow

altaria, -ium, n. pl.: altar

alter, altera, alterum: another, the other (of two); **alter . . . alter,** one . . . another

alterno, -are, -avi, -atum: do by turns, do in exchange

altilis, -e: fattened, full, large

altus, alta, altum: full grown, tall, high, lofty, deep

alumnus, -i, m.: foster-son, nursling

alvus, -i, m.: stomach, bowels, womb

amans, -ntis: fond, loving

ambitio, -ionis, f.: a going about, a desire for prestige and popularity

ambitus, -ūs, m.: a going around, canvassing for votes

amicus, -i, m.: friend, loved one (or as adj., friendly)

amitto, -ere, -misi, -missum: to send away, part with, lose

amo, -are, -avi, -atum: love, cherish, be fond of

amor, -oris, m.: love, affection, desire

amplus, -a, -um: great, ample, spacious, roomy

an: partc. introducing questions, can it be that?; **utrum . . . an,** whether . . . or

ancillula, -ae: a young female slave

angulus, -i, m.: angle, corner, nook

anguste: adv., at close quarters, with difficulty

anicula, -ae: little old woman

animal, -is, n.: animal, living thing

animose: adv., spiritedly, courageously, eagerly

animus, -i, m.: soul, mind; in pl., courage

annus, -i, m.: year

ante: adv. and prep. w./acc., before, in front of

antecedo, -ere, -cessi: go before, precede; excel, surpass

antequam: adv., before, sooner than

anticipo, -are, -avi, -atum: take before, anticipate

anxius, -a, -um: anxious, troubled, cautious; troublesome

aperio, -ire, -perui, -pertum: uncover, reveal, open, display

apertus, -a, -um: uncovered, open

apis, -is, f.: bee

apologo, -are, -avi, -atum: reject, spurn, forswear

apparatus, -ūs, m.: preparation, display, splendor

appareo, - ēre, -ui, -iturus: to appear, be evident, show oneself

appello, -are, -avi, -atum: call, name

applico, -are, -avi, -atum: join, attach

apricus, -a, -um: sunny

aptus, -a, -um: fitted, suited, proper

apud: prep. w/acc., at, at the house of, in the writings of

aqua, -ae, f.: water

arbiter, -tri, m.: spectator, witness, judge, umpire

arbor, -oris, f.: tree

ardeo, -ēre, arsi: to burn, blaze

arduus, -a, -um: steep, difficult

argentum, -i, n.: silver, money

argumentatio, -ionis, f.: reasoning, proof

argumentum, -i, n.: argument, ground, proof, evidence

aridus, -a, -um: dry, meagre, empty

arieto, -are, -avi, -atum: strike violently, ram; stumble

arma, -orum, n. pl.: equipment, implements, weapons

armatura, -ae, f.: armor, equipment

armo, -are, -avi, -atum: to arm, equip with arms

arrogantia, -ae, f.: arrogance, pride, insolence

ars, artis, f.: art, skill, craft

articulus, -i, m.: joint, member, part
artifex, artificis, m.: maker, creator, craftsman
as, assis, m.: a penny
aspectus, -ūs, m.: a seeing, glance; countenance
asper, aspera, asperum: rough, harsh
aspicio, -ere, spexi, -spectum: look at, notice, inspect, consider
at: disjunctive conj., but, however
atque: and, but, moreover
atqui: but, somehow, and yet, nevertheless
atrium, -ii, n.: forecourt, hall, foyer
auctor, -oris, m.: author, source, maker
audacter (audaciter): adv., boldly, rashly, courageously
audeo, -ēre, ausus sum: venture, dare, risk
audio, -ire, -ivi, or -ii, -itum: hear, attend
aufero, -ferre, abstuli, ablatum: take away, carry off, remove
augeo, -ēre, auxi, auctum: increase, enlarge, extend
aura, -ae, f.: air, wind, breath
auris, -is, f.: ear, hearing
aurum, -i, n.: gold
auspicor, -ari, -atus sum: begin, undertake, take the auspices, divinate
aut: or; **aut . . . aut,** either . . . or
autem: postpos. part., however, on the other hand,
auxilium, -i: aid, help, support; pl. troops
avaritia, -ae, f.: greed
averto, -ere, -verti, -versum: turn away, avert
aviditas, -tatis, f.: eagerness, longing, greed
avidus, -a, -um: eager, desirous, greedy
avis, avis, f.: bird
avocatio, -ionis, f.: diversion, distraction
avoco, -are, -avi, -atum: to call away, divert, distract

B

bacchor, -ari, -atus sum: rave like a Bacchant
balneum, -i, n.: bath, bathing place
barba, -ae, f.: beard
barbaria, -ae, f.: foreign country

barbarus, -a, -um: foreign, uncivilized
beatus, -a, -um: happy, blessed, prosperous
bellum, -i, n.: war
bene: adv., well, in a good way, correctly
beneficium, -ii, n.: benefit, favor, advantage
bibo, -ere, bibi: drink
blandior, -iri, -itum: fawn, caress, soothe, coax
blandus, -a, -um: flattering, fawning, agreeable
bonus, -a, -um: good, right, noble
botularius, -ii, m.: sausage seller
brevis, -e: short, brief, small, low
bruma, -ae, f.: winter time
bubulcus, -i, m.: ploughman, ox-handler

C

cado, -ere, cecidi, casurum: fall, befall, happen, die
caedo, -ere, cecīdi, caesum: cut, hew, cut off, strike
caelatura, -ae, f.: an engraving
caelum, -i, n.: sky, weather
Caesarianus, -a, -um: partisan of Caesar
calamitas, -tatis, f.: loss, damage, disaster
caligo, -are: be dark, gloomy, misty
callum, -i, n.: thick skin
campus, -i, m.: field, plain, expanse
cano, -ere, cecini: sing, perform music, resound
canto, -are, -avi, -atum: sing, perform music, resound
cantor, -oris, m.: singer, poet, harper
capio, -ere, cepi, captum: seize, take, grab, undertake, receive, have room for
capitalis, -e: of or pertaining to the head, capital
capto, -are, -avi, -atum: strive for, grasp at
caput, capitis, n.: head
carcer, -eris, m.: prison, jail
careo, -ēre, -ui, -iturum: be without, free from, lack (w/abl.)
carpo, -ere, -psi, -ptum: pick, pluck, enjoy, make use of
casa, -ae, f.: house

Vocabulary 135

castigatio, -ionis, f.: a correcting, censure, reproof
castra, -orum, n. pl.: army camp
casus, -ūs, m.: a falling, ruin, fate, chance, accident
catena, -ae, f.: chain
causa, -ae, f.: cause, reason, occasion, excuse; abl. w/prec. gen., because of
cavea, -ae, f.: the spectators' seats in a theater
cavus, -a, -um: hollow, concave
cedo, -ere, cessi, cessum: turn out, succeed, proceed; give place to, yield
celeber, -bris, -bre: much visited, frequented, crowded, distinguished
cella, -ae, f.: storeroom, cabinet, shrine
ceno, -are, -avi, -atum: dine
censorius, -a, -um: of or pertaining to the office of censor
censura, -ae, f.: office of censor
census, -ūs, m.: the value of one's estate, list of citizens
certe: adv., really, surely, certainly, of course, at least
certus, -a, -um: fixed, determined, certain, precise
cervix, -cis, f.: neck
ceterus, -a, -um: the rest (of), remaining
ceterum: adv., in other respects, otherwise, but
chorus, -i, m.: choir, chorus
cibus, -i, m.: food, nutriment
cingo, -ere, -nxi, -nctum: surround, encompass, gird
circa: adv. and prep. w/acc., at, around, about, near, nearly
circumago, -ere, -egi, -actum: turn around, wheel about
circumdo, -are, -avi, -atum: set around, surround, enclose
circumfero, -ferre, -tuli, -latum: carry around, spread around
circumsono, -are, -avi, -atum: resound
circumspicio, -ere, -spexi, -spectum: look around, survey
circumsto, -are, -steti, -statum: stand around, surround, attend
circumstrepo, -ere, -ui: make noise all around one
cito: adv., quickly, speedily, soon
civilis, -e: of or pertaining to citizens, civil, civic
civitas, -tatis, f.: city, the state; citizenship
clades, -is, f.: disaster, calamity, debacle
clamor, -oris, m.: shout, noise, clamor
clarus, -a, -um: famous, bright
classis, -is, f.: fleet, group

claudo, -ere, clausi, clausum: close, shut, restrict
clementer: adv., peacefully, calmly, with forbearance
cliens, -ntis, m.: a personal dependent, client
clunis, -is, m. and f.: haunch, rump
coacervatio, -ionis, f.: an accumulation, heap
coalesco, -ere, -alui, -alitum: to increase, unite, coalesce
coarguo, -ere, -ui: expose, refute, convict
coepio, -ere, coepi, coeptum: begin, commence
coetus, -ūs, m.: a joining, union, company, crowd
cogitatio, -ionis, f.: thought, thinking, reflection
cogito, -are, -avi, -atum: consider, ponder, weigh
cognitio, -ionis, f.: knowledge, acquaintance
cognosco, -ere, -gnovi, -gnitum: become acquainted with; in perf., know
cogo, cogere, coegi, coactus: force, compel
cohaereo, -ēre, -haesi, -haesum: cling together, be united, be composed of
colligo, -ere, -legi, lectum: gather, collect, assemble
collum, -i, n.: neck
colo, -ere, colui, cultum: till, tend, care for, frequent, esteem, adorn
comes, -itis, m.: companion, comrade
comitas, -tatis, f.: courtesy, kindness, affability
comiter: adv., affably, kindly, courteously
comitia, -orum, n. pl.: an assembly of the Roman people
commeo, -are, -avi, -atum: come and go, have recourse, make visits
commercium, i, n.: trade, commmerce, traffic
comminuo, -ere, -ui, -utum: lessen, diminish, reduce
commissio, -ionis, f.: a beginning of a contest, onset
commissura, -ae, f.: joint, seam, juncture
committo, -ere, -misi, -missum: join, connect
commodo, -are, -avi, -atum: lend, grant, allow
commodus, -a, -um: suitable, fit, easy, convenient, agreeable
communico, -are, -avi, -atum: impart, share, take a share in
communis, -e: shared, common
comparatio, ionis, f.: comparison, inquiry by comparison
compareo, -ēre, -ui: be evident, be plain, be visible
comparo, -are, -avi, -atum: furnish, provide, make ready
compesco, -ere, -pescui: hold in check, curb restrain
competo, -ere: agree, come together, coincide

complector, -i, -plexus sum: clasp, embrace, grasp, comprehend

complico, -are, -avi, -atum: fold together, fold up

compono, -ere, -posui, -positum: put together, connect, compose

comprendo, -ere, -i, -prensum: take hold of, arrest, comprise, include

comprensio, -ionis, f.: perception, comprehension

computatio, -ionis, f.: a calculation, computation, reckoning

concavus, -a, -um: hollow, concave

concedo, -ere, -cessi, -cessum: withdraw, retire, comply, yield, accede

concentus, -ūs, m.: choir, agreement, harmony

conchyliatus, -a, -um: dyed with purple

concido, -ere, -cidi: fall, crumble, fall dead

concilio, -are, -avi, -atum: reconcile, unite

concino, -ere, -ui: sing harmoniously, agree

concipio, -ere, -cepi, -ceptum: take hold of, imagine, conceive, understand

concito, -are, -avi, -atum: set into quick motion, excite, spur, agitate

concitatus, -a, -um: quick, fast

concoquo, -ere, -coxi, -coctum: digest

concordia, -ae, f.: harmony, agreement, concord

concors, -cordis: concordant, of the same mind, in agreement

concurro, -ere, -cucurri, -cursum: run together, engage in combat

concutio, -ere, -cussi, -cussum: shake, strike, disturb

condicio, -ionis, f.: condition, situation

condisco, -ere, -didici: learn thoroughly

conditivum, -i, n.: chamber, tomb

condo, -ere, -didi, -ditum: establish, found, build, hide, conceal

conferro, -ferre, -tuli, -latum: bring together, collect, match, compare

confragosus, -a, -um: broken up, rough, uneven

confundo, -ere, -fudi, -fusum: mingle, blend, combine, mix up

congero, -ere, -gessi: bring together, accumulate, pile up

congregatio, -ionis, f.: assembly, association

congrego, -are, -avi, -atum: collect in a flock, unite, assemble

conicio, -ere, -ieci, -iectum: throw together, apply, infer, surmise

coniunctus, -a, -um: connected

coniunx, -iugis, m. and f.: consort, spouse

conlatro, -are, -avi, -atum: bark at

conloco, -are, -avi, -atum: station, put in place, lay out

conluctor, -ari, -atus sum: wrestle with, struggle with

conor, -ari, conatus sum: try, attempt

conscendo, -ere, -endi, -ensum: mount, ascend, climb, embark

conscientia, -ae, f.: common knowledge, consciousness, conscience, sense of guilt

consecro, -are, -avi, -atum: consecrate, dedicate

consector, -ari, -atus sum: pursue eagerly, chase

consensus, -ūs, m.: an agreement, unanimity

consentio, -ire, -sensi, -sensum: agree

consequor, -sequi, -secutus sum: follow, press upon; reach, get, obtain

consero, -ere, -serui, -sertum: connect, join, entwine

conservo, -are, -avi, -atum: maintain, preserve, keep safe

conservus, -i, m.: fellow slave

considero, -are, -avi, -atum: think, consider

consilium, -ii, n.: advice, counsel, plan

consisto, -ere, -stiti, -stitum: come to a stop, stand; exist, occur

consolor, -ari, -atus sum: comfort, cheer, console

consono, -are, -ui: sound together, harmonize

conspicio, -ere, -spexi, -spectum: look at, observe, contemplate

conspiro, -are, -avi, -atum: breathe together, agree, be in accord

constantia, -ae, f.: steadiness, firmness, constancy

consto, -stare, -stiti, -staturum: persevere, edure; impers., be resolved/ agreed

consuesco, -ere, -suevi, -suetum: accustom oneself, be accustomed

consuetudo, -inis, m.: custom, habit

consularis, -e: of or pertaining to a consul

consulo, -ere, -lui, -ltum: deliberate, consult, advise

consummo, -are, -avi, -atum: accomplish, complete, perfect

consumo, -ere, -sumpsi, -sumptum: use up, eat, waste, squander

consuo, -ere, -i, -utum: sew up, stitch together

contamino, -are, -avi, -atum: corrupt, defile

contemno, -ere, -tempsi, -temptum: value little, despise, disdain

contemptus, -ūs, m.: contempt, scorn

contendo, -ere, -tendi, -tentum: strive for, hasten along; (w/dat.) reach

contentus, -a, -um: content, satisfied

contero, -ere, -trivi, -tritum: wear down, consume, exhaust

contextus, -ūs, m.: connection, context

conticesco, -ere, -ticui: become still, fall silent

contineo, -ēre, -tinui, -tentum: hold together, comprise, contain, restrain

continuo, -are, -avi, -atum: carry on without interruption, prolong

contra: prep. w/acc., against

contradictio, -ionis, f.: objections, counterargument

contraho, -ere, -traxi, -tractum: draw together, collect, assemble

contrarius, -a, -um: opposite, contrary, hostile

contristo, -are, -avi, -atum: sadden

contubernalis, -is, m.: tent companion, messmate

contumelia, -ae, f.: abuse, insult, invective

contumeliosus, -a, -um: full of abuse/insult

convalesco, -ere, -lui: regain health, recover

convenio, -ire, -veni, -ventum: come together, fit; impers., be agreed

conventio, -ionis, f.: agreement, compact, convention

conversatio, -ionis, f.: familiar intercourse, association, company

converso, -are: turn over

converto, -ere, -verti, -versum: turn, apply

convicium, -ii, n.: outcry, clamor, insult, reproach

convictus, -ūs, m.: a living together, company, banquet

conviva, -ae, m. and f.: dinner guest

convivium, -i, n.: meal, banquet, feast

convolvo, -ere, -volvi, -voluta: roll around, roll together

copulo, -are, -avi, -atum: join, connect

coram: adv. and prep. w/acc., in the presence of; openly

corpus, -oris, n.: body, a whole, a structure

corrigo, -ere, -rexi, -rectum: set straight, amend, reform

corripio, -ere, -ripui, -reptum: take hold of, snatch up, carry away

corruo, -ere, -ui: fall into a heap, collapse

cotidianus, -a, -um: daily, usual, customary

cotidie: adv., daily, every day

crastinus, -a, -um: of or pertaining to tomorrow

credo, -ere, credidi, creditum: believe, trust

crepitus, -ūs, m.: noise, din, sound

cresco, -ere, crevi, cretum: grow

crudelis, -e: unfeeling, hard, pitiless

cruor, -oris, m.: blood, gore

crustularius, -ii, m.: baker, pastry chef

cubiculum, -i, n.: bedroom

cubile, -is, n.: bed, couch

culmus, -i, m.: straw, thatched roof

cultus, -a, -um: well dressed, polished, cultivated

cultus, -ūs, m.: attire, dress, garb

cum: prep. w/abl., with (for uses as conj. and rel. adv. see Commentary ad loc.)

cunctus, -a, -um: all, whole

cupiditas, -tatis, f.: desire, lust, greed

cupio, -ere, cupivi, cupitum: want, desire

cur: why

cura, -ae, f.: care, concern, anxiety

curia, -ae, f.: senate house, senate

curiosus, -a, -um: full of anxiety

curo, -are, -avi, -atum: take care for, see to it

cursor, -oris, m.: runner, sprinter

cursus, -ūs, m.: course, journey, passage

custodia, -ae, f.: captive, prisoner

custodio, -ire, -ivi, -itum: guard, keep, protect

custos, -odis, m.: guard, jailor, watchman

D

damno, -are, -avi, -atum: condemn, convict, doom

damnum, -i, n.: injury, harm, penalty

de: prep. w/abl., from, down from, about, concerning

debeo, -ēre, -ui, -itum: owe, ought

debilis, -e: crippled, weak

December, -bris, -bre: the tenth, December

decenter: adv., properly, fittingly

decerno, -ere, -crevi, -cretum: determine, decide, judge

decerpo, -ere, -psi, -ptum: pluck off, tear away, gather

decet, decuit: impers., it is fitting/proper; suit

decipio, -ere, -cepi, -ceptum: entrap, beguile, deceive

decretum, -i, n.: decree, decision

decuria, -ae, f.: a division or lot of ten

decurro, -ere, -cucurri, -cursum: run down, hasten, traverse

dedecus, -oris, n.: disgrace, dishonor

deduco, -ere, -duxi, -ductum: lead/draw/drag down, reduce

defendo, -ere, -fendi, -fensum: ward off

defensor, -oris, m.: defender, averter, protector

deficio, -ere, -feci, fectum: fail, cease, be exhausted

deicio, -ere, -ieci, -iectum: throw down, lay low

deiectus, -us, m.: a throwing down, fall, descent

deinde: adv., then, next, thereafter

delecto, -are, -avi, -atum: please, delight, entertain

delego, -are, -avi, -atum: refer, assign

delenimentum, -i, n.: blandishment, allurement

delicatus, -a, -um: charming, pleasing, luxurious, effeminate

deliciae, -arum, f. pl.: delight, pleasure, charm, a sexual favorite

dementia, -ae, f.: insanity, folly

demo, -ere: reduce

demergo, -ere, -si, -sum: sink, submerge, plunge

deminutio, -ionis, f.: a lessening, decrease

demitto, -ere, -misi, -missum: send off/away, dismiss

demo, -ere, dempsi, demptum: subtract, remove, diminish

demum: adv., at last, at length, assuredly

densus, -a, -um: thick, close, crowded, compact

deorsum: adv., downward, down

depascor, -i, -pastus sum: eat up, consume, devour

depono, -ere, -posui, -positum: set down, lay aside, entrust

depravo, -are, -avi, -atum: distort, pervert, corrupt

deprecator, -is, m.: intercessor, mediator, advocate

deprehendo, -ere, -di, -sum: apprehend, catch, seize, comprehend

deprimo, -ere, -press, -pressum: press down, overwhelm

derideo, -ēre, -risi, -risum: laugh at, scoff at, scorn

derigo, -rigere, -rexi, -rectum: set straight, direct, steer

descendo, -ere, -di, -sum: climb down, fall, sink

desidero, -are, -avi, -atum: long for, ask for, desire

desino, -ere, -ii, -sistum: cease, leave off

despero, -are, -avi, -atum: be hopeless, despair

destino, -are, -avi, -atum: fix upon, appoint, select

desuetus, -a, -um: out of use, out of practice, unaccustomed, done with

desum, -esse, -fui, -futurum: be away, lack, fail

detergo (or -eo), -ere (or -ēre), -si, -sum: clean, wipe clean

deterreo, -ēre, -ui, itum: frighten off, deter, hinder
detineo, -ēre, -tinui, -tentum: hold back, keep in check, occupy
detraho, -ere, -traxi, -tractum: draw off, drag away, detract
deus, -i, m.: god, divinity
dicio, -ionis, f.: dominion, influence, authority
dico, dicere, dixi, dictum: say, speak, declare, mean
dies, diei, m.: day
differo, -ferre, -tuli, -latum: vary, differ
difficilis, -e: hard, difficulty
difficultas, -tatis, f.: difficulty, distressing circumstance, poverty
diffluo, -ere, -fluxi: flow in different directions, be dissolved, dissipate
digero, -ere, -gessi, -gestum: separate, divide, distribute, arrange
dignitas, -tatis, f.: worth, merit, rank, reputation, greatness
dignus, -a, -um: worthy, deserving, w/abl.
diligens, -ntis: attentive, diligent
diligenter: adv., attentively, diligently
diligentia, -ae, f.: attentiveness, diligence
diluo, -ere, -ui, -utum: wash away, dissolve, mix
discedo, -ere, -cessi, -cessum: leave, depart
discessio, -ionis, f.: division, divide; a unanimous vote
discipulus, -i, m.: student
disco, discere, didici: learn
discumbo, -ere, -cubui, -cubitum: recline at table, lie down
discurro, -ere, -cucurri, -cursum: run to and fro, wander, roam
discutio, -ere, -cussi, -cussum: dash in pieces, dispel, disperse, destroy
dispono, -ere, -posui, -positum: distribute, arrange, set in order
dispositio, ionis, f.: a regular disposition, arrangement, planning
disputo, -are, -avi, -atum: weigh, examine, argue, insist
dissentio, -ire, -sensi, -sensum: disagree, contradict, quarrel
dissideo, -ēre, -edi: sit apart, be at variance, disagree
dissimilis, -e: unlike, dissimilar, different
dissimilitudo, -tudinis, f.: unlikeness, difference
dissonus, -a, -um: dissonant, discordant
distendo, -ere, -ndi, -tentum: stretch apart, swell, stuff
distinguo, -ere, -nxi, -nctum: separate, make conspicuous, specify,
    distinguish
distringo, -ere, -tricti, -trictum: draw asunder, distract the attention of

diu: adv., for a long time

diversus, -a, -um: opposite, different, contrary

dives, -itis: rich, wealthy, costly

divido, -ere, -visi, -visum: divide, force apart, distribute, arrange

divitiae, -arum, f. pl.: riches, wealth

do, dare, dedi, datum: give, render

doceo, -ēre, docui, doctum: teach, instruct, show

doleo, -ēre, dolui: feel pain, grieve, take offense; cause pain/sorrow

dolor, -oris, m.: pain, suffering

domicilium, -ii, n.: dwelling, abode

dominicus, -a, -um: of or pertaining to a master

domino, -are, -avi, -atum: rule

dominus, -i, m.: master

domus, -i or -ūs, f.: home, house, family

dormio, -ire, -ivi, -itum: sleep

dos, -tis, f.: gift, endowment, talent, dowry

dubius, -a, -um: doubtful, hesitating, wavering, uncertain

duco, -ere, duxi, ductum: lead, draw, infer

ductus, -ūs, m.: a leading, a drawing motion

dudum: adv., a short time ago, before, once; w/*iam*, this long time, finally

dulcis, -e: sweet, agreeable, pleasant

dum: conj., while; provided that; until (for uses see Commentary ad loc.)

duplex, -icis: twofold, double

dupondius, -i, m.: two *asses*, twopence

duritia, -ae, f.: hardness, toughness

duro, -are, -avi, -atum: harden; endure

durus, -a, -um: hard, tough

dux, ducis, m.: general, leader

E

e, ex: prep. w/abl., from, out from, based on

ebrietas, -tatis, f.: drunkenness, intoxication

ebrius, -a, -um: drunk, sated with drink

ecce: lo! behold! look!

ecquis, ecquid: interrog. pron. and adj., any

erubesco, -ere, -bui: blush, feel ashamed

edax, -acis: greedy, voracious, devouring

edo, -ere, -didi, -ditum: bring forth, produce

edo, -ere, esi, esum: eat, consume

educo, -are, -avi, -atum: rear, raise, train

educo, -ere, -duxi, -ductum: lead out, bring forth, rear, erect

effectus, -ūs, m.: accomplishment, result, effect

efficax, -cacis: effective, effectual

efficio, -ere, -feci, fectum: produce, complete, accomplish

effluo, -ere, -fluxi: flow out, run out

effugio, -ere, -fugi: flee away, escape, avoid, escape the notice of

egero, -ere, -gessi, -gestum: bring forth, empty, discharge

egregius, -a, -um: outstanding, remarkable, eminent

elephantus, -i, m.: elephant

elido, -ere, -lisi, -sum: strike out, dash to pieces, destroy

eligo, -ere, -legi, -lectum: pick out, single out, choose, select

emendo, -are, -avi, -atum: free from faults, correct, improve

emergo, -ere, -si, -sum: come forth, emerge, appear

emineo, -ēre, -ui: stand out, project, be prominent, be conspicuous

emo, -ere, emi, emptum: buy, purchase, acquire

enervo, -are, -avi, -atum: weaken, deprive of vigor

enim: postpos. conj., for, namely, that is to say, in fact, truly

epistula, -ae, f.: letter

eques, -itis, m.: horseman, member of the equestrian order

equus, -i, m.: horse

ergo: then, therefore

erigo, -ere, -rexi, -rectum: raise up, arouse, excite

eripio, -ere, -ipui, -eptum: tear away, pluck, snatch, rescue

erro, -are, -avi, -atum: wander, err

error, -oris, m.: mistake, wandering

eruditio, -ionis, f.: learning, erudition

eruditus, -a, -um: instructed, learned, skilled, experienced

erumpo, -ere, -rupi, -ruptum: break out, burst forth

eruo, -ere, -ui, -utum: cast forth, root up, dig out; rescue

esseda, -ae, f.: two-wheeled Celtic chariot

esurio, -ire, -iturum: be hungry

et: and, even, yet; **et . . . et**, both . . . and

etiam: adv., yet, still, even, also, yes indeed, by all means

etiamnunc: adv., even now, still, even at this time
evado, -ere, -vasi, -vasum: go out, come out, escape, turn out, become
evello, -ere, -velli, -vulsum: tear out, eradicate, extract
evenio, -ire, -veni, -eventum: come out, turn out, happen
evito, -are, -avi, -atum: shun, avoid
evoco, -are, -avi, -atum: call out, summon, stir, raise
exactor, -oris, m.: expeller, exactor, tax collector
exagito, -are, -avi, -atum: rouse, disturb, harass
exanimo, -are, -avi, -atum: weigh, consider, examine, test
exardesco, -ere, -arsi, -arsum: blaze out, catch fire; be angry
exaudio, -ire, -ivi, -itum: hear clearly, heed
excandesco, -ere, -dui: grow hot, kindle
excellens, -ntis: towering, prominent, superior
excelsus, -a, -um: high, lofty, noble
excerpo, -ere, -psi, -ptum: pick out, extract, except
excido, -ere, -cī di, -cisum: cut out, extirpate
excipio, -ere, -cepi, -ceptum: take out, make an exception,
excito, -are, -avi, -atum: excite, rouse (from sleep), stir
exclamatio, -ionis, f.: shout
exclamo, -are, -avi, -atum: shout, cry aloud
excludo, -ere, -di, -clusum: shut out, hinder, prevent
excutio, -ere, -cussi, -cussum: shake off, cast out, throw, excite
execratio, -ionis, f.: curse, prayer
exemplar, -is, n.: image, likeness, model
exemplum, -i, n.: example, model
exeo, -ire, -ii, -itum: go out, perish
exerceo, -ēre, -ui, -itum: keep busy, train, practice
exhaurio, -ire, -hausi, -haustum: exhaust, tire, bring to an end
exhibeo, -ēre, -ui, -itum: show, display
exhilaro, -are, -avi, -atum: gladden, cheer
exhortatio, -ionis, f.: encouragement, exhortation
exigo, -ere, -egi, -actum: drive out, exact, demand
exiguus, -a, -um: scanty, small, petty, insignificant
exilis, -e: thin, slender, meager
exilium, -ii, n.: exile, place of exile
eximo, -ere, -emi, -emptum: take away, remove, deliver, except
existimo, -are, -avi, -atum: value, judge, suppose, consider, reckon

exitium, -ii, n.: exit, departure, death

exitus, -ūs, m.: way out, end, conclusion, death

expavesco, -ere, -pavi: be terrified, fear greatly

expecto, -are, -avi, -atum: wait for, expect

expeditio, -ionis, f.: an enterprise, campaign

expeditus, -a, -um: unfettered, free, easy, ready

expello, -ere, -puli, -pulsum: drive out

experimentum, -i, n.: proof, test, trial, experiment

experior, -iri, -pertus sum: try, test, undertake; in perf., to know by experience

explico, -are, -avi, -atum: unfold, disentangle, spread out, set free

exploro, -are, -avi, -atum: search out, examine, explore

exprimo, -ere, -pressi, -pressum: press out, express

exspectatio, -ionis, f.: expectation, longing, desire

extendo, -ere, -tendi, -tentum: stretch out, extend

exterior, -us: comparative adj., outer, exterior

externus, -a, -um: outward, external

extinguo, -ere, -nxi, -nctum: quench, extinguish

exto, -are: stand out, be prominent, exist

extra: adv. and prep. w/acc., on the outside, apart from, except, beyond

extremus, -a, -um: outermost, farthest, last

exulto, -are: leap up, rejoice, boast

exuo, -ere, -ui, -utum: draw/pull off, strip, despoil, cast off

F

faber, -bri, m.: craftsman (a smith or carpenter)

facilis, -e: easy

facio, -ere, feci, factum: do, make, achieve, attain, reach

facultas, -tatis, f.: capability, power, skill

falsus, -a, -um: false, unfounded

fama, -ae, f.: report, rumor, fame, renown

fames, -is, f.: hunger, famine

familia, -ae, f.: household, slaves in the household

familiaris, -e: of or pertaining to the household; friendly, intimate

familiariter: adv., on friendly terms

fastidio, -ire, -ivi, -itum: feel disgust, loathe, despise
fastidiosus, -a, -um: full of disgust, squeamish
fastigium, -ii, n.: the top of a gable, roof, peak
fateor, -ēri, fassus sum: admit, confess, acknowledge
fatigo, -are, -avi, -atum: to exhaust, weary, tire out
fatum, -i, n.: fate, destiny, death
fauces, -ium, n. pl.: jaws, throat
favor, -oris, m.: favor, goodwill, applause
favus, -i, m.: honeycomb
felicitas, -tatis, f.: luck, happiness, good fortune
felix, -cis: lucky, happy, fortunate
femina, -ae, f.: woman, female
fera, -ae, f.: beast, wild animal
feriatus, -a, -um: of or pertaining to a holiday, idle
ferio, -ire: strike, beat
fermentum, -i, n.: a fermenting, means of fermentation
fero, ferre, tuli, latum: bear, carry, endure, accept; say, report
ferreus, -a, -um: made of iron, hard, firm, unyielding
ferrum, -i, n.: iron, sword
festum, -i, n.: holiday, festival
fictilis, -e: made of clay, earthen; **fictilia, -orum:** earthenware
fideliter: adv., faithfully, honestly, with conviction
fidens, -entis: confident, courageous, bold
fiducia, -ae, f.: trust, confidence, assurance, pledge
figo, -ere, fixi, fixum: fasten, attach, fix, set
filius, -ii, m.: son
fingo, -ere, finxi, fictum: touch, handle, form, fashion, make
finio, -ire, -ivi, -itum: put an end to, terminate
finis, -is, m.: end, border, boundary, limit
fio, fieri: used as passive of *facio*, become, be made
firmitas, -tatis, f.: firmness, strength, endurance
firmo, -are, -avi, -atum: make firm, fortify, strengthen
firmus, -a, -um: strong, steadfast, reliable
fleo, -ēre, flevi, fletum: weep, cry
floreo, -ēre, -ui: bloom, blossom, flourish, abound
flos, floris, m.: flower

fluctus, -ūs, m.: flow, tide, wave, current
flumen, -inis, n.: river
fluo, -ere, fluxi, fluctum: flow
foedus, -a, -um: filthy, foul, loathsome, repulsive
folium, -ii, n.: leaf
foris: adv., out of doors
forma, -ae, f.: shape, form, beauty
formosus, -a, -um: shapely, beautiful
forsitan: adv., perhaps
forte: by chance, perhaps, by accident
fortis, -e: strong, stout, brave
fortiter: adv., bravely
fortuitus, -a, -um: accidental, happening by chance
fortuna, -ae, f.: luck, fortune, chance, fate
forum, -i, n.: marketplace, piazza, the Roman Forum
foveo, -ēre, fovi, fotum: keep warm, cherish, support, encourage
fragor, -oris, m.: a crashing, loud noise, din
frango, -ere, fregi, fractum: break, smash, crush
frater, -ris, m.: brother
fremitus, -ūs, m.: a murmuring, a resounding, loud noise
fremo, -ere, -ui: roar, resound
frigus, -oris, n.: cold, coldness
frons, -dis, f.: leafy branch, bough, foliage
frons, frontis, f.: forehead, brow, face, front, façade
frugalitas, -tatis, f.: thriftiness, economy
fruor, -i, fructus sum: enjoy, delight in (w/abl.)
frustum, -i, n.: bit, piece, chunk
fuga, -ae, f.: flight, escape, exile
fugax, -acis: fleeing, fleeting, transitory
fugio, -ere, fugi, fugiturum: flee, escape, avoid
fugo, -are, -avi, -atum: put to flight, cause to flee
fumosus, -a, -um: smoky
fungor, -i, functus sum: be engaged in, do, perform (w/abl.)
fur, -is, m.: thief
furor, -oris, m.: madness, rage, fury; inspiration, frenzy

G

gaudeo, -ēre, gavisus sum: rejoice

gemitus, -ūs, m.: groan, sigh, complaint

generosus, -a, -um: wellborn, noble

gens, -ntis, f.: clan, tribe, people, race, species

genu, -ūs, n.: knee

genus, -eris, n.: race, kind, type, sort

gero, -ere, -gessi, -gestum: carry, bear, exhibit, wear, conduct

gigno, -ere, genui, genitum: give birth to, produce

glaber, -bra, -brum: smooth, hairless

glacies, -ei, f.: ice

gladius, -ii, m.: sword

glomero, -are, -avi, -atum: roll up, bunch up, make into a ball, gather

gloria, -ae, f.: glory

glorior, -ari, -atus sum: boast, brag, exult in

grabatus, -i, m.: cot

gradus, -ūs, m.: step, gait, pace, approach

Graius, -a, -um: Greek

gratia, -ae, f.: favor, kindness; abl. with preceding gen., for the sake of

gratuitus, -a, -um: not for reward, free, voluntarily

gratus, -a, -um: welcome, dear, thankful, deserving of thanks

gravis, -e: heavy, serious, weighed down, bass-pitched

gravitas, -tatis, f.: heaviness, dignity, importance

grex, gregis, m.: flock, herd, swarm, throng

gubernaculum, -i, n.: helm, rudder

gubernator, -oris, m.: helmsman

gula, -ae, f.: throat, gullet

H

habeo, -ēre, -ui, -itum: have, hold, consider

habito, -are, -avi, -atum: dwell, inhabit

habitus, -ūs, m.: costume, garb, demeanor

haesito, -are, -avi, -atum: be irresolute, hesitate

haesitatio, -ionis, f.: irresolution, hesitation

harundo, -inis, f.: reed, stalk, cane
haurio, -ire, hausi, haustum: draw, devour, drink in
haustus, -ūs, m.: draught
herba, -ae, f.: an herb, grass
hīc: adv., in this place, here, in this matter, on this point
hic, haec, hoc: this
hiems, -emis, f.: winter
hilaris, -e: cheerful, merry
homo, -inis, m.: human being, person
honestus, -a, -um: respected, regarded with honor, noble
honor, -oris, m.: reputation, esteem; public office
hordeaceus, -a, -um: of or relating to barley
horrendus, -a, -um: dreadful, fearful, horrible
horridus, -a, -um: shaggy, bristly, rough; causing terror
hortus, -i, m.: garden, park
hortor, -ari, -atus sum: encourage, urge, incite
hospes, -itis: host, visitor, stranger
hospitalis, -e: of or pertaining to a guest or host
hostis, -is, m.: enemy, foe
huc: to this point, to this extent
humanus, -a, -um: human, refined, civilized
humanitas, -tatis, f.: human nature, civilization, refinement
humi: adv. (loc. of *humus*), on the ground
humilis, -e: lowly, insignificant, humble

I

iaceo, -ēre, -cui: lie, be recumbent, lie dead, be located
iacio, -ere, ieci, iactum: throw, cast, fling; build
iactatio, -ionis, f.: a tossing, shaking motion; boasting
iacto, -are, -avi, -atum: throw about, toss, consider, discuss, boast
iam . . . iamque: adv., once and again, continually
iam: adv., now, at last, again, presently, immediately
iamdudum: adv., long since, for a long time now
ianitor, -oris, m.: doorman, watchman
ibi: adv., there, in that place
ictus, -ūs, m.: blow, stroke, wound

īdem (isdem), eadem, idem: same, the very

ideo: adv., for that reason, on that account

idoneus, -a, -um: w/abl., suitable, sufficient

ieiunus, -a, -um: abstinent, unproductive, empty, insignificant

ignarus, -a, -um: ignorant, unknowing, unskilled

ignis, -is, m.: fire

ignominia, -ae, f.: disgrace, dishonor

ignoro, -are, -avi, -atum: not to know, be ignorant of, disregard

ille, -a, -ud: that, that well-known

illic: adv., in that place, yonder, therein

illuc: adv., to that place, to that end, thereto, to such an extent

imago, -inis, f.: representation, likeness, ghost, ancestral mask

imber, -bris, m.: rain, storm

imitor, -ari, -atus sum: imitate, copy, seek to resemble

immineo, -ēre: project over, hang down over, be near, strive for

immitto, -ere, -misi, -missum: send in, admit, enter into, introduce

immodicus, -a, -um: enormous, huge, immoderate, extravagant

immortalis, -e: deathless, immortal

immotus, -a, -um: unmoved, unmoving

imparatus, -a, -um: unprepared

impatiens, -ntis: impatient, unable to bear

impavidus, -a, -um: fearless, unafraid

impedio, -ire, -ivi, -itum: hamper, hinder, impede

impello, -ere, -puli, pulsum: strike against, urge, incite, drive forward

imperator, -oris, m.: commander, general, emperor

impendo, -ere, -ndi, -nsum: weigh out

imperitus, -a, -um: unskilled, inexperienced, unacquainted

imperium, -ii, n.: authority, command, dominion, control

impero, -are, -avi, -atum: command, enjoin, order

impetus, -ūs, m.: attack, assault, onset, impulse, impression

impingo, -ere, -pegi, -pactum: fasten upon, affix, throw on, thrust at

impleo, -ēre, -evi, -etum: to fill, make full

implico, -are, -avi, -atum: entwine, entangle, embrace, wrap, involve

imprimo, -ere, -pressi, -pressum: press upon, mark, stamp

in: prep. w/abl. in; w/acc. into, for, as, with regard to, for the purpose of

inaequaliter: adv., unequally, on unequal terms

inanis, -e: empty, useless, abandoned, vain

inbecillitas, -tatis, f.: weakness, feebleness

incedo, -ere, -cessi, -cessum: advance, proceed; happen, befall

incendium, -ii, n.: fire, flame, conflagration

incido, -ere, -cidi, -cisum: fall in with, rush at, light upon, happen, occur

incīdo, -ere, -cīdi, -cisum: cut into

incipio, -ere, -cepi, -ceptum: begin, start

inclinatio, -ionis, f.: leaning, tendency, inclination

inclino, -are, -avi, -atum: bend, incline, be inclined, divert

includo, -ere, -si, -sum: enclose, shut off, keep out, restrain

incola, -ae, f.: resident, inhabitant

incommodus, -a, -um: inconvenient, unsuitable, disagreeable

incomptus, -a, -um: unkempt, disheveled

inconcussus, -a, -um: unshaken, firm, unchanged

inconstantia, -ae, f.: fickleness, inconstancy

incorruptus, -a, -um: unspoiled, undefiled, genuine, pure

incumbo, -ere, -bui, -bitum: lean on, weigh upon, incline toward

inde: adv., from that place, therefrom, thence

indicium, -ii, n.: notice, charge, evidence, sign, mark

indico, -are, -avi, -atum: point out, show, accuse

indico, -ere, -dixi, -dictum: declare, proclaim

indifferens, -entis: not to be sought or avoided, neither good nor bad

indignus, -a, -um: unworthy, unfit, unbecoming (w/abl.)

induco, -ere, -duxi, -ductum: bring forward, introduce, present, exhibit

indulgeo, -ēre, -ulsi, -ulsum: give in, concede, indulge, be addicted

induo, -ere, -ui, -utum: assume, don, dress

induro, -are, -avi, -atum: harden, make tough

industria, -ae, f.: diligence, activity

ineo, -ire, -ivi and -ii, -tum: go in, enter, embark upon

iners, -ertis: without skill, incompetent; inactive

inertia, -ae, f.: lack of skill, inactivity

inexpertus, -a, -um: without experience, untested, unproven

inexpugnabilis, -e: not able to be fought off, unassailable

infamia, -ae, f.: bad repute, infamy, disgrace

infelix, -icis: unlucky, unhappy, unfortunate, miserable

inferior, -ius: lower down, inferior

infigo, -ere, -fixi, -fixum: fasten, implant, affix, impress

infirmus, -a, -um: weak, inconstant

infringo, -ere, -fregi, -fractum: break, inflict

ingenium, -ii, n.: natural talent, ability, capability, disposition

ingens, -ntis: huge, unnatural, remarkable, immense

ingenuus, -a, -um: freeborn, noble

ingero, -ere, -gessi, -gestum: pour in, heap upon, assail, load

ingratus, -a, -um: unpleasant, ungrateful, thankless

inhumanus, -a, -um: unhuman, unrefined, uncivilized

inicio, -ere, -ieci, -iectum: throw at, hurl upon, impose, apply

inimicus, -a, -um: unfriendly, inimical, hostile

iniquitas, -tatis, f.: inequality, unevenness

initium, -ii, n.: beginning

iniuria, -ae, f.: injury, harm

inlaesus, -a, -um: unhurt, unharmed

inlido, -ere, -si, -sum: strike against, push against

innato, -are, -avi, -atum: swim in, float in

innoxius, -a, -um: not harmful

inopia, -ae, f.: lack, scarcity, poverty, need

inopinatus, -a, -um: unexpected

inquam (inquis, inquit): say

inquietus, -a, -um: restless, disturbed

inquilinus, -a, -um: of foreign birth, non-native

inquiro, -ere, -sivi, -situm: seek, search after, inquire, examine

inritus, -a, -um: undecided, invalid, void, ineffetual

insania, -ae, f.: madness, frenzy

insatiabilis, -e: insatiable

inscribo, -ere, -psi, -ptum: write upon, inscribe, assign, attribute

insidiosus, -a, -um: deceitful, dangerous

insido, -ere, -sedi, -sessum: sit in/on, occupy, adhere to

insignio, -ire, -ivi, -itum: mark out, make conspicuous, distinguish

insolens, -ntis: excessive, immoderate, arrogant

insomnia, -orum, n. pl.: sleeplessness

inspicio, -ere, -spexi, -spectum: look at, inspect, examine, consider

instigo, -are, -avi, -atum: goad on, urge, incite

institor, -oris, m.: peddler, hawker

instituo, -ere, -ui, -utum: establish, arrange, ordain

instrumentum, -i, n.: tool, utensil, means, provisions, supply

instruo, -ere, -uxi, -uctum: set in order, prepare, equip, arrange

insum, -esse, -fui, -futurum: be in, be contained in, belong to

insuperabilis, -e: insurmountable

intectus, -a, -um: uncovered

integer, -gra, -grum: whole

intellego, -ere, -exi, -ectum: understand

intemperantia, -ae, f.: excess, extravagance

intentio, -ionis, f.: a straining, effort, exertion

intentus, -a, -um: intent, watchful, eager

inter: prep. w/acc. between, among, during

interdico, -ere, -dixi, -dictum: prohibit

interdum: adv., sometimes, occasionally, now and then

interim: adv., meanwhile, in the meantime

intermitto, -ere, -misi, -missum: suspend, interrupt, let pass, pause

interpello, -are, -avi, -atum: interrupt, object, disturb

interpono, -ere, -posui, -positum: place between, interpose, introduce

interrogo, -are, -avi, -atum: ask, inquire, interrogate

interrumpo, -ere, -rupi, -ruptum: break off, interrupt

interscindo, -ere, -scidi, -scissum: tear apart, divide

intersum, -esse, -fui, -futurum: be between, be different, matter

intervallum, -i: a space between two things, interval

intonsus, -a, -um: unshorn, unshaven

intrepidus, -a, -um: fearless, bold, brazen

intro, -are, -avi, -atum: enter

introrsus: adv., inward, inwardly, within

introsum: adv., toward the inside, inward, within

intueor, -ēri, -itus sum: look closely, gaze, regard, consider

intus: adv., on the inside

invenio, -ire, -veni, -ventum: come upon, find, discover

iudex, -icis, m.: judge

invicem: adv., by turns, alternately, reciprocally

invideo, -ēre, -vidi, -visum: envy, grudge

invidia, -ae, f.: envy

invidiosus, -a, -um: full of envy; exciting envy; hateful, odious

invitus, -a, -um: unwilling

iocus, -i, m.: joke

ipse, ipsa, ipsum: -self, by -self, the very

ira, -ae, f.: rage, anger

irascor, -ari, -atus sum: be angry
irrito, -are, -avi, -atum: stimulate, excite, provoke
is, ea, id: that
iste, -a, -ud: that (of yours)
istīc: there, in that place (where you are)
ita: adv., in this manner, thus, so; *ita   ut*, as . . . so
itaque: conj., and so, and thus, accordingly, therefore, consequently
iter, itineris, n.: journey
iterum: adv., again, a second time, once more
iubeo, -ēre, iussi, iussum: order, bid
iucundus, -a, -um: pleasant, pleasing, favorable
iudex, -icis, m.: judge
iudico, -are, -avi, -atum: examine, judge, determine
iugerum, -i, n.: an acre (gen. pl. = *iugerum*)
iugum, -i, n.: yoke
iumentum, -i, n.: beast of burden
ius, iuris, n.: right, law, authority
iuvenis, -is: young, youthful; as noun, youth, young men
iuvo, -are, -avi, -atum: help, assist, support

L

labo, -are, -avi, -atum: totter, be about to fall, sink
labor, -i, -psus sum: slip, slide, fall
labor, -oris, m.: work, toil
laboro, -are, -avi, -atum: work, take pains, work out
labrum, -i, n.: lip
labyrinthus, -i, m.: labyrinth
lacrima, -ae, f.: a tear, weeping
laedo, -ere, -si, -sum: hurt, harm, injure, insult
laetitia, -ae, f.: gladness, joy, delight
laetus, -a, -um: happy, glad
lamella, -ae, f.: a small plate or sheet of metal
langueo, -ēre: faint, be weary, sluggish
lascivio, -ire: be wanton, be lewd, be playful
lassitudo, -tudinis, f.: weariness, fatigue
lasso, -are, -avi, -atum: make weary, cause to faint, exhaust

latebra, -ae, f.: hiding place, retreat

lateo, -ēre, -ui: lurk, lie hidden, be concealed

latito, -are, -avi, -atum: hide, be hid, be concealed

latus, -a, -um: wide, broad, extensive

lautus, -a, -um: splendid, luxurious, elegant

laxus, -a, -um: spacious, wide, open, roomy, loose

lectio, -ionis, f.: reading, a selecting

legio, -ionis, f.: body of soliders, legion

lego, -ere, legi, lectum: gather, collect, choose, appoint, read

lenis, -e: soft, smooth, mild, easy

lentus, -a, -um: at rest, calm, motionless

levis, -e: smooth

libamenta, -orum, n. pl.: portion offered to the gods in sacrifice, firstfruits

libenter: adv., willingly, cheerfully, gladly

liber, libera, liberum: free

liberalis, -e: of or pertaining to freedom

liberalitas, -tatis, f.: the quality or characteristic of being free, generosity

libertas, -tatis, f.: freedom

libertinus, -i, m.: a freedman (ex-slave)

libet: impers., it is pleasing, is agreeable

libido, -inis, f.: pleasure, desire, longing, lust

libo, -are, -avi, -atum: sample, taste, touch lightly upon, extract

licet, -ēre, -cuit, -citum: it is permitted; although (see Commentary ad loc.)

limen, liminis, n.: threshold, border

limes, -itis, m.: path, passage, track, boundary

lingua, -ae, f.: tongue, language

liquens, -ntis: flowing, liquid

liqueo, -ēre, licui: be fluid, be clear, be apparent

lis, litis, f.: case, suit, action, dispute

litigo, -are, -avi, -atum: sue, go to law, prosecute

litterae, -arum, f. pl.: letter, literature

litura, -ae, f.: a smearing, a rubbing

loco, -are, -avi, -atum: place, put, position, locate, hire out

locuples, -etis: rich, opulent, well provided for

locus, -i, m.: place, position, topic, subject

longinquus, -a, -um: remote, far-off, long lasting, tedious

longus, -a, -um: long, extensive, distant, remote

loquor, loqui, locutus sum: speak, say, mention
lubricus, -a, -um: slippery
lucellum, i.: small gain, small profit
luceo, -ēre, luxi: be light, shine, be clear, be conspicuous
luctor, -ari, -atus sum: wrestle, strive, contend
ludo, -ere, lusi, lusum: play, make sport, delude, deceive
luo, -ere, lui: loose, free, pay off, atone for
lusus, -ūs, m.: play, game, sport
luxuria, -ae, f.: luxury, decadence
luxuriosus, -a, -um: excessive, luxurious

M

machina, -ae, f.: device, engine, machine
magis: adv., more, in a higher degree
magister, -tri, m.: teacher, master
magistratus, -ūs, m.: magistracy, office
magnificentia, -ae, f.: loftiness, splendor, grandeur
magnificus, -a, -um: distinguished, noble, august
magnitudo, -tudinis, f.: greatness, size, bulk
magnus, -a, -um: great, large
maiestas, -tatis, f.: grandeur, dignity, sovereignty
malignus, -a, -um: slanderous, spiteful, stingy
malitia, -ae, f.: ill-will, spite, malice
malivolentia, -ae, f.: ill-will, dislike, malevolence
malo, malle, -ui: prefer, incline toward
malus, -a, -um: bad, malicious, unwholesome, base
mancipium, -ii, n.: possession, property (particularly a purchased slave)
maneo, -ēre, mansi, mansum: stay, wait, remain, tarry
manifestus, -a, -um: clear, plain, apparent, exposed
manus, -ūs, m.: hand
marceo, -ēre: be faint, droop, be languid
mare, -is, n.: the sea
marmor, -oris, n.: marble
mater, -tris, f.: mother
materia, -ae, f.: stuff, matter, material, topic, source, opportunity
mature: adv., seasonably, at the right time, early, speedily

meditor, -ari, -atus sum: reflect on, give attention to, study, practice, rehearse

medius, -a, -um: in the middle of, in between

mehercules: by Hercules! assuredly

mel, mellis, n.: honey

memorabilis, -e: that which may be told/heard of, worth repeating, notable

memoria, -ae, f.: memory

mens, mentis, f.: mind, thought, intention

mensa, -ae, f.: table

mensis, -is, m.: month

mentior, -iri, -itus sum: lie, cheat, deceive, feign

merito: adv., deservingly, justly

merx, mercis, f.: goods, wares, merchandise

-met: intensifying suffix added to the oblique forms of the pers. pron.

meta, -ae, f.: cone, pyramid, turning point for chariots in the Circus

metior, -iri, mensus sum: measure, estimate, judge

meto, -ere, messui, messum: reap, mow, harvest

metus, -ūs, m.: fear, dread, terror

meus, -a, -um: my, mine

migro, -are, -avi, -atum: move location, depart

miles, militis, m.: soldier

militaris, -e: of or pertaining to military affairs

militia, -ae, f.: military service, warfare

mille (pl. milia): a thousand

mimus, -i, m.: a mimic actor, mime, farce

minime: adv., by no means, not in the slightest way

minimus, -a, -um: least, smallest

minister, -tri, m.: an attendent, minister, servant

ministerium, -ii, n.: office, occupation, employment

ministro, -are, -avi, -atum: attend, serve, wait upon

minor, -ari, -atus sum: threaten, menace

minor/minus, -oris: smaller, less, shorter, younger

mirator, -oris, m.: admirer

miror, -ari, atus sum: wonder, be amazed at, admire

misceo, -ēre, miscui, mixtum: mix, mingle, blend

miser, -era, -erum: wretched, miserable, unfortunate

mitto, -ere, -misi, -missum: send, launch, direct, let go

mobilis, -e: prone to movement, quick, fleet
moderatio, -ionis, f.: guidance, regulation, moderation, temperateness
modeste: adv., moderately, with discretion, with temperance
modicus, -a, -um: of proper measure, ordinary, of a tolerable size
modo: adv., only, merely, just (other uses, see Commentary ad loc.)
modulatio, -ionis, f.: melody, rhythm, pitch
modus, -i, m.: manner, measure, method, limit; sort, kind
moles, -is, f.: mass, bulk, pile, greatness, strength
molestia, -ae, f.: trouble, annoyance, distress
molestus, -a, -um: annoying, bothersome, harmful
mollio, -ire, -ivi, -tum: soften
mollis, molle: soft, flexible, pliant
mora, -ae, f.: delay
morbus, -i, m.: sickness, disease
morior, -i, mortuus sum: die, perish
moror, -ari, -atus sum: delay, linger, stay, reside
mors, -tis, f.: death
mortuus, -a, -um: dead
mos, moris, m.: habit, custom; pl., character
motus, -ūs, m.: movement, motion
moveo, -ēre, movi, motum: move, cause to stir, set in motion, disturb
muliebris, -e: female, feminine, effeminate
mulio, -ionis, m.: mule-driver
multus, -a, -um: much, many
munditia, -ae, f.: cleanness
mundus, i, m.: world, universe
munus, -eris, n.: function, duty, gift
murmur, -uris, n.: murmuring, rumbling, hum
mutatio, -ionis, f.: a changing, exchange, mutation
muto, -are, -avi, -atum: change, alter
mutus, -a, -um: silent, mute

N

naevus, -i, m.: birthmark, mole, wart
nam: for, for instance, but
narro, -are, -avi, -atum: tell, expound, relate

160   *Vocabulary*

nascor, nasci, natus sum: be born, arise
natura, -ae, f.: nature, Nature, one's natural disposition
naturalis, -e: natural, one's own, produced by nature
nauseabundus, -a, -um: on the verge of vomiting
navigium, -ii, n.: ship, boat
navigo, -are, -avi, -atum: sail, steer
navis, -is, f.: ship
ne: not; **ne . . . quidem,** not . . . even
nec: and not, nor; **nec . . . nec/neque,** neither . . . nor
necdum: not yet, still not
necessarius, -a, -um: necessary, pressing, unavoidable
necesse: n. adj., unavoidable, necessary, needful
necessitas, -tatis, f.: necessity, compulsion, fate, destiny
necessitudo, -tudinis, f.: want, need, distress, necessity
nectar, -aris, n.: drink of the gods, balm, honey
neglegens, -ntis: careless, negligent
neglego, -ere, -legi, -lectum: neglect, disregard, slight, despise
nego, -are, -avi, -atum: deny
negotium, -ii, n.: business, occupation, toil
nemo, neminis, m.: no one
nempe: conj., certainly, without a doubt
nescio, -ire, -ivi, -tum: not to know, be ignorant
nihil: nothing, adv., in no way, not at all
nil: see *nihil*
nimius, -a, -um: too much, excessive, beyond measure; adv. **nimium**
nisi: if not, unless, except
nitidus, -a, -um: bright, polished, shiny, gleaming
nobilis, -e: noble, good
nobilitas, -tatis, f.: nobility, good character
noceo, -ēre, -ui, -turum: harm, hurt
nodus, -i, m.: knot
nolo, nolle, -ui: not want, be unwilling, refuse
nomen, -inis, n.: name, title
non: not
nondum: adv., not yet
nosco, -ere, novi, notum: know, to come to know
noster, -tra, -trum: our

notabilis, -e: notable, noticed, remarkable
notitia, -ae, f.: knowledge, familiarity
novitas, -tatis, f.: novelty, strangeness
novus, -a, -um: new, strange
nox, noctis, f.: night
nullus, -a, -um: none, not any
num: interr. part. introducing a question expecting a negative answer
numeratio, -ionis, f.: a counting, a tally
numero, -are, -avi, -atum: count, enumerate
numerus, i, m.: number
numquam: never
nunc: now, then
nutrix, -icis, f.: nurse, caretaker

O

obeo, -ire, -ivi, -tum: go to meet, engage in, encounter
obicio, -ere, -ieci, -iectum: throw in one's way, present, object, oppose
obiratus, -a, -um: angered, angry
obiurgo, -are, -avi, -atum: scold, blame, reproach, exhort
obliviscor, -i, oblitus sum: forget, neglect, disregard
oboedio, -ire, -ivi, -itum: obey, heed, be subject to
obsecro, -are, -avi, -atum: beseech, implore, supplicate
obsero, -ere, -sevi, -situm: sow, plant, cover over
observo, -are, -avi, -atum: watch, note, attend to, comply with
obsideo, -ēre, -edi, -essum: occupy, besiege
obsonator, -is, m.: grocery shopper
obsonium, -ii, n.: sauce, side dish
obsto, -are, -avi, -atum: block the way, hinder, thwart
obstrepo, -ere, -ui: roar at, clamor against
obstupefacio, -ere, -feci, -factum: amaze, astound, strike dumb
obvenio, -ire, -veni, -ventum: go to meet, come one's way, fall to one's lot
occasio, -ionis, f.: occasion, opportunity
occido, -ere, -cidi, -cisum: strike down, kill, slay
occultus, -a, -um: hidden, secret, obstructed from view
occupatio, ionis, f.: busyness, employment, occupation
occupo, -are, -avi, -atum: seize, occupy, busy, engross

occurso, -are, -avi, -atum: run out to meet, present oneself, charge, attack

oculus, -i, m.: eye

odi, -isse: hate

odiosus, -a, -um: hateful, offensive, unpleasant

odium, -ii, n.: hatred, ill-will, animosity

offendo, -ere, -fendi, -fensum: find fault with, shock, provoke, offend

officium, -ii, n.: duty, function, service, business

olim: adv., at that time, now and then, once upon a time

omitto, -ere, -misi, -missum: let go, pass over

omnis, -e: every, all, whole

onero, -are, -avi, -atum: load up

onus, -eris, n.: load, burden, weight

opera, -ae, f.: work, effort, labor, pains

opimus, -a, -um: fat, plump, sumptuous, abundant

opinio, -ionis, f.: opinion, fancy, belief

oportet, -ēre, -uit: impers., it is proper, it is fitting, it behooves

oppono, -ere, -posui, -positum: set against, set before, lay bare

ops, opis, f.: wealth, riches, substance, means

optimus, -a, -um: best, noble

opto, -are, -avi, -atum: pray for, wish for, choose

opus, -eris, n.: work, labor, toil; **opus est:** there is need (w/abl.)

oratio, -ionis, f.: speech, discourse

orbitas, -tatis, f.: bereavement, orphanage, childlessness

ordinatus, -a, -um: arranged, ordered, appointed

ordo, -inis, m.: row, line, series, rank

organum, -i, n.: musical instrument

origo, -iginis, f.: origin, source

oriundus, -a, -um: born from, sprung

ornatus, -a, -um: furnished, fitted out, decorated, ornate

ortus, -ūs, m.: a rising, birth, beginning, origin

os, oris, n.: mouth

osculor, -ari, -atus sum: kiss

ostendo, -ere, -di, -tentum: show, point out

ostium, -ii, n.: door

otiosus, -a, -um: at ease, idle, unconcerned

otium, -ii, n.: leisure, relaxation

P

paedagogium, -i, n.: a school for servant boys
paedagogus, -i, m.: tutor, pedagogue
paenitentia, -ae, f.: repentence, remorse
palatum, -i, n.: palate, taste
pallesco, -ere, pallui: turn pale
palus, -i, m.: a wooden stake or post
panis, -is, m.: bread
pantomimus, -i, m.: an actor, pantomime
papula, -ae, f.: pustule, pimple
par, -is: equal, matched, adequate
parabilis, -e: easy to be had, at hand
paratus, -a, -um: prepared, equipped
parco, -ere, peperci, parsum: spare, abstain, use moderately
parens, -ntis, m. and f.: parent
pareo, -ēre, parui: obey
paries, -ietis, m.: a wall, partition
pariter: adv., equally, in like manner, at the same time
paro, -are, -avi, -atum: make ready, fit out, prepare
pars, -tis, f.: part, share, portion, piece; party, faction, side
parsimonia, -ae, f.: thrift, frugality
particula, -ae, f.: a small part, particle
parum: adv., too little, not enough, in insufficient quantity
parvulus, -a, -um: very small, tiny
parvus, -a, -um: small, insignificant
pasco, -ere, pavi, pastum: feed, nourish, graze
pascuum, -ii, n.: pasture, pasturage
passim: adv., scattered about, in every direction, without order
pastor, -oris, m.: shepherd
pateo, -ēre, -ui: lie open, be allowable, be plain/manifest
pater, -tris, m.: father
patientia, -ae, f.: patience, endurance, suffering
patior, -i, passus sum: suffer, experience
patria, -ae, f.: homeland, one's country
patricius, -a, -um: of senatorial rank
patrius, -a, -um: of or pertaining to a father

pauculus, -a, -um: very few
paucus, -a, -um: few
paulatim: adv., little by little, gradually
paulo: adv., a little, somewhat
pauper, -eris: poor
paupertas, -tatis, f.: poverty
pausarius, -i, m.: rowing master, coxswain, barker
pavor, -oris, m.: trembling, fear, dread
pax, pacis, f.: peace
pecco, -are, -avi, -atum: make a mistake, err
pectus, -oris, n.: breast, chest
pecunia, -ae, f.: money
pecus, -oris, n.: cattle
peior: comp. of *malus*
pendeo, -ēre, pependi: hang down, be suspended, float
penitus: adv., inwardly, deeply, from the depths
penso, -are, -avi, -atum: weigh, weigh out, compare, pay for, purchase
per: prep. w/acc. through, across, by, on account of
perdo, -ere, -didi, -ditum: destroy, lose, ruin, squander, waste
perduco, -ere, -duxi, -ductum: lead through, lead all the way
perduro, -are, -avi, -atum: last, endure
peregrinatio, -ionis, f.: wandering, travel abroad
peregrinor, -ari, -atus sum: travel abroad, wander, roam
pereo, -ire, -ii or -ivi, -iturum: die, perish, waste
perficio, -ere, -feci, -fectum: accomplish, complete
pergo, -ere, -rexi, -rectum: go on, press on
periculum, -ii, n.: danger
peritus, -a, -um: skilled, experienced, practiced
permaneo, -ēre, -mansi, -mansum: remain, last
permitto, -ere, -misi, -missum: let go, allow, permit
perniciosus, -a, -um: hurtful, harmful, destructive
perpetuus, -a, -um: continual, everlasting
persequor, -i, -secutus sum: follow after, pursue
persevero, -are, -avi, -atum: adhere strictly, continue, persist
persona, -ae, f.: mask, person
persto, -are, -avi, -atum: endure, last, stand firm
persuadeo, -ēre, -suasi, -suasum: persuade, convince

persuasio, -ionis, f.: a convincing, conviction
persulto, -are, -avi, -atum: leap about, prance
pertinaciter: adv., stubbornly, with determination
pertineo, -ēre, -ui: apply, belong, pertain
pervenio, -ire, -veni, -ventum: reach, arrive at, attain
perversus, -a, -um: crooked, wrong, perverse
pervideo, -ēre, -vidi, -visum: survey, see through, discern
pervigilo, -are, -avi, -atum: keep watch all night, remain awake
pervius, -a, -um: passable, accessible
pes, pedis, m.: foot
pessimus, -a, -um: superl. of *malus*
peto, -ere, -ivi, -itum: seek, require of, beseech, aim at, head toward
philosophia, -ae, f.: philosophy, philosophical lifestyle
philosophus, -i, m.: philosopher
piger, -gra, -grum: unwilling, reluctant, lazy, slow
pigritia, -ae, f.: laziness, sloth
pila, -ae, f.: ball
pilicrepus, -i: one who calls balls
pilleatus, -a, -um: wearing the cap of a freedman
pilleum, -i, n.: the close-fitting felt cap of a freedman
pinguis, -e: fat, rich
piscina, -ae, f.: fishpond, pool
placeo, -ēre, -ui, -itum: please, satisfy, be sufficient; impers., be pleasing
placidus, -a, -um: calm, smooth, unperturbed
planus, -a, -um: even, level, flat, plain, clear
plausus, -ūs, m.: clapping, applause
plebeius, -a, -um: plebeian, common, low-class, cheap
plenus, -a, -um: full, w/abl.
plerumque: adv., generally, in general, for the most part, often
plumbum, -i, n.: lead, a lead weight
plurimum: adv., very much so, for the most part (superlative of *multum*)
plus, pluris: more, too much, greater
podagra, -ae, f.: gout
polenta, -ae, f.: peeled barley
pondus, -eris, n.: weight, load
pono, -ere, posui, postium: put, place, establish, set forth
popina, -ae, f.: eatery, tavern

popularis, -e: of or pertaining to the people

populus, -i, m.: the people, populace

porrigo, -ere, -rexi, -rectum: stretch out, extend, reach for

porro: adv., forward, afterward, futhermore

porto, -are, -avi, -atum: carry, transport

portorium, -ii, n.: tax, toll, tariff, fee

posco, -ere, poposci: ask, demand, request, seek

possessio, -ionis, f.: a seizing, occupying, possession

possideo, -ēre, -sedi, -sessum: possess, occupy, be master of

possum, posse, potui: be able, have power

post: prep. w/acc. behind, after

postmodo: adv., afterward, later

postremum: adv., at last, finally

potestas, -tatis, f.: power, ability

potior: comp. of *potis*, possible, capable, powerful; preferable

potius: adv., rather (w/*quam*), preferable

praebeo, -ēre, -ui, -itum: offer, hold forth, grant, exhibit, present

praeceptum, -i, n.: maxim, rule, injunction, precept

praecipio, -ere, -cepi, -ceptum: advise, enjoin, direct, teach

praecipito, -are, -avi, -atum: throw headlong, rush headlong, hasten

praecludo, -ere, -si, -sum: shut off, close, hinder

praeco, -onis, m.: herald, auctioneer

praecordia, -orum: heart, chest, the seat of emotion

praemitto, -ere, -misi, -missum: send forward, dispatch in advance

praeoccupo, -are, -avi, -atum: seize upon beforehand, preoccupy

praeparo, -are, -avi, -atum: make ready beforehand, equip

praeruptus, -a, -um: steep, rugged

praescriptum, -i, n.: rule, precept

praesens, -ntis: present, at hand

praesto, -are, -avi, -atum: stand out, show, render, exhibit, prove, excel, surpass

praesum, -esse, -fui, -futurum: be before, be preeminent, have charge of

praeter: prep. w/acc. besides, beyond, except, apart from

praetereo, -ire, -ii, -itum: go past, pass by, leave out, avoid, surpass

praetor, -oris, m.: praetor, magistrate

pravus, -a, -um: crooked, deformed, perverse

premo, -ere, pressi, pressum: press, push, oppress

pretiosus, -a, -um: costly, precious, valuable
pretium, -ii, n.: price, cost, expense
primum: adv., at first, first of all
primus, -a, -um: first, the first to
principalis, -e: first, primary, leading, imperial
principium, -ii, n.: beginning, commencement
prior, -oris: previous, superior, elder, earlier
prius: comparative adv., sooner, before, earlier
pro: prep. w/abl., for, on behalf of, instead of, as
proavus, -i, m.: great-grandfather
probo, -are, -avi, -atum: approve, commend, prove, test, show
procedo, -ere, -cessi: go before, march forward, advance, result
procerus, -a, -um: high, tall
procul: far-off, away, distant
procumbo, -ere, -bui, -itum: fall prostrate, lean forward, incline
produco, -ere, -duxi, -ductum: lead forth, expose for sale
profero, -ferre, -tuli, -latum: carry forth, produce, make known
professio, -ionis, f.: public acknowledgment, avowal, declaration
proficio, -ere, -feci, -fectum: make progress, help, be successful, be useful
profiteor, -ēri, professus sum: to profess, declare publicly
profligo, -are, -avi, -atum: conquer, ruin, finish off, dispatch
progenies, -iei, f.: offspring, progeny
prohibeo, -ēre, -ui, -itum: hold back, prevent
proicio, -ere, -ieci, -iectum: throw forth, let go, cast off
promitto, -ere, -misi, -missum: promise, offer
pronus, -a, -um: bent over, inclined, disposed, prone
prope: adv., near, nearly, almost, about
propero, -are, -avi, -atum: hasten, hurry, speed
propono, -ere, -posui, -positum: propose, put before, imagine, lay down
proprietas, -tatis, f.: a property, peculiar nature, quality
prorsus: adv., forward, right onward, by all means, absolutely
prosequor, -i, -secutus sum: follow, escort, accompany
prosum, -esse, -fui, -futurum: be of use, do good, benefit
protinus: adv., right onward, directly, continuously,
prout: conj., according as, just as, in proportion to
proverbium, -i, n.: proverb, saying
providentia, -ae, f.: forethought, providence

provideo, -ēre, -vidi, -visum: see in front, foresee
provincia, -ae, f.: province, territory
provoco, -are, -avi, -atum: call forth, summon, challenge
proximus, -a, -um: very close, closest, adjoining, most recent
prudentia, -ae, f.: good sense, good judgment, discretion
publicus, -a, -um: public, open to view
puer, -i, m.: boy, slave
pueritia, -ae, f.: boyhood, childishness
pugna, -ae, f.: fight, battle, contest
pugno, -are, -avi, -atum: fight, contend
pulcher, -chra, -chrum: beautiful, handsome, fine
pulpitum, -i, n.: platform, stage
purus, -a, -um: pure, clean, plain
pusillus, -a, -um: very small, petty
puto, -are, -avi, -atum: think, imagine, suppose

Q

quā: adv., at which (place), by what (way), in what (manner), as
quadragies: adv., forty times
quaero, -ere, -sivi, -situm: seek, beg, search, ask
qualis, -e: of what sort, what kind of, of such a sort, of such a kind
qualiscumque, quale-: of what quality whatsoever, of whatever kind
qualitas, -tatis, f.: quality, state, property
quam: adv., as, how, than; w/superl., most, as . . . as possible
quamdiu: adv., how long, as long as
quamvis: adv. and conj. as you will, as much as you want, although
quantulus, -a, -um: how little, how small
quantus, -a, -um: of what size, how great, how much, as much as
quantuslibet, quanta-, quantum-: how/as much as you like
quare: why, in what manner
quasi: as if, just as if, as though, almost, just about
quatriduum, -i, n.: period of four days
quattuordecim: fourteen
quemadmodum: in what manner, as, just as, how
querella, -ae, f.: complaint, accusation
queror, -i, questus sum: complain, express indignation

qui, quae, quod: who, which
quia: because
quicumque, quae-, quod-: whosoever, whatsoever, any whatever, every
quidam, quae-, quod-/quid-: a certain, some
quidem: certainly, in fact, indeed, what is more; **ne . . . quidem,** not even
quidni: why not
quies, -ietis, f.: peace, quiet, stillness, repose
quiete: adv., calmy, quietly, peacefully
quilibet, quae-, quod-: who-/whatever, who/whatever you please
quin: why not, how not, indeed, in fact
quis, quid: who, what
quisquam, quicquam: any, any one, any person/thing
quisque, quaeque, quidque: who-/whatever; each one, every
quisquis, quicquid (quidquid): whoever, whatever, everyone who, everything which
quomodo: in what manner, how, as
quoniam: since, because
quoquam: to any place, in any direction, whithersoever
quoque: also, too, as well
quot: how many, as many as
quotiens: how often, how many times, as often as
quousque: until what time, how long

R

rabies, -iei, f.: rage, madness, frenzy
rarus, -a, -um: not dense, thin, scattered, far apart, uncommon
ratio, -ionis, f.: reason, rationality
reliquiae, -arum, f. pl.: remainder, remnants, fragments
recedo, -ere, -cessi, -cessum: give way, recede, be distant
recipio, -ere, -cepi, -ceptum: take back, receive, get, obtain
receptus, -ūs, m.: retreat, withdrawal
recognosco, -ere, -gnovi, -gnotum: recall, recognize, review, inspect, examine, prove
recondo, -ere, -didi, -ditum: store up, lay away
recrudesco, -ere, -dui: break out afresh, crop up again
rectus, -a, -um: straight, upright, correct

rector, -oris, m.: director, guide, governor
reddo, -ere, -didi, -ditum: give back, return, answer, render, impart
redigo, -ere, -egi, -actum: collect, reduce
reduco, -ere, -duxi, -ductum: bring/lead back, escort, restore, reduce
refero, -ferre, -tuli, -latum: bring back, return, restore, answer
refert: impers., it matters/concerns, makes a difference
reficio, -ere, -feci, -fectum: make again, restore, refresh
rego, -ere, rexi, rectum: guide, direct, control, rule
regio, -ionis, f.: region, area, territory
regnum, -i, n.: realm, kingdom, rule
reiculus, -a, -um: that which is to be rejected, worthless
reicio, -ere, -ieci, -iectum: throw back, reject
relinquo, -ere, -liqui, -lictum: leave behind, abandon
remeo, -are, -avi: go back, flow back, return
remedium, -ii, n.: cure, remedy
remex, -igis, m.: oarsman
remitto, -ere, -misi, -missum: send back, relax, remit
renuntio, -are, -avi, -atum: bring back notice, renounce
reor, -ēri, ratus sum: reckon, think, judge, decide
repeto, -ere, -petivi, petitum: seek/go after again
reprehendo, -ere, -ndi, -ensum: blame, censure, reprove
res, rei, f.: thing, matter, fact, event, property
resono, -are, -avi, -atum: resound, echo
respicio, -ere, -spexi, -spectum: regard, notice, pay attention to, contemplate
respiratio, -ionis, f.: breathing, breath
respondeo, -ēre, -spondi, -sponsum: answer, reply, resemble
respuo, -ere, -ui: spit out again, discharge, reject
retineo, -ēre, -tinui, -tentum: hold back, restrain, retain
retraho, -ere, -traxi, -tractum: drag/draw back
retritus, -a, -um: scraped off, rubbed away
retro: adv., backward, behind, in past times
revello, -ere, -velli, -vulsum: tear off, peel back, strip
revertor, -i, -versus sum: turn back/about, return
revoco, -are, -avi, -atum: call back, summon again, turn back
rex, regis, m.: king
rideo, -ēre, -si, -sum: laugh, ridicule

ridiculus, -a, -um: amusing, laughable
rigo, -are, -avi, -atum: water, irrigate
ritus, -ūs, m.: ceremony, rite; in abl. w/ gen., in the manner of
rixa, -ae, f.: quarrel, contest, brawling
rixor, -ari, -atus sum: wrangle, brawl, struggle
robur, -oris, n.: oakwood, strength, vigor
rogo, -are, -avi, -atum: ask, demand, implore, insist
Romanus, -a, -um: Roman
ros, roris, m.: dew, drops, moisture
ruo, -ere, -ui, -atum: rush/fall down, hasten, hurry, cast down
ruina, -ae, f.: downfall, a crumbling, ruin
rursus: adv., back, again, on the other hand, in turn
rus, ruris, n.: countryside

S

sacer, -cra, -crum: dedicated, consecrated, regarded with reverence
sacrifico, -are, -avi, -atum: make/offer a sacrifice
saeculum, -i, n.: generation, age, era
saepe: often
saevio, -ire, -ivi, -itum: be fierce, rage
sagino, -are, -avi, -atum: fatten, cram full
sagum, -i, n.: military cloak, blanket
salio, -ire, -ui, saltum: leap, jump, spring
salubris, -e: healthful, wholesome, salubrious
salus, -utis, f.: health, soundness
salutaris, -e: of or pertaining to well-being, wholesome, salutory
salutatio, -ionis, f.: greeting, well-wishing
salutator, -oris, m.: a salutor, one who makes complimentary visits
saluto, -are, -avi, -atum: greet, pay respects, visit
sanctus, -a, -um: consecrated, inviolable, upright, chaste
sanguis, -inis, m.: blood
sanitas, -tatis, f.: health, sanity, good sense
sano, -are, -avi, -atum: make sound, restore to health
sapiens, -ntis: wise
sapientia, -ae, f.: wisdom
sapor, -oris, m.: taste, flavor

sarcina, -ae, f.: package, bundle, load
sat: indecl., enough, sufficient, content
satietas, -tatis, f.: sufficiency, abundance, satiety
satio, -ionis, f.: a planting, cultivated land
satis: indecl., enough, sufficient
satur, -ura, -urum: full, satisfied, sated
saturitas, -tatis, f.: fullness, abundance, plenty
Saturnalia, -iorum, n. pl.: feast of the Saturnalia (beginning December 17)
saucius, -a, -um: wounded
scabies, -iei, f.: mange, scab, rash, itch
scientia, -ae, f.: knowledge, know-how, expertise
scindo, -ere, scidi, scissum: cut, tear, rend, divide
scintilla, -ae, f.: spark
scio, -re, -ivi or -ii, -itum: know, understand, be skilled in
scordalus, -a, -um: cocky, pugnacious
scribo, -ere, -psi, -ptum: write
scrutor, -ari, -atus sum: search carefully, examine, investigate
secedo, -ere, -cessi, -cessum: withdraw, retire
seco, -are, -cui, -ctum: cut off, carve; cut through, traverse
secundus, -a, -um: second, following, favorable
securitas, -tatis, f.: freedom from anxiety, composure
securus, -a, -um: free from care, unconcerned
sed: but
sedes, -s, f.: seat, habitation, abode
seditio, -ionis, f.: uprising, insurrection, revolt
segnis, -e: slow, sluggish, lazy
segnitia, -ae, f.: slowness, inactivity
semel: once, a single time
semen, -inis, n.: seed, offspring
seminudus, -a, -um: half-nude
semper: always
senatorius, -a, -um: senatorial
senectus, -tutis, f.: old age
senesco, -ere, -nui: grow old
sensus, -ūs, m.: sense, perception, feeling, sentiment
sententia, -ae, f.: opinion, judgment
sentio, -ire, sensi, sensum: feel, perceive

separo, -are, -avi, -atum: separate, divide
sepositus, -a, -um: distant, remote, removed
sequor, -i, secutus sum: follow, pursue
series, -ei, f.: succession, series, sequence
serius, -a, -um: serious, earnest
sermo, -onis, m.: conversation, discourse, discussion
serrarius, -i, m.: saw sharpener, saw maker, sawyer
servilis, -e: slavish, servile
servio, -ire, -vi, -itum: serve, be enslaved
servitus, -tutis, f.: slavery, servitude
servo, -are, -avi, -atum: keep, save, preserve, protect
servus, -i, m.: slave
sestertium, -i, n.: a sum of money equal to one thousand sesterces
severus, -a, -um: sober, grave, severe, austere
si: if, when, since
sibilus, -i, m.: hissing sound
sic: thus, in this way, just so
siccus, -a, -um: dry
sicut: so, as, just as, like
silentium, -ii, n.: stillness, silence
silva, -ae, f.: forest
similis, -e: similar, resembling, like, alike
similitudo, -inis, f.: similarity, resemblance, likeness
simul: at the same time
simulo, -are, -avi, -atum: imitate, copy, pretend
sine: prep. w/abl., without
singuli, -ae, -a: one at a time, separate, several, individual
singultus, -ūs, m.: sobbing, burp, hiccup
sinus, -ūs, m.: fold (of a garment), lap, bosom
sobrius, -a, -um: sober, moderate
socius, -i, m.: associate, partner, comrade, ally
soleo, -ēre, solitum: be used to, be acccustomed, (do) usually
solidus, -a, -um: solid, whole, intact
solitudo, -inis, f.: loneliness, solitude, a solitary place
sollemnis, -e: religious, sacred
sollicito, -are, -avi, -atum: stir up, shake, trouble, disturb
sollicitudo, -inis, f.: dis-ease, disquiet, anxiety

sollicitus, -a, -um: agitated, troubled, disturbed

solum, -i, n.: ground

solus, -a, -um: sole, alone, only

solvo, -ere, solvi, solutus: loosen, release, dissolve, discharge, pay

somnus, -i, m.: sleep

sono, -are, -avi, -atum: sound, make noise, express

sonus, -i, m.: noise, sound

sordeo, -ēre: be dirty

sordidus, -a, -um: dirty

spargo, -ere, sparsi, sparsum: sow, scatter, spread

speciosus, -a, -um: beautiful, splendid, for show, pretentious

spectaculum, -i.: a sight, spectacle

spectator, -oris, m.: onlooker, spectator

specto, -are, -avi, -atum: look at, behold, gaze at

sperno, -ere, sprevi, spretum: to spurn, reject, despise

spes, spei, f.: hope, expectation for the future

spiramentum, -i, n.: breathing-hole, breathing space

spiritus, -ūs, m.: breath, breathing, spirit, life, courage

spiro, -are, -avi, -atum: breathe

splendeo, -ēre: shine, gleam

splendidus, -a, -um: gleaming, illustrious

spolia, -orum, n. pl.: booty, spoils

sponte: abl., of one's free will, of one's own accord, spontaneously

sputum, -i, n.: spittle

squalor, -oris, m.: dirtiness, filth

stabilis, -e: stable, steady, firm

stagnum, -i, n.: standing water, lake, pond

statio, -ionis, f.: post, position

statura, -ae, f.: height, stature

stemma, -atis, n.: garland, family tree

sterilis, -e: unfruitful, barren

sternumentum, -i, n.: sneezing

stilus, -i, m.: stylus, pen

stimulus, -i, m.: stick, goad, stimulus

stipo, -are, -avi, -atum: compress, stuff full, pack

sto, -are, steti, statum: stand

stomachus, -i, m.: stomach

strages, -is, f.: mass, pile, heap

stratum, -i, n.: saddle

stridulus, -a, -um: grating, creaking

struo, -ere, struxi, structum: heap up, pile, arrange, construct

studeo, -ēre, -ui: give attention to, be eager for, apply oneself, study

studlosus, -a, -um: eager for, studious

studium, -ii, n.: pursuit, study

stultus, -a, -um: stupid, unthinking

stupeo, -ēre, -ui: be dumbfounded, be aghast, be stunned

suadeo, -ēre, -si, -sum: urge, persuade, induce

subdo, -ere, -didi, -ditum: put under, subject

subduco, -ere, -duxi, -ductum: lead away, remove

subeo, -ire, -ivi, -itum: enter, come under, submit to

subiacens, -ntis: lying beneath, underneath

subinde: from time to time, presently, forthwith

subministro, -are, -avi, -atum: aid, serve, furnish, supply

subsido, -ere, -sedi, -sessum: settle down, subside

subtilis, -e: fine, delicate, subtle

subveho, -ere, -vexi, -vectum: transport, conduct

succingo, -ere, -cinxi, -cinctum: gird about, dress, surround

sucus, -i, m.: juice, secretion

sudo, -are, -avi, -atum: sweat

sudor, -oris, m.: sweat

sufficio, -ere, -feci, -fectum: suffice, be enough

sum, esse, fui, futurum: be, exist

summa, -ae, f.: summit; sum (as in arithmetic)

summitto, -ere, -misi, -missum: offer, submit

summus, -a, -um: highest, topmost, last, final, extreme

sumo, -ere, sumpsi, sumptum: take up, take in hand, acquire

supellex, supellectilis, f.: furniture

super: prep. w/abl. and acc., over, above, on top of, beyond, besides

superbia, -ae, f.: pride (both good and bad)

superbus, -a, -um: proud, haughty, arrogant

superior, -ius: higher, superior, stronger

supero, -are, -avi, -atum: rise above, overcome, conquer

supersum, -esse, -fui, -futurum: be above, be left, remain

supervacuus, -a, -um: useless, needless, superfluous

supervenio, -ire, -veni, -ventum: come upon, enter in the midst
supplicium, -ii, n.: punishment
supra: prep. w/acc., above, over, beyond
surdus, -a, -um: deaf
surgo, -ere, surrexi: rise, arise, surge, ascend
sursum: up, upward
suspensus, -a, -um: raised, pressing lightly, anxious, hesitating
suspicio, -ere, -spexi, -spectum: look up, respect, admire
suspicio, -ionis, f.: mistrust, suspicion
sustento, -are, -avi, -atum: support, maintain
sustineo, -ēre, -tinui, -tentum: uphold, support, sustain, bear, endure
suus, -a, -um: his/her/its/their own (belonging to the subject of a sentence)

T

taceo, -ēre, -cui, -citum: be silent
taedium, -ii, n.: boredom, loathing, disgust
taeter, -tra, -trum: foul, hideous, disgusting
talis, -e: such, of such a kind
tam: as much, so, so much; **tam . . . quam,** as . . . as, so much . . . as
tamen: nevertheless, however, yet, still; with *si*, if at least, if only
tamquam: as, so, in the same way as
tango, -ere, tetigi, tactum: touch
tantum: to such an extent/degree, only
tantummodo: only, merely
tantundem: just so much, to the same extent
tantus, -a, -um: so great, so large
tarde: slowly, late
taurus, -i, m.: bull
tego, -ere, texi, tectum: cover, hide, conceal
telum, -i, n.: weapon
temere: rashly, boldy
temperans, -ntis: sober, moderate
temperatus, -a, -um: moderate, calm, steady
tempero, -are, -avi, -atum: be moderate, combine suitably, regulate
tempestas, -tatis, f.: season, storm, weather
tempto, -are, -avi, -atum: try, attempt

tempus, -oris, n.: time, occasion

temulentus, -a, -um: drunk, intoxicated, tipsy

tendo, -ere, tetendi, -ntum: stretch, aim, direct, hold course

teneo, -ēre, -ui, -tentum: hold, keep, comprehend

tener, -era, -erum: soft, young, delicate, tender

tenuis, e: thin, drawn out, trifling

tergiversatio, -ionis, f.: a turning of the back, retreat, refusal

terminus, -i, m.: end, limit, boundary

terra, -ae, f.: land, earth, country

terreo, -ēre, -ui, -itum: frighten, scare

territo, -are: frighten, scare, alarm

testis, -is, m.: witness

theatrum, -i, n.: theater

tibia, -ae, f.: pipe, flute

timeo, -ēre, -ui: be afraid, fear

timidus, -a, -um: fearful, skittish, timid

timor, -oris, m.: fear

tiro, -onis, m.: rookie, beginner, new military recruit

titulus, -i, m.: label, title, placard

toga, -ae, f.: toga

tolero, -are, -avi, -atum: tolerate, endure, support

tollo, -ere, sustuli, sublatum: raise up, nourish, educate

tormentum, -i, n.: anguish, pain, torment, torture

torpeo, -ēre: be numb, be inactive, idle, dull

torpesco, -ere, -pui: grow numb, stiff, become torpid, grow slothful

torqueo, -ēre, torsi, tortum: turn, twist, bend, contort, torture

tot: so many, such a number

totidem: just so many, the same number of

totus, -a, -um: all, whole, entire

tractatio, -ionis, f.: a handling, management, treatment

tracto, -are, -avi, -atum: drag, draw, conduct, practice, handle, manage

trado, -ere, -didi, -ditum: hand over, pass down, entrust

traho, -ere, traxi, tractum: drag, draw, pull

traicio, -ere, -ieci, -iectum: cross over, pass through

trames, -itis, m.: footpath, by-way

tranquillitas, -tatis, f.: calmness, peace, quiet

tranquillus, -a, -um: calm, quiet, tranquil, unperturbed

transcendo, -ere, -di: pass beyond, climb over, transcend
transcurro, -ere, -cucurri, -cursum: run through, traverse
transeo, -ire, -ivi, -itum: go/pass through
transfero, -ferre, -tuli, -latum: transfer, transport, transform
trepido, -are, -avi, -atum: be frightened, tremble, hasten with worry
tribuo, -ere, -ui, -itum: assign, impart, attribute
triduum, -i, n.: three day period
triginta: thirty
tristis, -e: sad, downcast
tristitia, -ae, f.: sadness, grief, depression
tritus, -a, -um: well-trod, frequently traveled, worn down
tubula, -ae, f.: tube, pipe
tueor, -ēri, tutus sum: take care for, watch over, regard, consider
tum: then, at that time
tumidus, -a, -um: swollen, puffed up
tumultuosus, -a, -um: bustling, confused, disorderly
tumultus, -ūs, m.: bustle, uproar, commotion
tunc: then, at that time, in that case
turba, -ae, f.: crowd
turbidus, -a, -um: stormy, churned up, crowded
turbulentus, -a, -um: full of commotion, disordered
turpis, -e: base, mean, foul, dirty
tussis, -is, f.: a cough
tutus, -a, -um: safe, unharmed
tuus, -a, -um: your (s.)
tyrannus, -i, m.: tyrant, king

U

ubi: where, when
ubicumque: wheresoever
ulcus, -eris, n.: ulcer, sore
ullus, -a, -um: any
ultimus, -a, -um: farthest, most remote, last, utmost, highest
ultra: prep. w/acc., beyond
umbra, -ae, f.: shade
umerus, -i, m.: shoulder

umor, -oris, m.: fluid, liquid
umquam: ever, at any time
unctio, -ionis: a besmearing, anointing
unde: whence, from which place, from which source
undique: on all sides, all around, in all respects
unitas, -tatis, f.: unity
universus, -a, -um: all, whole, entire
unus, -a, um: one, a single
unusquisque, -quaeque, -quidque: each individual, each one, every single
urbs, urbis, f.: city
urgeo, -ēre, ursi: urge, press, push, press forward
usitatus, -a, -um: customary, usual, ordinary
usque: continuously, as far as, up until
usus, -ūs, m.: use, practice, value, benefit, profit
ut: that, as, when (for particular uses see Commentary ad loc.)
uter, -tra, -trum: which of two, whichever one
uterque, utraque, utrumque: each, either, both
uterque . . . uterque: the one . . . the other
utilis, -e: useful, beneficial
utique: certainly, in any case, especially, in particular
utor, -i, usus sum: use, utilize, enjoy, w/abl.
uxor, -oris, f.: wife

V

vaco, -are, -avi, -atum: be idle, have time
vado, -ere: go quickly, rush
vagor, -ari, -atus sum: stroll about, wander, range, roam
vagus, -a, -um: wandering, nomadic
valens, -intis: strong, vigorous, healthy
valeo, -ēre, -ui, -iturum: be strong, be well, succeed; **vale:** farewell, good-
    bye
valitudo, -inis, f.: a condition of health (including sickness)
vallum, -i, n.: wall, fortification, rampart
vanus, -a, -um: empty, void, unsubstantial
ventosus, -a, -um: like wind, changeable, puffed up
varietas, -tatis, f.: diversity, variety, a change

varius, -a, -um: multicolored, diverse, changeable, versatile

vastus, -a, -um: huge, immense, enormous, empty, deserted

vatis, -is, m. and f.: bard, poet, prophet

vehemens, -intis: eager, violent, impetuous

vel: or, even, indeed, whether; **vel . . . vel**, either . . . or

vello, -ere: pluck

velocitas, -tatis, f.: speed

velut: adv., as, just as, as it were

vendo, -ere, -didi, -ditum: sell, vend

venio, -ire, veni, ventum: come, go

venter, -tris, m.: belly, paunch

ventus,-i, m.: wind

verber, -eris, n.: lash, whip, rod, scourge

verbero, -are, -avi, -atum: whip, beat, flog

verbum, -i, n.: word

verminor, -ari, -atus sum: ache

verruca, -ae, f.: wart

verso, -are, -avi, -atum: turn, whirl about, consider

vertex, -icis, m.: eddy, whirlpool, vortex

verto, -ere, -ti, -sum: turn, change

verus, -a, -um: true, real

vescor, -i: feed upon, eat (w/abl.)

vester, -tra, -trum: your (pl.)

vestibulum, -i, n.: courtyard, porch

vestigium, -i, n.: footstep, trace, track

vestis, -is, f.: clothing

veteranus, -a, -um: old, veteran

veto, -are, -ui, -itum: forbid, oppose, prohibit

vetus, -eris: old, aged, ancient, long-standing

vetustus, -a, -um: old, ancient

vexo, -are, -avi, -atum: harry, trouble, harass, annoy

via, -ae, f.: way, path, route, journey

vibro, -are, -avi, -atum: brandish, shake, agitate

vicinia, -ae, f.: neighborhood, vicinity

vicinus, -a, -um: neighboring, nearby

victus, -ūs, m.: sustenance, provisions, means of living

video, -ere, vidi, visum: see, observe; pass., seem, think

vilis, -e: cheap, base, vile
vinco, -ere, vici, victum: conquer, overcome
vindex, -icis, m.: avenger
vinum, i, n.: wine
vir, -i, m.: man, hero
vireo, -ēre,: be fresh, be green, flourish, bloom
virga, -ae, f.: rod, whip, scourge
virtus, -tutis, f.: virtue, manliness
vis, vis, f.: force, power; pl., strength
viscera, -um, n. pl.: innards, bowels
vita, -ae, f.: life, way of life
vitium, -ii, n.: fault, vice
vito, -are, -avi, -atum: avoid, shun
vivo, -ere, vixi, victum: live
vix: adv., scarcely, with difficulty
volo, velle, volui: want, wish
voluntarius, -a, -um: voluntary, willing, self-sought
voluntas, -tatis, f.: will
voluptas, -tatis, f.: pleasure, luxury
vomito, -are, -avi, -atum: spew out, vomit
vox, vocis, f.: voice, sound
vulgo: everywhere, universally, commonly, publicly
vulgus, -i, m.: mob, the common people
vulnus, -eris, n.: wound

the journey to which you refer — journey that shake the lazine out of my system — I hold it to be profitable both for my health & my studies. You see why they benefit my health, since my passion for literature makes me careless & lazy about my body, & can take exercise my deputy; as for my studies, I shall show you why my journies help them

Pliny is born in 61 or 62. Called Pliny the Younger. So he is born as Seneca is writing these letters. Dies in 113. Was appointed consul suffectus (substitute consul). In 111 he app't legate in Bithynia (near Ovid's Black Sea exile. Dies there 2 years later. Epistulae. Book 10 are the letters from Pliny to Trajan.